American Classic Screen Profiles

EDITED BY
JOHN C. TIBBETTS
JAMES M. WELSH

Preface by Ray Bradbury

THE SCARECROW PRESS, INC.
Lanham • Toronto • Plymouth, UK
2010

Published by Scarecrow Press, Inc.
A wholly owned subsidiary of The Rowman & Littlefield Publishing Group, Inc.
4501 Forbes Boulevard, Suite 200, Lanham, Maryland 20706
http://www.scarecrowpress.com

Estover Road, Plymouth PL6 7PY, United Kingdom

British Library Cataloguing in Publication Information Available

Library of Congress Cataloging-in-Publication Data

American classic screen profiles / edited by John C. Tibbetts, James M. Welsh.
    p. cm.
  Collection of profiles previously profiles in the periodical, American classic screen.
  Includes index.
  ISBN 978-0-8108-7676-7 (pbk. : alk. paper) — ISBN 978-0-8108-7677-4 (ebook)
  1. Motion pictures—United States—History—20th century. 2. Motion picture actors
and actresses—United States—Biography. 3. Motion picture producers and directors—
United States—Biography. I. Tibbetts, John C. II. Welsh, James Michael. III. American
classic screen.
  PN1993.5.U6A8585 2010
  791.4302'80922—dc22
  [B]   2010013537

Printed in the United States of America

Contents

PART II: ACTRESSES

PART III: HOLLYWOOD PAIRS

PART IV: BEHIND THE CAMERA: THE DIRECTORS

PART V: BEHIND THE CAMERA: THE CRAFTSMEN

Foreword

A FILM STUDIES PROLOGUE: RECONNECTING THE FANS TO THE CULTURE

Henry Jenkins

Film studies in the 1970s and 1980s was deeply invested in establishing itself as an academic field and this too often, unfortunately, meant defining academic film scholarship as something different from the writing of film buffs. In some cases, this occurred through the embrace of theoretical models or language which closed off their work from larger conversations that were taking place elsewhere about cinema. In some cases, this meant adopting a critical stance which denied the theorists' own emotional investments in their object of study. In both cases, there was a real loss. There was a thriving film culture in the 1970s—as people were rediscovering Hollywood's past, embracing the global art film movements, and debating the merits of the "New American Cinema," film societies and retro houses were helping to educate people about film's past. Critics like Andrew Sarris and Pauline Kael were debating contemporary film practices. Film buffs and collectors were building informal archives that protected aspects of our film heritage from destruction and conducting oral histories which would yield great insights for future generations of film scholars. Film studies lost contact with both the fans and the industry and as a result, accepted a much diminished place in the world. Today, we are trying very hard to rebuild bridges, to open larger conversations, and to join forces with fans and industry alike as we explore the new directions being taken within media culture. As I look back on the history of our discipline, I value all the more the small pockets where real conversation about cinema was taking place between the many diverse groups who care about the movies.

Preface

THE EYES OF TIME

Ray Bradbury

I've seen almost every film ever made, starting when I was three. I have always identified with movies, because as a boy I felt so alienated from the rest of the world. My education comes from movies, books, and libraries.

I was born in Waukegan, Illinois, on 11 South St. James Street. On the corner, just to the right of us, at 619 Washington Street, was my grandparents' house. Around the block, on Glenrock Avenue, my Uncle Bion lived with his family. I came out of the womb a 10-month baby. I could *see* when I came forth. That's very unusual. The fact that I stayed in the womb an extra month caused all my senses to be heightened. My mind is full of stuff I poked into my eyeballs as a kid. I have an education in all the major films, starting with *The Hunchback of Notre Dame* when I was three, and *The Lost World* and *The Phantom of the Opera* when I was five. Lon Chaney was my idol. I remember one night after seeing *The Phantom of the Opera* walking back with my brother through the ravine that cut through the town. That place used to scare the hell out of me. I wouldn't go down there now at night for anything. It's not all that deep, you know, but it's deep enough and there's a lot of wild shrubbery and trees (that path has since been named for me!). All those films between my third birthday and my sixth birthday really helped me change forever.

Meanwhile, there were all the Tarzan and John Carter books by Edgar Rice Burroughs I found at my Uncle Bion's house. Like John Carter, I raised my hands to Mars and cried for it to take me home. In a special bookcase at my grandmother and grandfather's house, on one side of the parlor, my Aunt Neva had all of her fairy tale books and all of the Oz books.

Now, why would I identify with all these strange characters and movie monsters, so fantastic and deformed, so put-upon, huh? I accepted them for what they *are*, impossible but wonderful! They were wonderful companions for boys! When I started to write stories I already knew I wanted to write sympathetically about them. Ordinarily, they would be looked on with horror, you know? But I understood the Frankenstein monster and the Hunchback and the Phantom.

And I put that into all those stories about Timothy and his wonderful vampire family in Green Town, Illinois.

When I was in my last year at L.A. High School, *Snow White and the Seven Dwarfs* came out. I saw it four or five times. I made the mistake of telling my friends, and I was labeled a "pansy" immediately. Boys were not supposed to like that sort of thing, then. To them I was the alien who watched weird movies and read strange stories. I talked strangely. I cared for the wrong things. Everything's changed since, thank god. But the boys were merciless in making fun of me for liking *Snow White*, but I just thought it was the greatest film ever made at the time. And then when *Fantasia* came along three or four years later, I dubbed *that* the greatest film ever made, and I have no reason to change my mind, except for *Citizen Kane*.

This was my education. I have all the metaphors I got from movies, books, and comics. If you look at the average page of any of my novels or short stories, it's a storyboard, a shooting script. You can shoot the paragraphs—the close-ups, the long shots, what have you. If you have a complete history of cartoons in your head, you're all set to write motion picture screenplays! That puts me ahead of almost every screenwriter, because they didn't collect comic books! Look at "Prince Valiant," "Flash Gordon," "Mickey Mouse," "Brick Bradford," "Mandrake the Magician," etc. They're all storyboards for movies, aren't they? When you get all these things in your head, then you can begin to think about things. And you can learn certain techniques, certain shortcuts to being yourself, to explode every morning and pick up the pieces at noon.

I've written screenplays for movies and television from almost all my novels and stories. I wrote a treatment but not the screenplay for *It Came from Outer Space*. I wrote for *Alfred Hitchcock Presents*. I brought my *Halloween Tree* and *The Wonderful Ice Cream Suit* to the screen. My novel, *Something Wicked This Way Comes*, actually began as a screenplay, then later became a novel, then finally ended up as my screenplay for the movie! I got script control for the 65 scripts I wrote for my television series [*The Ray Bradbury Theater*]. But a lot of projects are still to come. I wrote a screenplay for Mel Gibson for *Fahrenheit 451*, but nothing's happened with it so far. I've been working through different versions of *The Martian Chronicles* for forty years! But, what the hell. I love my own style, and I have fun with it. My screenplays, like my stories, are a collection of metaphors. Only I can know them and know how to use them and create from them.

It's all about *seeing*, huh? Movies are a part of that. I said in my screenplay for *The Martian Chronicles* that all of us are the Eyes of Time, born to witness and to celebrate. We are travelers, on our way to Eternity. Mars and the planets are but a way station to all Time and Space. We come like water and like wind we go. Our destination? Forever. Our occupation? To know the Universe. To be Immortal. To live forever.

ॐ

This interview with Ray Bradbury was conducted by John C. Tibbetts in Kansas City in October 1997. It is published here for the first time with the permission of Ray Bradbury and Don Congdon Associates, Inc.

Acknowledgments

Our gratitude goes to the many people who remember *American Classic Screen* and are now helping to bring it to a new generation of readers . . . to Randy Neil, who foresaw many years ago the importance of involving amateur and professional enthusiasts, filmmakers, and historians in the preservation of America's film heritage; to Allyn Miller, who as president of the National Film Society ably managed the magazine's membership and organized the annual awards ceremonies; and to her Kansas City staff and West Coast assistants, including Tom Hartzog, Gene Nelson, John Gallagher, Gary Spink, Vic Pettibone, Romayne Hoffman, Alice Becker, Frank Hoffman, and Frank Edwards; and, of course, to the many contributors who became close and personal friends, along the way, Gene D. Phillips, Frank Thompson, and Stan Singer (who also helped to orchestrate the West Coast Movie Expos) in particular, to name just a few. We especially want to thank three remarkable women at the Digital Media Services Department at the University of Kansas for their unstinting assistance in the preparation of this book. Pam LeRow, Paula Courtney, and Gwen Claasen contributed many hours of their time in scanning and retyping articles from the back issues of *American Classic Screen*. Without them this volume would not have been possible. But our debt of gratitude also extends to our extraordinarily patient and helpful editors, first to Stephen Ryan, our acquisitions editor at Scarecrow Press, who saw the true potential of this material and then worked endless hours helping us to shape it appropriately; and, finally, to our Rowman & Littlefield production editor, Jessica McCleary, who also was splendid in helping to worry us through the production process by staying in good cheer.

Introduction

John C. Tibbetts and James M. Welsh

We knew we weren't in Kansas anymore . . .

We were looking into a little book entitled *When the Smoke Hit the Fan: A Reminiscence of the Theater, Movies and T.V.,* inscribed "with Best Wishes" by the author in Los Angeles in 1979. In 1936 he served on the first board of directors of the Screen Actors Guild, and, in fact, was one of the founders. He later served as president of Actors Equity Association from 1952 until 1964. On Broadway, he earned both a Tony Award and the New York Drama Critics Award for his portrayal of FDR in *Sunrise at Campobello* in 1958. But we remember him best for playing a fellow who looked like Ralph Bellamy in the classic screwball comedy *His Girl Friday* (1940), sharing the playbill with Rosalind Russell and Cary Grant. We met Ralph Bellamy at a book signing in Los Angeles quite by accident. We immediately invited him to stop by the "Movie Expo" convention we were running across the street, and he generously agreed to share his time and experience with us. This led us to believe that stars of his age and magnitude were more approachable than we might have thought.

Of course, such happenstance encounters don't occur much in Kansas, but they were surprisingly common for us back then in Southern California, thanks to the National Film Society and *American Classic Screen* magazine. We never really took them for granted, but as editors of *American Classic Screen* we could find ourselves discussing convention plans while sitting at the Brown Derby, for example, next to the great Victor Jory, president of the Screen Actors Guild at that time and who we remembered well for his portrayal of an astonishingly menacing King Oberon in *A Midsummer Night's Dream* (1935).

On another occasion we tossed down beers with stuntman Richard Farnsworth (*The Grey Fox*) at a nearby Burbank bar. Disney veteran animator Bill Justice showed us the miniature Magic Castle that he had built for his kids in his backyard. Another Disney veteran, Ollie Johnston, talked with us in his living room about the love of trains he shared with the immortal Walt. We joined in the applause of a standing ovation when "Stepin Fetchit" rose from his wheelchair in an impromptu shuffle. Director King Vidor and historian Kevin Brownlow fled the crush of their fans and sought refuge for interviews in our hotel room. Leonard Bernstein got lost backstage while searching for a restroom before paying tribute to Betty Comden and Adolph Green. Francis Ford Coppola left an Italian feast to pay tribute at an awards luncheon to Gwen Verdon. The venerable producer/director John Houseman—more dazzling to us for his historic association with Orson Welles than for his recent acclaim in *The Paper Chase*—took a snooze on the sofa in our guest suite before submitting to the ordeals of a celebrity panel. At a Western Film Awards panel, we were surrounded by the likes of Ben Johnson, Yakima Canutt, Woody Strode, Farnsworth, Sunset Carson, Don "Red" Barry, and Doug McClure.

In other circumstances, we found ourselves doing video interviews with Peter O'Toole, from one generation of stars, and with Cyd Charisse, Jane Withers, and Jack Palance, from another. Or later that same evening, we sat at a banquet table between everybody's favorite film director, Frank Capra, along with Jimmy and Gloria Stewart.

We offer no apology for our name dropping. During the tenure of the National Film Society and *American Classic Screen*, from 1976 to 1985, scholars, performers, and enthusiasts alike all succumbed to the siren song of celebrity.

And then, after the better part of a decade, it just stopped. With the demise of the National Film Society and *American Classic Screen*, we returned to Kansas and points east. Although much of what was happening in those days has become a blur, we know it wasn't a dream. The selections in this volume amply document that trajectory.

The first volume in this series from *American Classic Screen* covered interviews. This second volume offers a selection of "Profiles." In the best tradition of Hollywood's "Coming Attractions," we invite you, stargazers all, to turn these pages in search of the those actors, actresses, directors, and others whose work once constituted the Golden Age of Hollywood and, at the same time, prefigured the pursuits, activism, and obsessions of today's fan culture.

We're on the set with Boris Karloff and that wonderful cycle of RKO horror films, as remembered by the great screenwriter who was there, DeWitt Bodeen; with Mae Clarke as she recounts the famous "grapefruit" scene with Jimmy Cagney in *The Public Enemy* (1931); and with beloved character actor Beulah Bondi while shooting Leo McCarey's legendary *Make Way for Tomorrow* (1937), a film that Orson Welles claimed "would make a stone cry." The same year that film was released, McCarey won the Best Director Oscar for *The Awful Truth*, and noted, in his acceptance speech, that the Motion Picture Academy had given him the award for the wrong film. In a recent review of the Criterion DVD release, *The Washington Post* described *Make Way for Tomorrow* as "an exceptional American film that most Americans have probably never heard of, let alone seen."

We learn why George M. Cohan's promising film career (yes, *that* Cohan) took a dive after his spoof of the fiery evangelist Billy Sunday, *Hit-The-Trail Holliday* (1917); why Mickey Rooney considered *The Human Comedy* (1944) his finest film; how Kenneth Strickfaden fashioned those remarkable electrical effects for the gruesome laboratory scenes in the *Frankenstein* films; and how George Bancroft's off-screen exploits surpassed anything he did on screen. Katharine Hepburn shares with writer Gene D. Phillips her half-century partnership with director George Cukor; and Marilyn Monroe's dance partner, Frank Radcliffe, recalls working with her on *Gentlemen Prefer Blondes* (1953). ("She was not the easiest person to lift!") We investigate the trauma of completing Natalie Wood's last film, *Brainstorm*, in the weeks after her untimely death; probe the desperately suicidal lifestyle of one-time screen goddess, Barbara La Marr; and review the facts in the rape trials of Roscoe "Fatty" Arbuckle.

There's more, of course, to be found inside these pages. So, read on, dear reader, but with caution. So many of these figures of renown ended up fleeing our gaze in their real lives, as much as they courted it in their screen lives. Know that we stargazers sometimes bear an awful responsibility. Whether you live in Kansas or not.

Part I
ACTORS

Roscoe "Fatty" Arbuckle

FILMDOM'S FORGOTTEN FUNNYMAN

Bob Young Jr.

Originally appeared in vol. 2, no. 2 (November/December 1977),
no. 4 (March/April 1978), and no. 5 (May/June 1978)

His full name, bestowed at birth on March 24, 1887, in a sod house on the outskirts of Smith Center, Kansas, was Roscoe Conkling Arbuckle. He weighed in at fourteen pounds, and was never less than chubby throughout his life. Fatty was an early nickname awarded by schoolmates, but he preferred Roscoe and was always so-called by his friends and close associates.

Fatty Arbuckle: singer of songs with illustrated slides, vaudeville mono-logist, juggler, and musical comedy star; actor, writer, producer, director—accomplishments for which he is little remembered (except for dedicated silent film buffs and screen historians). Rather, he is recalled, inaccurately, as the vil-lain of a 1921 sex scandal in San Francisco that eclipsed his versatile motion picture career for eleven years, until 1933 when death, at 46, deprived him of his comeback he worked hard to earn, justly deserved, and had just begun.

When I was a boy in Hollywood I lived in back of what was then Educa-tional Pictures' production lot. Educational was the studio that employed an art-ist's conception of Aladdin's Lamp as a trademark. Nearby, bordering on Mel-rose and Formosa Avenues, was United Artists, organized in January, 1919, by Mary Pickford, Douglas Fairbanks, Charlie Chaplin, and D. W. Griffith. The move provoked what quickly became one of the film industry's most enduring wisecracks when Richard A. Rowland, president of Metro Pictures, remarked: "So the lunatics have taken charge of the asylum."

Rowland came to rue his *mot.* But, in a way, he was right. Hollywood in its early days was something of an asylum, and those who made films, on both sides of the camera, were viewed as lunatics by many outsiders. Indeed, those motion picture people wanted the moon, reached for it, and often came as close to getting it as artistic and financial success can bring anyone.

My first memories of Hollywood are of the way it appeared to be in the early 1930s, an area seemingly apart from Los Angeles, less bustling than the city itself, more residential than commercial, despite the studios it hosted. In those days, on Saturday mornings, I went to the movies at the Oriental Theatre on Santa Monica Boulevard. Admission was a dime. For it, I saw two long features, a comedy short, three cartoons, and the latest thrilling chapter of a fast-paced serial.

Sitting in the darkness of the Oriental's tiny auditorium, I watched the images of Hoot Gibson, Colonel Tim McCoy, Tom Mix, Andy Clyde, Edgar Kennedy (who, one Sunday at the beach in Santa Monica, bought me a hamburger—for five cents?), Laurel and Hardy, and, although sound in films was five years established, all the great silent screen comedians: Harold Lloyd, Charlie Chaplin, Harry Langdon, Charlie Chase, Buster Keaton, and Fatty Arbuckle. Then as now, I enjoyed Keaton and Arbuckle the most. Chaplin and Langdon were superb, but neither really played to children. They were too subtle (Chaplin by design, Langdon by fortuitious accident). The brilliant nuances I later discovered in their work then escaped me. The rough-and-tumble brand of slapstick practiced by Keaton and Arbuckle appealed more to my unsophisticated mind. I now find subtle nuances galore in Keaton and Arbuckle comedies, both those made together and separately. I view them with sharper eyes honed by forty-five years of going to the movies. Back at the Oriental, pies in the face, kicks in baggy pants, breakneck train and automobile chases, and incredible physical feats made credible by trick photography were more than enough. I was seeing early Keaton and Arbuckle, cheap to rent and run. Their later work incorporated subtleties and bits of business still being imitated today.

Years after those memorable morning-into-afternoon hours at the Oriental I learned that in seeing Arbuckle comedies I saw films that the rest of the country, and the world, were going without. Fatty Arbuckle's films had been banned for years in every city and town in the United States. They are still banned in Great Britain, and most likely are only screened *sub rosa* in Sweden where strict Puritan censorship still keeps a number of Chaplin's early pictures from being seen. Exhibitors in the Hollywood of my childhood, however, regularly filled out their "kiddie" programs with Arbuckle's antics. The ban, issued by Will Hays, former Postmaster General of the United States, shortly after he answered the call of movie moguls to be their official watchdog, just sort of faded away and died by common consent. It had taken effect on April 18, 1922. A decade later the public approbation that greeted it, along with a loud sigh of relief from a spineless industry that put self–financial preservation before ethics and truth, were less than faint echoes. Anyway, in 1932, Fatty had been given a new lease on film life. A contract by Warner Brothers, and his first "new" films were favorably received by a public that seemed willing to forgive and forget, oblivious to the fact that it was Fatty who should really forgive; he had already done his best to forget.

Arbuckle's pictures, unreeled at the Oriental, were wholesome and funny. Nothing in them offended. There was no smut, no daring display of bare skin. In his films he displayed a talent that saw him second only to Chaplin in U.S. rank. Abroad, especially in Germany, Fatty was Number One. Once barred from appearing in films, there was nothing he could do but suffer arrested growth while he was out-distanced by his contemporaries, especially Buster Keaton, whom he introduced to film work, teamed with, and who, years later in an interview with film historian Kevin Brownlow, said simply with respect, "I learned it all from him."

Whatever Fatty Arbuckle's popularity with children, the mention of his name around adults when I came home reliving one of his films produced knowing looks and a pointed change of subject. I was told, finally, that Fatty Arbuckle, wonderful, fat, funny Fatty, whose gyrations seemed to defy gravity, supposedly injured a young lady during a party in San Francisco. The girl, sometimes actress Virginia Rappe, later died. Fatty was indicted, first for murder, then for manslaughter, pilloried by the press hellbent on sensation, renounced by religious groups and women's clubs, repudiated by the industry, tried three times and acquitted. But only by a jury.

I first heard this account of why Arbuckle's film career ended some forty years ago. The incident that led to his fall from grace took place more than fifty years ago. The telling and retelling of the story, with little attention to fact, for five decades, has brought it to the point of being a legend. Only last year, after long and careful research by British film writer David Yallop, was the story finally brought into focus and the true facts pinned down. Fatty Arbuckle was not responsible for Virginia Rappe's death. While twelve of his peers determined his innocence in 1922, the public, his fans, inflamed by biased newspaper reports, lies, slander, hearsay, and innuendo, threw the fear of economic reprisal into Hollywood which quickly shut Fatty out. He was thirty-five years old. He had been in pictures for thirteen years.

Most writers about silent film comedy and the industry's beginning years credit Fatty Arbuckle as having entered pictures when Mack Sennett hired him at Keystone in April, 1913. In his as-told-to-Cameron Shipp memoirs, *King of Comedy*, the custard pie pioneer says that Arbuckle skipped up the stairs to his office and announced: "Name's Arbuckle. Roscoe Arbuckle. Call me 'Fatty.' I'm with a stock company. I'm a funnyman and acrobat. Bet I could do good in pictures. Whatcha think?"

This is more fiction than fact. Mabel Normand, Sennett's greatest star, was present when Arbuckle introduced himself. The producer's reaction was negative. All he saw was a fat man with a beaming smile in a boyish face. Mabel sensed Fatty's potential and persuaded Sennett go give him a chance. In time, Mabel Normand and Fatty Arbuckle were teamed together in a series of pictures.

As a matter of film history, it was Mabel who tossed the first custard pie and Fatty who got it in the face. "Splurch" is the word Sennett coined to describe the sound a pie makes when it connects.

Although it was in Keystone films that Fatty made his first marks, by the time Sennett signed him he had already appeared in five pictures made by the Selig Polyscope Company whose studio was near Sennett's (three in 1909 and one each in 1910 and 1913), and also had worked four weeks for Al Christie with the Nestor Comedies company of Universal on its lot at Sunset Boulevard and Gower Street in Hollywood. These ventures before the camera he kept secret from his wife, Minta Durfee, whom he had married in 1908, when both were members of a stock company in Long Beach. He said later that he kept quiet about it because he didn't think she would approve. "He was ashamed," Minta Durfee Arbuckle told me during one of the long series of interviews I had with her in 1957. "He considered making films a long step down from the show business we both knew and loved, and only did it because we needed the money.

"Roscoe did not willingly take to moving pictures," she said. "They baffled him at first. He missed the roar of the audiences acclaiming his stage performances. 'This kind of work is like dropping from grand opera to burlesque,' he told me one evening. He looked upon picture making as stop-gap work, and spent his free time hunting for a stage engagement. I was lucky enough to be booked to sing at Clune's Auditorium in Los Angeles for six weeks. The strain, however, destroyed my voice and I had to take a long rest.

"Meanwhile, Roscoe"—Minta never called him Fatty—"slowly reconciled himself to working in moving pictures. His initial dissatisfaction was eventually swept away by his interest as he began to learn more about the business and to get the 'feel' of performing before a camera. However, he continued to seek stage work. I'm sure if he had been successful in finding any, he would have quit the movies without the slightest hesitation."

Sennett's studio was located in Edendale, a small settlement near Tropico (later to become Glendale), east of Los Angeles. "Anything on film made money," Sennett said, and his "fun factory" turned out pictures at an incredible rate. Arbuckle is known to have appeared in 106 Keystone films between April, 1913 and July, 1916, and it is presumed that many more featuring him were made during that period. His rise in popularity with the public was meteoric.

It was not Mack Sennett's belief that anyone else should shepherd his flock. But, once Fatty's abilities had changed his initial dubious view, Sennett came to trust the comedian's suggestions and ideas. Eleven months and 46 pictures after he joined Keystone, Arbuckle was writing and directing his pictures, and repaying Sennett's confidence with fast, dependable results. Sennett let him spend money, a sure sign he had arrived.

Once performing for the camera began to pay well and steadily, Arbuckle took pains to learn how pictures were made: how the camera operated and what it could and could not do, how lighting was handled, and the intricacies of editing. He had a gift for improvisation and for embroidering and expanding the suggestions of others as to how a scene should be played, and how to get the most out of situations. Chaplin was another who pursued this route, as did, later—taught by Arbuckle—Buster Keaton. Sadly, it is often at Fatty Arbuckle's expense that film historians and other writers on motion pictures emphasize their admiration for the contributions of Chaplin and Keaton.

The noted critic Walter Kerr, a serious yet adoring student of silent film comedy, in his paean to its funnymen, *The Silent Comedians,* says that the Arbuckle repertory of original gags and bits of business was not large. Forgetting the personal tragedy that cost Fatty more than a decade of creative growth, Kerr overshadows him with Chaplin, Keaton, Langdon, and Harold Lloyd. He makes Arbuckle someone who helped rather than led. Fatty's talents, however, as an actor and as a director, were large enough to bring him to the pinnacle of his profession within six years of joining Keystone Studios.

In *Mabel and Fatty Adrift,* for example, directed by Arbuckle at Keystone in 1916, there is a scene in which Fatty tenderly tucks Mabel Normand in bed by candle, blows the flame out, and retreats to the doorway. Standing there, as his huge shadow is thrown on the wall above her head by the light behind him, he slowly bends so the shadow bends and kisses her forehead as she stares at him out of large luminous eyes. It's an inventive bit of business that works in turn what would otherwise be cliche into a memorable film moment. Arbuckle grew into such subtleties over the years as he came to understand that motion picture audiences were not locked into the eleven-year-old mentality that Mack Sennett was fond of preaching that they were. He learned that audiences were clever; that they picked up on the little things and appreciated them as much as they responded to the broad strokes for which silent comedy is remembered best.

In Chaplin's 1925 milestone film, *The Gold Rush,* a memorable sequence (admittedly one of many) is that in which he pokes forks into Parker House rolls and manipulates them as dancing feet in a dinner table ballet which is at once pathetic and comic. Arbuckle originated and used the bit years before Chaplin. It was Fatty's on-the-spot idea, too, in *The Rounders,* a rough-and-tumble film centering on the misadventures of a pair of drunks, to pull the plug in the rowboat the two wind up lying in at the close of the picture. As they lie in a stupor, the boat fills and sinks. The gag had Chaplin gritting his teeth. He hated getting wet.

Most comedians zealously guard their routines and ideas—claiming patent by first use if copyright cannot be procured. Fatty was usually too interested in what was coming next to establish any proprietorship. He used the dancing buns in *The Rough House,* released in June, 1917, in which he also sliced salami by feeding it into the blades of an electric fan. Chaplin appropriated the first bit and made it his by using it in another context. The second regularly pops up as a visual gag in films. Since he was the most inventive of Arbuckle's contemporaries, many film buffs are ready to swear that both ideas came from him. He supported Fatty in the picture, and was on his own making film history less than three years later.

Perhaps Fatty Arbuckle would enjoy greater stature (the tragedy in San Francisco aside) if he had been more self-serving and professionally aggressive. He was neither. "He was the best friend I ever had," Keaton said, early and late. "The longer I worked with Roscoe," he said years after Arbuckle's death, "the more I liked him. Arbuckle was that rarity, a truly jolly fat man. He had no meanness, malice, or jealousy in him. Everything seemed to amuse and delight him. He was free with his advice and too free in lending and spending money. I could not have found a better-natured man to teach me the movie business, or a more knowledgeable one." How strongly this characterization contrasts with what is generally known and recalled about Fatty Arbuckle.

෴

One of the tourist attractions of Hollywood is the "Walk of Fame," initiated by the Hollywood Chamber of Commerce in 1950. It is a trail of brass stars embedded in the concrete sidewalks bordering Hollywood Boulevard and Vine Street, the intersection of which is, perhaps, the most well-known address in the nation. Enclosed in each star is the name of a screen, radio, television, or recording "great." Some *are* honored with more than one star: Mickey Rooney, Robert Young, and Danny Kaye are among those. Even Lassie and Rin-Tin-Tin have stars.

Of the hundreds of entertainment personalities commemorated in the "Walk of Fame," by far the most nostalgic names to be seen are those of the old-time stars, the pioneers of the art when it was silent: Mary Pickford, Douglas Fairbanks, Francis X. Bushman, Theda Bara, Rod La Rocque, Clara Bow, William S. Hart, Gloria Swanson, Buster Keaton, Harold Lloyd, and Roscoe Arbuckle. These are but a few, of course.

Marred by chewing gum ground into the porous cement, the star honoring Roscoe Arbuckle is opposite the doorway of Swenson's Ice Cream Parlour at 6701 Hollywood Boulevard, a few feet short of where the throughfare meets Las Palmas Avenue.

Roscoe's star is third from the corner, flanked by stars honoring Mary Livingston and Mary Astor. Thousands of feet tread upon the star daily. The young who pause to read it shrug. The name is not recognized. The memories of the middle-aged are mixed. They know he was in the movies. They may vaguely recall he was involved in some scandal. One really has to be seventy years in age, or more, to clearly remember Roscoe Arbuckle.

The tarnished, gum-stained star on Hollywood Boulevard is the only complimentary public notice of "Fatty" Arbuckle extant in Hollywood today. Dusty and decaying, his prized teak-wheeled, custom-built Pierce-Arrow phaeton is a curiosity in the Movieworld Cars of Stars museum, in the shadow of Disneyland, in Buena Park, California. The sprawling Tudor-style mansion he owned on West Adams Boulevard in Los Angeles, with its six-stall garage and $15,000 front door, is presently owned by the Catholic Church Authorities, but it is not on the list of meccas for tourists. Moldering records and fading still photographs dealing with his film career sleep in the files of the Academy of Motion Picture Arts and Sciences. Unknown are the whereabouts of the souvenirs of their life and careers together cherished for years by his first wife, Minta Durfee. She died, at 85, on September 9, 1975, of heart failure, at the Motion Picture and Television Country House and Hospital in Woodland Hills, California.

"I always called him Roscoe, never 'Fatty,'" Minta said during her last interview for publication, given two years before her death. Always to her, although she divorced him, Roscoe Arbuckle was "a man I loved so much that I never remarried, a man who means so much to me that I'm still proud to bear his name."

From the day they were divorced, in 1925, until her last days, Minta always gave her name as Minta Durfee Arbuckle. The world put him out of mind, but she did not, ever.

When Roscoe Arbuckle was born in the geographical center of the United States, Smith Center, Kansas, on March 24, 1887, his brother Arthur is said to have cursed in disbelief at the baby's size (he weighed in at fourteen pounds), and fled the sod house that was home. Their father, William Goodrich Arbuckle, a confirmed Democrat, effected the first of a number of contradictions in Roscoe's life by naming him after Roscoe Conkling, a founder of the Republican Party!

From birth, Roscoe was destined never to be less than chubby. He was viewed as fat, but the blubber was deceiving in appearance. He was extremely strong, and his endurance under physical exertion was tremendous. His chest always looked as if it had slipped, but he could run fast and long, and was an excellent swimmer. Schoolmates early tagged him with the nickname, "Fatty." "It was inevitable," he said, "and not very original." He did not like the nickname, though he made it world-famous. No one close to him ever used it in his presence. Mabel Normand christened him "Big Otto." Alice Lake called Roscoe "Arbie." On the set, when he was directing films, the crew called him "Chief." In conversation with others, Buster Keaton referred to him as "the Chief," and always addressed him directly as Roscoe. "Fatty" was strictly for marques, newspaper articles, advertisements, publicity, and the public which adored him.

Now and then, the unknowing, seeking to be familiar, would call Roscoe "Fatty." He would wince and a hurt look would cloud his gaze as he said, "I've got a name, you know." He never raised his voice or was impolite, no matter what the slight or insult. His patience appeared to be infinite, whatever the situation. He could, however, swear like a sailor, but took pains to edit himself when in mixed company. He did not like dirty stories told when women were present. There was a distinct air of Puritanism about him. Yet, Roscoe Arbuckle came to be the victim of the most sordid of accusations, of lies that have become legend, of injustice, and of slanders still repeated and enlarged upon today.

There is no denying, however, that Roscoe Arbuckle was anything but large. His adult weight has often been pegged at 300 pounds, but only once or twice in his lifetime did he ever tip the scares at that figure, and then for days only. His usual weight was 275. Little of that poundage was fat. He was mostly muscle, had the coordination of a trained athlete, and hair-trigger reflexes. In 1915, *Bioscope,* a British film trade publication, described Roscoe as being made of "watch springs and elastic."

For a heavy man whose circumference made him appear to be much shorter in height than five feet, ten inches (Roscoe towered over Chaplin and Keaton in the films they made with him, and in turn was towered over by Mack Swain, a fellow clown on the Keystone lot), Arbuckle was exceptionally light on his feet. He was a superb dancer, juggler, and acrobat. He possessed an acute sense of timing and an unerring eye. Especially when it came to throwing things, a standard Sennett ploy. The late Gene Fowler, a lover of madcap slapstick comedy, waxed well beyond lyric in his acclaim of Roscoe's slinging prowess. In his biography of Mack Sennett, *Father Goose,* Fowler saw Roscoe as the "greatest custard slinger of all time, the mightiest triple-threat man that ever stepped on the waffle-iron, the All-American of All-Americans, the supreme grand lama of the meringue, the Hercules of the winged dessert, the Ajax of the hurtling fritter, the paragon of patty-casters . . ."

Piling it on, Fowler said "he had all the qualifications that a champion must possess: form, speed, power, co-ordination, temperament and an ability to take as well as give pastry. . . Fatty Arbuckle could deliver a bake-oven grenade from any angle, sitting, crouching, lying down with a good book, standing on one leg or hanging by his toes from a pergola. He was ambidextrous and could hurl two pies at once in opposite directions."

Buster Keaton never tired of telling of his first encounter with the Arbuckle expertise in trajectory. In his first film, *The Butcher Boy,* shot early in 1917, Keaton steps into a country store *just* as Roscoe lets fly with a brown paper bag of flour. Al St. John was the target, but he ducks.

Keaton recalled that Arbuckle "could put his whole heart and every ounce of his weight into throwing a flour bag with devastating accuracy. There was enough force in that thing to upend me completely. It put my feet where my head had been, and with no cooperation from me whatever."

It was with *The Butcher Boy*, filmed at the Colony Studios in New York City, that Arbuckle began a phase of his movie career away from Keystone. He left Sennett following a disagreement over salary and production philosophy and technique. After more than a hundred pictures marked by fast, furious gags aimed at the eleven-year-old mentality, Arbuckle decided the audience was more clever than he had initially thought, that it was time for him to thicken plots, introduce depth, and be more subtle. Mack Sennett wanted to continue pursuing the tried and true formula, so they parted. Roscoe's departure triggered the end of Keystone. He signed with Joseph Schenck, one of the most powerful men in the burgeoning film industry. The contract guaranteed Arbuckle $1,000 a day, twenty-five percent of the profits, complete artistic control over his pictures, and his own production company—the Comique Film Corporation. The arrangement was a milestone in the business. Not until twenty years later, when Orson Welles went to Hollywood, did a contract approach what Roscoe was given. To boot, Schenck, well aware of the one great luxury Arbuckle allowed himself, an indulgence in expensive automobiles, gave the comedian a brand-new Rolls Royce.

Roscoe's rapid rise in films played havoc with his marriage. Minta objected to the Schenck deal which, among other things, put the damper on her film career. They separated—Roscoe moving to New York's Friars Club in which Minta had given him a membership as a gift. But the two were often seen together.

Minta said it was a man, Lou Anger, Roscoe's manager acquired in the wake of the Schenck contract, who drove them apart. Up to then, her brother-in-law, Herbert Maclean, handled Roscoe's affairs. Those who thought the cause of the break was another woman were deceived by the traditional cliché. Roscoe Arbuckle was a shy man when it came to women. He never played around. Minta Durfee, whom he approached impulsively during a streetcar ride from Los Angeles to Long Beach the summer of 1908, was his first love, and remained so, although he was to marry twice between their divorce in 1925 and his death in 1933.

The Comique Film Corporation was an adjunct of Paramount, affiliated with Famous Players-Lasky. Comique productions were listed as Paramount-Arbuckle Comedies. For his new company, Roscoe went to work with all the vigor and zest of independence. Before 1917 was over (beginning with *The Butcher Boy* in April), he wrote, directed, and starred in eight two-reelers—six at studios and on location in and around New York and two back in California, where he shifted operations near the close of the year.

The films were: *The Butcher Boy, A Reckless Romeo, The Rough House, His Wedding Night* (in which he used the Rolls Royce Schenck gave him), *Oh, Doctor!,*

Fatty at Coney Island (with which he revived the series in which he had made his mark at Keystone), *A Country Hero*, and *Out West*. Each reveal an increasing sophistication and artistic and creative growth. They also reflect expense. Roscoe was not frugal when it came to getting what he wanted. A sequence in *A Country Hero* called for the destruction of two Model T Fords by a locomotive. Retakes boosted the cost of the scene to $20,000. For *A Reckless Romeo*, Roscoe hired and imported the 28-member cast of a New York cabaret show, engaged a large orchestra, and signed on dozens of extras for an elaborate restaurant scene that cost more than $10,000 and was later scrapped. Whatever the expense, Paramount did not object. Fatty Arbuckle comedies earned record profits.

The Comique Film Corporation produced twenty-one Arbuckle comedies from April, 1917 until December, 1919. *Out West* was followed by *The Bell Boy*, a film containing one of the finest examples of the comedian's comic creative ability. The locale is a resort hotel in a rural village. Roscoe is the bellboy, but quickly becomes a barber when a heavily bearded guest looking like Rasputin demands immediate attention. In a twinkling he scissors the subject into a duplicate of President Lincoln. Then, after considering his handiwork for a few moments while the audience grasps what he has done, Roscoe resumes cutting and Lincoln suddenly becomes General Grant.

Another outstanding Arbuckle film of this period is *The Sheriff,* a hilarious burlesque of the films of Douglas Fairbanks, whose trademark was strenuous physical action—leaping from balconies, jumping from roof to roof, climbing up buildings hand over hand. Roscoe imitated the great athletic star feat for feat as an Old West sheriff in a lone battle against bandits. Fairbanks, a close friend, loved the satire. Roscoe showed himself to be every bit as fine an athlete as the original.

In looking back over his career, 1919 stands out as Roscoe Arbuckle's banner year. Although he continued to make two-reel comedies throughout 1919, his success convinced Adoph Zukor, head of Famous Players-Lasky, parent of Paramount, that a major change was in order. The change would be to feature-length films, a compliment not paid to any comedian, including Chaplin, up until this time. After conferring with Schenck, then with Jesse Lasky, Zukor approached Arbuckle with an offer to purchase his next twenty-two pictures—the two-reelers set for 1919, after which all his films would be features of five reels or more. Financially, the offer entailed the payment of $3 million over a period of three years. This meant a daily income of nearly $3,000—600 times the five dollars a day Roscoe received when he joined Keystone as an extra six years previously.

Arbuckle's deal with Schenck had been sealed with a handshake. This time for money that in the era of low taxes made him a millionaire with a stroke of a pen, Arbuckle signed on the dotted line.

Until this contract was signed, Arbuckle, although his income easily allowed it, eschewed high living. Only his taste in automobiles reflected his wealth. But now, at Schenck's urging, he moved to live in a style commensurate with his earnings. He spent $250,000 to buy a Tudor mansion set deep among trees on Los Angeles's West Adams Boulevard and settled in splendor in a location previously rented by Alla Nazimova and Theda Bara. Another $33,000 was spent on redecoration. Into the garage went his Rolls Royce, a Stevens-Duryea, a Cadillac town car, a White, a Renault roadster, and a custom-built Pierce-Arrow phaeton that featured a bar and toilet. Other makes he owned included an Alco, a MacFarlan, a Locomobile, and a Hudson limousine. Characteristically, one of the house's first visitors was Minta. "He was like a child as he showed me through it," she recalled. "He even pulled his bureau drawers open to display his monogrammed dress shirts."

Roscoe capped the year by taking a trip to Europe. His fans in England and France went wild. The crowds were enormous. Their size and frenzy recalled the jubilation that marked the end of World War I. He got little rest, returned to California in a state of euphoria, and prepared to make his first feature, *The Round Up*, at the Famous Players-Lasky studio on Vine Street in Hollywood. Rich, internationally famous, beloved by millions, he was at the pinnacle of his profession, but would remain there only eighteen months.

༈

Ten years after he first stepped before a motion picture camera lens for Selig Polyscope, six years after he joined Mack Sennett's Keystone Studios as an extra, Roscoe "Fatty" Arbuckle began filming his first feature-length picture in December, 1919. It was a western romance titled *The Round Up*, based upon a successful Broadway play by Edmund Day.

Playing Slim Hoover, the sheriff, in *The Round Up*, gave Arbuckle his first opportunity to act, not just play the prat-falling buffoon. His portrayal showed characterization and depth, and the public loved him.

He followed it with *The Life of the Party*. Critics who had been dubious about Arbuckle's acting ability had to admit, as one writer put it: "Fatty Arbuckle, unlike most comedians, is an artist, and his artistry is manifested with pleasing frequency." Of the films that followed—*Brewster's Millions, The Dollar a Year Man, The Traveling Salesman, Gasoline Gus, Crazy to Marry, Leap Year*, and *Freight Prepaid*— all filmed in 1921, each was better than the last. So great was Roscoe's success, and so eager was Paramount to capitalize upon it, that the last three films were made concurrently. This was a money-saving tactic dictated by Roscoe's astronomical salary and zooming production costs.

The last of the three films made in tandem was completed on Thursday, Sept. 1, 1921. Arbuckle was drained and days of relaxation away from Hollywood were in order. The comedian had promised his friends, director Fred Fischbach and actor Lowell Sherman, that the three of them would drive north to San Francisco in his Pierce-Arrow to spend the holiday at the St. Francis Hotel, a Bay City landmark and Arbuckle's favorite. The trio arrived at the St. Francis late Saturday afternoon, enjoyed cocktails and dinner at the hotel, and went to bed. Twenty-four hours later, in a twelfth-floor corner luxury suite composed of rooms 1219, 1220, and 1221, events were put into motion that brought the fabulous film career of Roscoe "Fatty" Arbuckle to an unwarranted 11-year halt.

When the mammoth Pierce-Arrow rolled to a stop in front of the St. Francis Hotel, word quickly spread that Roscoe Arbuckle was in town.

Fred Fischbach found tall, pretty, 26-year-old Virginia Rappe and a woman she introduced as Bambina Maude Delmont in the lobby of the Palace Hotel. He told them Arbuckle was staying at the St. Francis and invited Virginia to drop by. She did so, Sunday afternoon, Sept. 4, bringing Bambina Delmont with her.

Arbuckle knew Virginia Rappe as a sometime model and Keystone bit-player who spent more time in bed than before the camera. He liked her and felt sorry for her. She lived with Henry "Pathe" Lehrman, a film director who had no intention of entering into the marriage Virginia desperately hoped for.

Virginia Rappe told Arbuckle her troubles, including the news that she was pregnant and wanted an abortion. He promised financial help, but did not like the idea. He and his estranged wife, Minta, had longed for children, but her one pregnancy had ended tragically; the baby was born dead.

Virginia drank too much gin and orange juice and became ill. Attempts to revive her proved fruitless, so Roscoe booked another room down the hall from his and had her put to bed. Her illness persisted, and after one physician, then a second, were called, she was taken to Wakefield Sanatorium, a maternity hospital. Medical authorities confirmed her pregnancy, and also learned that she was suffering from a venereal disease and had a ruptured fallopian tube, which had become infected. She was to die.

Bambina Maude Delmont was a woman of few scruples and fewer morals whose past included prostitution, swindling, and blackmail. She sensed an opportunity to make big money out of Virginia's condition and began telling all who would listen that Arbuckle had raped the drunken girl, rupturing her bladder with his great weight. Her lies fell upon eager ears.

Ignorant of Virginia's severe illness and the budding scandal, Arbuckle had returned to Los Angeles on Tuesday, Sept. 6. Three days later, Virginia Rappe died. At no time during her illness did she accuse Roscoe of any misconduct, and she loudly denied it when questioners tried to put accusations in her mouth.

Lost in the uproar, but to surface later, was the information that Bambina Delmont had telegraphed confederates in Los Angeles and San Diego two days before Virginia's death: "We have Roscoe Arbuckle in a hole here. Chance to make some money out of him."

First the newspapers, then the civic-minded, then women's clubs, and finally, the law, all began howling for Arbuckle's head. Arbuckle, secure in his innocence, voluntarily returned to San Francisco—there to endure questioning without the benefit of counsel. He was first charged with murder. Then, after a farce of a coroner's inquest, booked for manslaughter and jailed.

In Hollywood, Sid Grauman, a friend of Roscoe's from his pre-film San Jose and San Francisco vaudeville days, was running the comedian's latest release, *Gasoline Gus*, to packed houses at his theater. Half a day after he learned that Roscoe had been indicted, Grauman withdrew the film and began a run for cover that eventually involved most of the film industry on the West Coast. Too much was at stake for Grauman, who would build his famous Chinese Theater in 1927. The "cut" hurt Roscoe deeply.

The enemies of movie pictures and the newspapers had a field day. Now, out in the open, was the supposedly seamy side of Hollywood. Whipped by newspaper sensationalism splashed across every front page, the public's love for Roscoe turned to hatred.

Matthew Brady, San Francisco's district attorney in 1921, was a very tenacious man. He succeeded in trying Roscoe three times between Nov. 18, 1921 and April 12, 1922. The third stanza of the *People of the State of California vs. Roscoe Arbuckle* ended in acquittal.

Proving what had been evident from the very beginning cost Roscoe close to $1,000,000 and put him deeply in debt. Paramount had stopped his salary the day he was arrested and suspended him until he was cleared. Further, the withdrawal of his films and the shelving of his final three erased about $600,000 in profit-sharing income.

But Roscoe remained determined. "I want to go back to work," he said.

ॐ

However, the film industry, running scared and sensing ruin, hired U.S. Postmaster William Hays to front for it. Into being came the "Hays Office," a censorship bureau. Six days after Arbuckle was acquitted, on April 18, 1922, Will Hays announced his first major decision as guardian of public morals for motion pictures. He banned Roscoe Arbuckle from the screen. That Arbuckle had been exonerated was of no importance. Throughout the country, Hays' decision was applauded and in Hollywood tensions relaxed.

For the next decade, Roscoe Arbuckle earned his living by trial and error. He returned to vaudeville, starred in a Broadway musical, opened a restaurant, wrote and directed films under a pseudonym—William Goodrich, his father's first and middle names, and hoped.

As the twenties wore on, the American public mellowed regarding Arbuckle, although "bluenoses," as Jackie Coogan termed them—ministers, politicians, and bigoted women's clubs—still reviled him. There were thousands, however, who wanted him back on their neighborhood screens. They made their wishes known to such an extent that Will Hays lifted his ban. But at the local level, opposition mushroomed anew. Typical were the reactions of the mayors of Boston, Detroit, and Indianapolis, each of whom said the ban would continue in their cities. Nevertheless, the Park Music Hall in New York City was jammed when an old Fatty Arbuckle film was announced and shown. But the ban, though officially lifted, remained in effect.

Arbuckle did appear in one film following Hays' lifting of the ban—*Hollywood*. Ironically, it was produced by Paramount. Film scholar emeritus Lewis Jacobs wrote of it in his milestone account of films, *The Rise of the American Film*: "The film's story—partly satirical, partly straightforward—of a small-town girl who does not make good in Hollywood was probably the truest picture of the industry yet made . . . An allusion to the current Arbuckle scandal was the pointed scene in which the heroine seeking a place in a crowded line before a casting director's window, is politely given room by a fat man. She is rejected . . . then he applies. The window slams in his face: upon it is the word 'Closed.' The fat man turns to the cameras: he is 'Fatty' Arbuckle, outlawed from further movie activity."

The years rolled by. Arbuckle, divorced by Minta in 1925, but still on the best of terms with her, married Doris Deane, a girl he had met on the steamship trip down from San Francisco following the fateful Labor Day weekend in 1921. The fight to come back and the constant rejection he carried led to divorce in mid-1928. In 1930 he signed to direct a young actress named Addie McPhail in a picture for Educational Film Exchanges. They were married in 1932.

Beginning in 1930, a groundswell favoring Arbuckle's return to film began to grow. Buster Keaton had never flagged in his devotion. An article in *Motion Picture* magazine asking justice for Arbuckle produced letters and petitions asking for his return to pictures.

In February, 1932, mogul Jack Warner invited Arbuckle to appear in a Big V Comedy for Warner Brothers' Vitaphone Corporation. The film, a two-reeler produced at the Vitaphone studio in Brooklyn, New York, put him back where he had started with Sennett. The picture, *Hey, Pop*, was an immediate hit. He followed it with five more, completing the last, *Tomalio*, June 28, 1933, and signing that day to make a feature. He had weathered the storm and returned.

After passing the evening talking with friends, he and Addie retired to their room in the Park Central Hotel. He went to bed laughing, fell asleep almost at once, and never woke, dying of heart disease at 2:15 a.m., June 29.

Charlie Chaplin sent red roses to the funeral. Will Rogers said publicly: "Those who demanded their pound of flesh finally received their satisfaction.

Roscoe 'Fatty' Arbuckle accommodated them by dying, and from a broken heart." Actor Humphrey Bogart and comedian Bob Hope, then on the early rungs of their careers, were to recall years later that Roscoe had helped and encouraged them both.

Many Americans old enough to recall the Arbuckle scandal still believe he was guilty of causing Virginia Rappe's death. A number of film historians have written that he died broke and in obscurity. Those who recall his comeback films put them down as flops. Others trumpet Keaton and Chaplin at Arbuckle's expense, denying him his niche in the development of film comedy. Perhaps the day will come when Arbuckle's contribution to films, unclouded by references to his personal trouble, will be put into proper perspective. Then he will finally receive the respect and credit he deserves, and emerge from the neglect of years no longer to be filmdom's forgotten funnyman.

George Bancroft

Raymond G. Cabana Jr.

Originally appeared in vol. 6, no. 6 (November/December 1982)

Who was George Bancroft?

According to writer Budd Schulberg, even grand masters of motion-picture trivia draw a blank on that question. His answer: "He was the world's number one box-office star, bigger than Gilbert and Colman, Beery and Barthelmess and all the rest of them!" And Schulberg goes on to devote an entire chapter of his recent book, *Moving Pictures,* to this man whose name had once "risen like a surfer's dream-wave and then had come pounding down across America and on around the world." George Bancroft was also the world's number one fan of George Bancroft.

Budd Schulberg's father, B. P. Schulberg, was vice-president-in-charge-of-production at the studio where Bancroft held sway: Paramount. Thus, young Schulberg became acquainted with many movie stars, among whom was George. Another individual who was there and knew George was the late John Cromwell—one of Hollywood's finest directors. What follows represents a conversation I had some years ago with him about "this man whose name had once . . . "

Cromwell: He must have been very over-developed physically because it was either when he was 14 or 16 that he was a turret gunner on one of the cruisers in Dewey's fleet when he fought the Battle of Manila. Now that shows that Bancroft probably didn't come anywhere near finishing high school; he may not even have gone to high school. And a little later, after the war was over, he was on the famous battleship, *Oregon,* and they hit a rock in Peking Bay, and they asked for volunteers to dive into the water and swim under the ship to take a quick look and come up and tell them how badly the ship was damaged—and Bancroft volunteered. As a reward for this, they gave him an appointment to Annapolis, which, you know, must've elated him enormously; but, in thinking it over, it seems to me it was either a gag, or the officer who did it had his tongue in his cheek because it must've been so obvious that Bancroft could *never* get into

Annapolis, and if he were put in by the Navy itself, he would last two or three months, then he'd be out. And this is exactly what happened.

Available data corroborates Cromwell. George Bancroft was born in Philadelphia, Pa., on September 30, 1882. Vital statistics: 6'2" tall; brown eyes and hair; 195 pounds. Education: Tomes Institute, Post Depost, Maryland; U.S. Naval Academy, Annapolis. George went to sea on merchant ships at the age of 14. In the Navy he was apprenticed on the frigate Constellation *(sister ship of the* Constitution*). He served aboard the U.S.S.* Essex *on an 8-month cruise to South America and the West Indies and was a gunner on the U.S.S.* Baltimore *at the Battle of Manila Bay in the Spanish-American War. During the Boxer Rebellion in 1900, Bancroft swam beneath the hull of a damaged ship, anchored off the China coast, and was rewarded with the Annapolis appointment. He left the Academy after one year for a theatrical career.*

Cromwell: He was probably 18 or so then and he drifted to New York and got interested in the theatre, and went into it. Several years later, after he'd had some experience, he became the leading man of a star [June Walker] who toured the country in a play called *The Trail of the Lonesome Pine*, which afterwards made a very famous silent picture. He was the leading man so he had some stature; he wasn't the New York leading man but he was a leading man. Sometime after that I suppose because he wanted a job and all (he had gotten married), he got a hold of a vaudeville act for himself and his wife, and it was touring out toward the West: California—and he must've come to Los Angeles and got a glimpse of the motion-picture industry and said, "This is us; this is where we can make a future and a lot of money." So he either finished his tour, or left his tour, and went into silent pictures.

George Bancroft purportedly made his theatrical debut at the age of two when he was brought on stage in one of the shows presented by the Forespaugh stock company of Philadelphia, Pa. He began his performing career actively in 1901, touring in plays like Uncle Tom's Cabin *and doing juvenile leads in musical comedies. In vaudeville, George was noted for his comical blackface routines and impressions of personalities such as Ulysses S. Grant, Mark Twain and Eddie Foy; a ragtime number also constituted part of his repertoire and, for a finale, he and his wife, Octavia, performed a cakewalk. Then came the movies. George Bancroft played the male lead in his first film,* The Journey's End *(W. W. Hodkinson; 1921). As "a photoplay without subtitles" it anticipated F. W. Murnau's famous German feature,* The Last Laugh *(1924) and, as "The Ironworker," George had the kind of vigorous yet sympathetic role which would later become his standard. Appearing as "The Child" was Bancroft's own daughter, whom the actor—characteristically—had named after himself, Georgette.*

Cromwell: Now in a very short time he worked up quite a reputation for himself in silent pictures. When 1928 came, and the change was made to sound, this was a very precarious time for everyone in the profession because no one knew how they were gonna come out—and it was with that same feeling that I was picked up as one of the recognized New York stage directors because they didn't know what to do with dialogue and they immediately turned to the stage—men who knew how to handle dialogue—and fell down and said "Allah!" and gave them contracts. The third picture they gave me to do, *The Mighty*, starred Bancroft. I was quite excited about it. . . Bancroft was then Paramount's biggest star.

The Mighty (1929) had smashed all records at New York's Rivoli Theatre by $19,300 and was in its third week of packing the 2,100-seat house when Variety's *annual poll showed George to be "the greatest drawing card on the screen." Although Joseph von Sternberg claimed in his autobiography,* Fun in a Chinese Laundry, *to have "launched" Bancroft to stardom, and Budd Schulberg labeled the actor "a mere feature player" prior to his association with B.P. Schulberg, George's ascension to stardom had begun prior to knowing either man. Be it a bestial hillbilly villain in* Driven *(Universal; 1922) or a murderous outlaw heavy in a Tom Mix western such as* Teeth *(Fox; 1924), George Bancroft generated an atavistic excitement. In* The Pony Express *(1924), he portrayed Jack Slade, stepping forth in top-boots, frock coat, black wide-brimmed hat and two long-barreled pistols. What particularly stirred viewers and critics alike about this Bancroft villain was the smile — ". . . not an ingratiating smile," observed* The New York Times, *"but one that forebodes ill." He stole the picture and became known as "the smiling villain." Ironically enough, the device seemed to increase in proportion to the recognition it brought George until, with the release of his most famous film—*Underworld *(Paramount; 1927)—The* New York Times *commented "that one does not care so much about his guffawing when a smile would be more effective."*

Cromwell: Well, I got along fine with George because he was, as I say, their biggest star, and he was very confident, having been on the stage. He wasn't worried about any problem; he had an excellent voice—wonderful voice—and knew pretty well how to use it. And he had great confidence in me because I was from the New York stage, and he knew, more or less, of my reputation. So we made this first picture, which was quite successful, and I think I made three in succession. Well, I discovered a lot about George very quickly. He was a very agreeable fellow on the surface; not very gregarious, but agreeable enough—but you almost immediately encountered this terrific ego. At one time the studio warned me; they told me this story that as they developed him as a star, and he began to, as we say, feel his oats, he got rather temperamental . . . and you'll hardly credit this story because it sounds so ridiculous: There would be a call in the morning for four hundred extras on the set at nine o'clock, you know, and Bancroft wouldn't show up until one in the afternoon. Well, this is an enormously expensive business, and after talking to him all they could and getting nothing out of him, they finally appealed to his wife, and she came down to the studio and had an interview with them and she said: "Gentlemen, you don't understand how sensitive George is. In the morning, when he is working, I go in to see if he's awake, and when I can't tell, I take a slice of peach and put it on his lips, and if he eats this, then I know he's awake—otherwise I won't disturb him." Well, I know the studio people saw this incredulous expression on my face and said, "We know it sounds absolutely crazy but this is the truth!"

Von Sternberg, writing of George's role in Underworld, *stated: ". . . I had heard him compared to Attila the Hun, despite his wife having told me that she woke him up each morning by wafting orange blossoms under his nose." Wrote Schulberg: "Stardom had made George so sensitive, his wife Octavia confided to us, that she lulled him to sleep by stroking his cheek with peach fuzz." Budd's father's reaction to Mrs. Bancroft's plea for understanding: "Peach fuzz! His head is so thick I don't think Gene Tunney could put him to sleep with a straight right to the jaw!"*

Cromwell: Well, George and I got along fine for a while. When I saw him in silent pictures I noticed this laugh that he had—he opened his mouth and threw back his head and this roar came out like a lion. Well, even in silent pictures he had capitalized on this. It was sort of a trademark with him. So when I started working with him it gave me the collywobbles because it was so false and he would do it at the slightest provocation. So I made up my mind that he wouldn't do it in any picture of mine. So when he tried it once, I drew him aside and said, "George, I wouldn't laugh there at that point," and then I went into a very intricate psychological discussion on how the man felt, *et cetera,* and why he wouldn't laugh. He swallowed this at first—and then I found out that his friends got to him finally and said, "You know, you may think Cromwell is fine, but he's toning you down—you *don't laugh anymore!"* And this began to work on him because I noticed his cooperation getting less and less.

In his book, Schulberg recalls the lack of cooperation George gave von Sternberg in a scene for The Drag Net *(Paramount, 1928) in which—at the director's command of "Bang!"—the actor was supposed to feign getting shot and slip down a staircase. But instead the huge man kept on climbing, seemingly oblivious to the repeated shouts of "Bang!—Bang!" "God damn it, George!" von Sternberg finally screamed. "What's the matter with you? Are you deaf?" To which George quietly responded, "Don't shout at me, Joe. Of course I heard you. But just remember this: One shot can't stop Bancroft!"*

Cromwell: So finally, after we had done three pictures—and I was scheduled for another one—I went to the studio and said, "Look now—I'm very dissatisfied at becoming Bancroft's director, so I'll do this one, but I want some kind of assurance from you that this will be the last; let somebody else work with him."

The man I dealt with mostly at Paramount was Ben Schulberg, who is Buddy Schulberg's father. He was a very fine man—had a weakness for gambling, to his own detriment—but he was a very honest fellow and we got along beautifully. He had promised me the Hemingway story, *A Farewell to Arms,* for doing all these Bancrofts, and we started on the picture and then something happened and they decided to take him out and turn the studio over to somebody else. And then the producer on this picture evidently felt that I was not the fellow to do this (he wanted a bigger name), so he persuaded them to take me off it and got a very good director named Frank Borzage. Well, this infuriated me so that I got my contract cancelled. My agent then was Myron Selznick, who was the biggest agent in Hollywood, and he knew that his brother, David Selznick, was going over to RKO to be in charge of the studio, so when I phoned him and said I just had a big fight with Sam Katz—who was then the head of Paramount—he said, "Well, good for you. In a few weeks I'll have you over at RKO." After this, Bancroft started to go off and was less and less successful. And I think it was mostly due to the fact that the industry was improving so fast, and he wasn't smart enough to keep up to it. He was still this egotistical guy who thought he was so good that he didn't have to worry.

According to von Sternberg, who was "Bancroft's director" before John Cromwell inherited that rather dubious distinction, George once said to him, "I know why you are fond of directing me. You want to be like me, don't you?" According to Schulberg, von Sternberg's "defense" was simply to ignore the antics of his star, who—frustrated by this "freeze"—turned to B.P. with his complaints. The executive, in turn, got back to the director, saying: "Sure, we know he's a moron, but after all, his popularity is helping to pay our salaries." At home B.P.—an otherwise "tower of charm and patience"—would shout to himself, "That stupid sonofabitch George is driving me out of my goddamn mind!"—and, finally, to his wife: ". . . If I don't get away from George for at least a couple of weeks, I'm going to crack." At this juncture, the Schulbergs decided to take a European vacation. The consternation the harried studio boss must have experienced shortly before departing requires little imagination—for George had strutted into the former's office and joyfully announced: "B.P., I've got great news. We're going with you."

Cromwell: There was a story—a wonderful story—about him, just to give an idea the way his mind worked . . . and Schulberg himself told me this story. Schulberg was going with his wife on a trip to Europe in the summer, and he happened to mention it to Bancroft. And Bancroft said, "Oh! Mrs. Bancroft and I would love that—we'll join up with you." Well, nothing could have appealed to Schulberg less than the prospect of this trip. But then, on second thought, he knew Bancroft's contract was coming up and he said to himself, "Well, it's a good time for me to negotiate this contract." So, fine—they all took off for Europe. They were in a big restaurant in Germany somewhere, and all this German was being spoken around them. And they knew then that sound was coming on, so Schulberg, thinking to make a point about the terms of this contract for the studio, said: "You see, George, we lose all this business in Germany because you speak English—they don't understand English, we don't get the release, we don't get the money we do on silent pictures." George thought for a minute and he said: "Ben, when they know it's Bancroft, *they'll learn English!*"

Budd Schulberg recalls the itinerary of that vacation well. Bancroft's arrival at Southampton caused a tumult. Asked by a reporter what he most wanted to see in England, George—after pausing dramatically—answered: "I have come here to see your underworld." In Paris, Prague, Budapest and Vienna, the world-famous star made the same statement, occasioning, each time, the same expression on the face of the elder Schulberg—what son Budd termed the "I'm going to murder George Bancroft" look. In Berlin, George visited von Sternberg—there to direct The Blue Angel—*and reproached him bitterly "for not having been at the terminal to witness the furor at his arrival."*

Cromwell: I'd always felt that, boy, if this chap had had the proper background and education, and his mind had developed, he would've made a magnificent actor, really would. He was a big, strong-looking fellow . . . but we found, oddly enough after reading his early history in the Navy, *et cetera*, that despite this reputation of being a big he-man, he really acted anything but. There's an amusing story I tell about the last picture I did with him, *The World and the Flesh* [1932], which was about a big Russian sailor who, when the Revolution came, got a very quick reputation as a fighter and was an idol of the people. The story was laid in a famous port on the Black Sea. When the Bolsheviks took possession of the town, Bancroft, in his character, rescued a party of refugees from the royal palace, and among them was a princess, you see, and of course he fell in love with the princess, and the princess fell in love with him. The last shot in the picture called for George to turn with the princess [the leading lady, Miriam Hopkins] and start down this long, circular staircase. George said to me, "John, how do you see this exit?" and I said, "Oh, I don't know, George—I think I'd just throw my arm over her shoulder and walk down the steps." "Well," he said to me, "I thought, John, as I turn at the door there I'd pick her up in my arms and carry her down." Well, this seemed to me, you know, what we used to refer to as "ham," and unnecessary, but I was determined not to get into any arguments with him so I said, "All right, George." He said, "You know, years ago I had a horse step on my wrists and so they're kind of weak, but Miriam only weighs about 90 pounds and I think I can handle that. When I was doing *The Docks of New York* with von Sternberg I had to carry Betty Compson around and von Sternberg arranged a little shelf that was tied onto my belt here in front and

I just rested her on this shelf." Picture this! I restrained my amusement over it because this was all serious business; he was talking *seriously*—he wasn't kidding! So I said, "All right, George, pick her up. She's not heavy; you can manage that all right." So they came through the door, Bancroft with the girl, and they start down these stairs, and about halfway down, just up on the curve, I saw her begin to droop—*down she went!* So I said, "Cut!"

In those days, you shot with several cameras—I had three on this shot—my cutter, who incidentally, was a funny little guy who *hated* Bancroft (mostly on account of his conceit, you know), said to me, "Where you gonna watch it?" And I said, "Oh, I don't know, George [George Nichols, Jr.]; I think I'll go up on that fly gallery there." And he said, "I'll go along with you." So we saw this and we almost burst into laughter. I said, "What's the trouble, George?" And he said, "Well, the curve of these stairs goes around like that, and these big boots— I couldn't get any purchase." I said, "Well, that's easy, George—we will never see your feet at any of these angles so just take the boots off." He said, "That's a good idea, John." So he went back and took the boots off—and down they come again. And they get about the same place and—*down she goes!* Well, Nichols, my cutter, and I are almost hanging onto the rails to keep from laughing. And I said, "What was it now, George?" And he said, "Well, this carpet here—the carpet slips!" So I said, "That's easily fixed, George." I called, "Props! Get some tacks and nail that carpet all the way down the stairs." So we waited until they got it nailed and, finally, third take—down they come. They get about the same place and she begins to slip—and by this time she was almost in hysterics. George stopped for a moment, placed his knee under her and—with a loud grunt—boosted her up to where he could regain his hold . . . and then resumed his descent.

George's powerful screen persona enthralled the public but, as Schulberg put it, "Their idol had feet of clay that went all the way up to his head." Von Sternberg credited himself in large measure for establishing this persona by filming George bending coins in his bare hands (the coins were made of pliant lead), lifting a beer keg over his head and drinking from it (the keg was suspended from a chair—"and what he drank would not have intoxicated a parrot") and handling a sub-machine gun as if it were a toy ("the lights were so adjusted that when the popgun went off his eyes were not seen to blink"). George supposedly hid under a shipboard barrel when a storm came up during the filming of Old Ironsides *(Paramount; 1926). And, in a subsequent production, he ruined a fist-fight scene by actually getting knocked out by Fred Kohler when it was Bancroft's character scripted to emerge victorious. Whether this knock-out was unintentional is subject to conjecture since, on another occasion, the entire cast and crew tip-toed away when George dozed off in the steel cell of a jail set—to be released by the night watchman after having shouted in vain for over an hour. George's name even got kicked around by George Burns and Gracie Allen in some of their Paramount short subjects: In one, Gracie referred to him as "George Bankrupt" and, in another, when asked if she liked the actor, her reply was, "I don't know—I've never been out with a horse."*

Cromwell: The makeup of Hollywood, and how it slowly changed during the time I was there, interested me a great deal. Now there was Bancroft, practically like everybody else in silent pictures. They came from all over the country, from all sorts of vocations—but they were, you know, like carnival people, and they had no qualifications. The industry was really growing beyond them. And George was one of these. So I was always struck by what he might have done if he'd had the advantages he should've had.

⅋

George Bancroft's career peaked in 1930 but the intervening years between that and 1942, when he retired from acting to work his 48-acre ranch in the San Fernando Valley, were hardly the nadir described by Josef von Sternberg and Budd Schulberg. He appeared in a good number of motion pictures, all major releases, always with prominent billing (with an occasional starring vehicle), and working for such well-known directors as Frank Capra, Michael Curtiz, John Ford, Frank Lloyd, Lloyd Bacon, James Whale and Norman Taurog. George Bancroft, the "tower of strength" who, on film could go "to his doom with a loud guffaw," succumbed to a three-week illness on October 2, 1956; he was 74 years old and reportedly a millionaire. His favorite word had been "facsimile"—which he invariably used incorrectly. Since his movies were such that *The New York Times* could criticize one of them simply because, in it, an actor of *ordinary* physical attributes had *dared to* look "threateningly at George Bancroft!"—and in light of what is now known about the former star's true nature—George would have used his favorite word correctly had he admitted that, in reality, he was the antithesis of his screen image rather than a facsimile thereof.

Warner Baxter

DeWitt Bodeen

Originally appeared in vol. 7, no. 1 (1983)

In 1928 Warner Baxter felt that after being in the business as a film actor for eleven years, he wasn't really going to hit the top. He had worked hard and consistently, and had built up some good credits like *Those Who Dance* with Blanche Sweet; twice he had been leading man to Betty Compson in *The Female* and *The Garden of Weeds*; he had given the best male performance in DeMille's *The Golden Bed*; he had been stunning as the civilized native lover of Aida Gray in *Aloma of the South Seas*; he had been miscast, but was appealing as Jay Gatsby in the first version of *The Great Gatsby*; he had been leading man to Pola Negri in *Three Sinners* and to Dolores del Rio in *Ramona*. He had played Walter Craig to Irene Rich's Harriet Craig in William C. deMille's *Craig's Wife*; and he had been outstanding with Lon Chaney in Tod Browning's *West of Zanzibar*. He had made 43 features, and he was now seriously thinking of sticking it out for maybe one more film, for by then it was obvious that talking features were going to be the thing, and he felt—because of his age—that he'd never have a chance at a good role in them at his age.

And then the gods smiled, and passed a miracle.

Fox was making the first outdoor talking picture, *In Old Arizona*. Raoul Walsh was directing and also appearing in the leading role of The Cisco Kid, a romantic, gay-hearted bandit. One night when Walsh was driving home from location in Zion Canyon, Utah, a startled jackrabbit leaped through his windshield, shattering glass everywhere. Walsh was permanently blinded in one eye, and production was temporarily halted on the picture. Irving Cummings was called in to take over direction, and his immediate task was to replace Walsh as The Cisco Kid. Some dozen actors were tested for the role, but the minute Baxter acted a test scene for Cummings, Baxter was hired.

It was the second year of the Academy Awards, and the five nominees in the 1928/29 year for Best Actor were George Bancroft (for *Thunderbolt*); Warner Baxter (for *In Old Arizona*); Chester Morris (for *Alibi*); Paul Muni (for *The Valiant*); and Lewis Stone (for *The Patriot*). Baxter was the winner. It was clearly a case of the talkies not only saving his career, but making a new career for him, and, now aged 37, he could hardly believe his luck. In the theatre he had been one of the best actors in stock. For some years he had alternated with Richard Dix and Edmund Lowe as leading man in Oliver Morosco's L.A. stock company. He was trained in acting a part vocally, and he also had a pleasant singing voice. His whole personality changed with a talking role. He knew how to play it, giving it every nuance of speech. He was a master of accents, for in stock some of the best roles require an authentic foreign or regional accent. He was to have 21 more years as a film star.

His fan mail jumped immediately to leading figures at his studio; he was even ahead of Gaynor and Farrell. Because he spoke with such a winning Mexican accent in *In Old Arizona*, and had jet-black eyes and raven black hair, most people didn't associate him with his silent roles; they wanted to know if he was a true Hispanic.

Not at all.

He was born in Columbus, Ohio, on March 29, 1892. His mother, Jane Baxter (*nee* Barrett) and her family were all Virginian, and had been prominent citizens of the Old Dominion since early Colonial times, emigrating from Ireland and Scotland. Edwin Baxter, his father, and his people were pioneer settlers of the old commonwealth of Ohio, all pure English.

When Baxter was only five months old, his father suddenly died of influenza, and his mother took her baby son to live with her brother, Warren L. Barrett, in the family home on High Street in Columbus. When he was 10, young Warner and his mother moved to New York City, where he took an active part in school dramatics, and became an ardent theatre goer. Baxter and his mother moved again, this time to San Francisco, where he, like George O'Brien and Janet Gaynor, graduated from Polytechnic High School. On the morning of April 18, 1906, an earthquake hit the city, and a large part of it was consumed by fire. Baxter and his mother spent eight days and nights living with other refugees in Golden Gate Park before they could get across the bay to Alameda, where they lived with friends for three months. Young Baxter secured a position with the Underwood Typewriter Co., but in 1908 he and his mother returned to Columbus to the family home on High Street.

He worked as a salesman for farm implements, but when he got a chance to go on as the partner of Dorothy Shoemaker in her Keith circuit act, he tried out and traveled with the vaudeville act for four months. When the season was over, he went back home to Columbus and the old job selling farm implements. When he went on to work for the Traveler's Insurance Co., he met a girl from Philadelphia named Viola Caldwell. They fell in love and married. They moved to Tulsa, where his young bride had a brother who owned a garage. Baxter was persuaded to invest all his savings in his wife's brother's business, which promptly went broke, leaving him penniless.

He sent his wife back to her Philadelphia family, and then went looking for a new job. He found one—in a stock company, where he was engaged as the juvenile for *Brewster's Millions* at $25 per week. He always deplored the fact that he had spent so much time making a living in businesses in which he was not really interested. Acting intrigued him, anything theatrical. He progressed to leading man at $35 a week. His wife had had no interest whatsoever in the theatre. He acted a full season with the stock company, and then resigned, and went to Hollywood, where he was confident he could get a job as an actor either on the stage or in the film studios. He never again saw his wife, and eventually she divorced him.

The year was 1914, and Baxter, canvassing the studios, decided that the best way to get them to notice him was to act in a play. He was glad to be signed by Oliver Morosco at the Burbank Stock Co. for leads, because Morosco's name was the most prestigious among theatre managers in L.A. His first play opened on a Sunday matinee, and was *Under Cover* by Roi Cooper Megrue, with Edmund Lowe and Frances Ring, wife of Thomas Meighan. On the first day of rehearsal, Baxter had spotted a girl in the lobby; he learned her name, Winifred Bryson; she was an actress who frequently played second leads at the Burbank. They became friends, and four years later were married. It was a union that lasted until his death.

There were a lot of stage performances before that happened, however; Morosco sent out his very successful production of *Lombardi, Ltd.* with Baxter and Miss Bryson. They played in key cities all over the U.S. and were two years traveling on the road. They were married in a Bronx church on Jan. 29, 1918, went on to the theatre for a special rehearsal, and played their regular engagement that night.

Back in L.A., they rented a bungalow on Gramercy Place, and Morosco set them up for another transcontinental tour in *A Tailor-Made Man*. Film casting directors were now very much aware of Warner Baxter, and he found the studio doors opening to him. He had played romantic leads in several silent films, and wanted an opportunity to play others. Morosco gave him a leave of absence, and he got appointments and leading roles in pictures at Realart, Paramount, Vitagraph, Fox, and Metro.

Ernst Lubitsch had asked for him for *The Marriage Circle*, his second film in the U.S. But Baxter either didn't like the part or wasn't impressed with the prestige of playing in *any* Lubitsch picture, so he turned it down, and Lubitsch gave it to Monte Blue. *The Marriage Circle* was an instant hit; it began the legend of "the Lubitsch touch." Casting directors looked the other way when the name of Warner Baxter was mentioned; they thought him more than a little erratic for having bowed out of a Lubitsch film.

1924 started as a lean year for Baxter; he only did two nondescript films, both released by FBO. Then Thomas H. Ince, who didn't give a damn about gossip, cast him in an excellent melodrama, *Those Who Dance*. Other directors followed suit—Sam Wood, George Archainbaud, James Cruze. By the time '24 ended, Baxter was working at Paramount for Cecil B. DeMille in *The Golden Bed*. Paramount liked him so much that they awarded him with a non-exclusive contract that lasted until '27.

In 1928 Baxter learned that director Edwin Carewe was interviewing actors to play opposite Dolores del Rio in *Ramona*. The role was for Alessandro, the tragic California mission Indian hero who falls in love with Ramona. Carewe could not see him in the part. Nothing daunted, Baxter went to the studio wardrobe, selected the kind of costume suitable for Alessandro, made himself up for the character, and then went back to confront Carewe. He sold himself to the director on sight, and he came to regard *Ramona* as the breakthrough for him into the big leagues.

Ramona also brought him a completely different kind of role in *Craig's Wife*, the adaptation of George Kelly's Pulitzer Prize–winning play, which William C. deMille directed with Irene Rich as the wife who loved her home more than her husband (Baxter).

Baxter's last silent release was as "Doc," the alcoholic hero in Lon Chaney's *West of Zanzibar*, who saves Mary Nolan from Chaney's degradations, inflicted upon her without his knowing that she was really his own daughter.

Then in January of 1929, *In Old Arizona* was released, and shortly afterward Baxter won his Oscar and began getting the star treatment.

Baxter, at first, did not get the choice roles he deserved at Fox. He had some interestingly different parts, as in *Thru Different Eyes*, which has a kind of *Rashomon* twist in which the viewer sees three different versions of a crime as witnessed by three pairs of eyes; there was the melodramatic *Behind That Curtain*, in which he played an out-and-out fortune hunter; there was a real charmer, *Daddy Long Legs*, which he played with Janet Gaynor; and there was the fascinating bizarre story told in *Six Hours To Live*, in which the hero lives and dies twice.

But it was the loan-outs that brought him the real gutsy roles. He went to Warner Bros. to play the harrassed stage director, Julian Marsh, in *42nd Street*, one of the first really memorable musicals. Everything in it in '33 was fresh and invigorating, but it has since been copied in so many run-of-the-mill musicals that it often seems hackneyed now. But not Baxter's performance, which is apart from all the hysterical pace of the story. The director is the one tragic character in the show. He brings in a hit, and the last one sees of him he is sitting in the stage alleyway, unnoticed, near to suffering a heart attack, the one man who changed failure into success. Everybody is talking about the actors in his show; they don't even know who he is.

There was the stylish melodrama he did with Myrna Loy for MGM from a Goodrich-Hackett screenplay, *Penthouse*. There was also *Broadway Bill*, the

Capra racehorse story which he also did with Miss Loy at Columbia; and there was *Robin Hood of El Dorado*, in which he played the well-known bandit, Joaquin Murietta, directed by William A. Wellman at MGM, with Margo looking, as always, enchanting.

Over the years he did do two more charming comedies at Fox with Janet Gaynor—*One More Spring*, from Robert Nathan's novel, and *Paddy, the Next Best Thing*. Baxter played exceptionally well with Gaynor.

His favorite role, however, was one back on his home lot in '35, *Prisoner of Shark Island*, in which he was directed by John Ford in one of Ford's best films, the story of a grave miscarriage of justice. Baxter played Dr. Samuel Mudd, who sets the broken leg of John Wilkes Booth, without knowing the identity of the man, and from that time on, life becomes a nightmare. In fact, it was only very recently that Congress passed an act completely exonerating Dr. Mudd from any conspiracy in the matter of Lincoln's assassination. Baxter made Dr. Mudd a kind of American Jean Valjean, a man both hunted and haunted. Incidentally, the picture was Baxter's first release under the new 20th Century-Fox banner.

Immediately thereafter he played for Howard Hawks in a very gripping and bitter war story, *The Road to Glory*, in which he, Fredric March, and Lionel Barrymore did some of the best work of their careers.

For John Cromwell he played a very pleasantly romantic love story, *To Mary with Love*, which he did with two fine actresses, Myrna Loy and Claire Trevor. Popular at the box office, too, were the twin triangles—*Wife, Doctor and Nurse* (Baxter with Loretta Young and Virginia Bruce); and *Wife, Husband and Friend* (Baxter with Loretta Young and Binnie Barnes).

There were also two big adventure features he did at 20th—*Slave Ship*, in which Baxter played with Wallace Beery and Mickey Rooney; and Robert Louis Stevenson's admirable *Kidnapped*, in which he played Alan Breck (to Freddie Bartholomew and C. Aubrey Smith).

There was the inevitable *Return of the Cisco Kid*, a role which he subsequently turned over to other actors more capable of playing the part now that it was '39 and he was ten years from his original triumph as The Cisco Kid.

His contract ended, and he did not play in another important picture until '41—*Adam Had Four Sons* with Ingrid Bergman at Columbia. It was very early American Bergman, but she was lovely as the governess of a father's four sons, and Baxter was, as usual, always sincere and good to see.

He was perfectly happy and made considerable money in several real estate deals but he was persuaded to return to Columbia in '43, where he made a series of *Crime Doctor* melodramas, in which he played Dr. Ordway, an ex-gangster turned psychiatrist. Over the next seven years he filmed ten of the *Crime Doctor* programmers, which nowadays are sometimes screened at impossible early morning hours on TV. He also played other action melodramas at Columbia, but his only other real class performance was with Ginger Rogers in Paramount's Moss Hart–Kurt Weill musical, *Lady in the Dark*, in which he played a wealthy suitor, Kendall Nesbitt, about whom Miss Rogers, as Jenny, couldn't make up her mind. Neither could the audience decide what they really thought of the picture. It was lavish, but it was certainly not the *Lady in the Dark* that had entertained American audiences onstage with Gertrude Lawrence and Danny Kaye.

Baxter suffered from chronic arthritis, which every year grew more agonizing. The last year of his life he was in such great pain that he could not eat and suffered from vitamin deficiency and malnutrition. He was slowly starving to death when, mercifully, bronchial pneumonia took his life. He died in his Beverly Hills home on May 7, 1951, with his wife and mother at his bedside. He was only 58 years old.

Ralph Bellamy

James Bawden

Originally appeared in vol. 7, no. 1 (1983)

The streets that run through Laurel Canyon are steep and winding. Behind the carefully manicured lawns and dense foliage are the mansions of the very rich and the very famous. My taxi stops almost at the top of Mulholland Drive and there spread out behind the hills, is Los Angeles in all its smoggy grandeur. One massive home, with a garage as the first story, seems precariously perched on the edge of the hill. A buzzer opens the front door even before I can knock and there, standing on the second floor rotunda, is Ralph Bellamy.

It's his voice you first notice—rich and firm like a cello but warm and instantly friendly. And when he motions you to come up you notice his physical appearance—a towering 6'1" frame that does not stoop with age but walks tall and proud. He's wearing a simple blue polo shirt, slacks and white loafers, but the way he pumps your hand and exchanges pleasantries is, well, presidential. There's still a lot of FDR in the man.

His study is cozy and uncluttered. "You said you'd be here at 2:00," he says. "You just made it. I like to be on time—I guess it stems from my years in the theatre when I had that curtain to make every night at 8:30 sharp. Today, with TV work, I like to get in and out of makeup early."

Indeed Bellamy, in recent years, has celebrated something of a renaissance. He suddenly seemed to be appearing in every other prestigious mini-series and TV movie, including *Wheels* and *The Moneychangers* and such teleflicks as *The Boy in the Plastic Bubble*, *McNaughton's Daughter*, *Search for the Gods* and *Nightmare in Badham Country*. "It's like I tell the producers," he laughs. "They're paying for 50 years of experience. The role might be a juicy cameo. Just as long as they don't pay cameo salaries. We shoot twice as fast for TV as in the old Grade B movie days. But I've always been a quick study. I took over from Ray Massey in *Moneychangers* on a day's notice when he got ill."

Bellamy's movie past goes back to the first year of the talkies. And he starred in one of television's first long-running series, *Man Against Crime*, back in 1949. "I've lost count of the movies I did but they rarely let me get the girl except in

32

the B's. I always considered myself a character actor even when I was 17 years old and just starting out in stock. I'd be playing one role, rehearsing a second and memorizing a third."

Born in Chicago in 1904, Bellamy decided he wanted to act while still in high school. After he was kicked out of school for smoking in the auditorium, he joined a touring stock company and spent the next nine years touring the Midwest. By 1925 he had formed the Ralph Bellamy players in Des Moines, Iowa, and they traveled as far east as Providence, Rhode Island. Bellamy made his delayed Broadway bow in something called *Town Boy* on October 4, 1929, but the show closed after one day. His next Broadway attempt—*Roadside*—lasted for only eleven performances, but it brought him offers to try out for the talkies. He weighed the offers, signed with Joe Schenk for $650 a week and was promptly loaned to M-G-M for *The Secret Six* (1931).

"I remember sitting in a speakeasy owned by Chaplin after we finished filming *The Secret Six* and in comes Clark Gable. He was very down, telling me he wouldn't last and how he'd earned $11,000 for his first film *The Painted Desert* [1930] with Bill Boyd." (Although Bellamy played his baby-faced gambler role in the film with style, the studio concentrated their star buildups on Jean Harlow and Gable.) "I felt really sorry for Johnny Mack Brown who was supposed to be the star and found his part gradually decreasing as Gable's was expanded."

Following *The Secret Six*, Ralph was loaned to Paramount for *The Magnificent Lie* and was soon after dropped by Joe Schenk who didn't think he was an exciting enough actor for the screen.

On the set of *West of Broadway* in 1932, Bellamy met a despondent John Gilbert. "He had a tenor's voice which was too reedy for the primitive cameras. He had signed a $3 million deal with Metro just before talkies came in and the big bosses were doing everything to make him break it. They'd call him in the middle of the night for set-ups. But Jack told me he'd clean spittoons to keep going. I was vocal in disapproving such treatment and that studio never called me back.

"You know in those days there was no actor's guild. On the B's we'd work Saturdays until Sunday morning dawned. I finally got mad and told Harry Cohn—I was at Columbia by then—that I was going to walk out every day at 6:00. I was a fast worker so Cohn had to agree, but he sputtered, 'Don't tell Jack Holt.' Holt was his big star who often had to work all night to finish scenes."

Bellamy eventually worked with most of the big stars of the time including Barbara Stanwyck in *Forbidden* (1932) and James Cagney in *Picture Snatcher* (1933). "I only remember how efficient Missy Stanwyck was. But Jimmy and I became close friends. On *Picture Snatcher* I permanently changed his appearance. I was the drunken city editor and he the hot reporter. I'm strong and he's so small and light I misjudged during a fight scene and knocked a chip off one of his teeth. But he could take it and we even had to retake the shot because it looked so tame."

Katharine Hepburn chose Bellamy as her co-star in *Spitfire* (1934). "Kate is incredible, but the movie was a stinker and I avoid watching it today. She played a backwoods gal with a Bryn Mawr accent and it was terribly bucolic. Her contract with RKO was a big one guaranteeing her a certain cut-off date to go to Broadway to do a play. There were troubles and at midnight she walked off the set and director John Cromwell was fuming. Kate said her contract had a $10,000-a-day penalty clause and she wanted the money, so the big bosses came down to see her. Presently, she reappeared on the set in her little gingham gown. Just as I came in for the clinch she pulled the check out of her pocket and winked."

Bellamy made dozens of B movies in succession "because I had a family and they needed new shoes. I wasn't choosey enough, but I hate to be idle." One film he did do was *The Awful Truth* (1937) for which he won his only Academy Award nomination as best supporting actor. He played Irene Dunne's stupid Oklahoman suitor so well he almost became typecast in such parts. "Irene hated the script—or what script there was. Cary Grant kept muttering he'd be ruined. One day director Leo McCarey asked me if I could sing and I said 'No' and he asked Irene if she could play the piano and she said 'No.' So he had me singing "Home on the Range" and Irene banging away and that's the moment Harry Cohn dropped by to see what was going on. He hit the roof, but we actually finished the film ahead of time because there were so few retakes."

Bellamy went on to play the same type of role in such films as *Carefree* (1938), *His Girl Friday* (1940) and *Brother Orchid* (1940). "I remember Howard Hawks phoned me up and said he was doing a remake of *The Front Page*. I asked what part and he said 'The girlfriend, stupid.' I told him how we'd done it in stock by overlapping dialogue and it certainly speeded the movie up. I remember the line in the film where Cary, trying to describe me to a friend says, 'Sort of ordinary looking. Like that guy in pictures, Ralph Bellamy.'"

Bellamy had high hopes for the Ellery Queen series co-starring Margaret Lindsay. "We had the writers on the set but the product was very ordinary indeed. I withdrew because they were shot too fast and Bill Gargan took over for awhile." Over at Universal he tried his luck with horror films, *The Wolfman* and *The Ghost of Frankenstein* in 1941. "Everybody did them for the money. On *Ghost* we were on *The Phantom of the Opera* set for the last shot and an officious assistant director came up. Sir Cedric Hardwicke and Evelyn Ankers were there and we had to go down a balcony—that was all. But here's how that assistant director set up the shot: 'Now Evelyn, your mother's been carried off by Frankenstein, your father got his from the wolfman, your lover is being chased across the moors by dogs and the servants have left you at 4:00 a.m. in this oozing, slimy castle. What I want is reaction. Evelyn, show me that you're fed up with it all.' Of course that started Cedric off and there were tears of laughter in his eyes all night and whenever we'd meet he'd yell, 'Fed up with it?'"

In the early '40s, Bellamy signed with independent producer Hunt Stromberg. His favorite film from that period cast him in a cunning dual performance in *The Great Impersonation* (1942). Soon after, while in producer Mark Hellinger's office, he came upon a script with this penciled notation: "The second lead is a charming but naive fellow—a typical Ralph Bellamy part."

"That did it," says Bellamy. He left Hollywood to appear in *Tomorrow the World* which ran for a year in New York (Fredric March did the film). Then, after supporting Deanna Durbin in *Lady on a Train* (1945), he left Hollywood, living in New York for 15 years and returning only to appear in the 1955 *The Court-Martial of Billy Mitchell*. During his years in New York he starred in the Pulitzer Prize–winning *State of the Union* opposite Ruth Hussey and Kay Francis (old pal Spencer Tracy took the movie version). Then came two years in *Detective Story* (he was replaced by Kirk Douglas in the film). "I always wanted to make the movie versions, too, but I was out of sight and out of mind as far as the producers were concerned."

In 1949 he started a TV series called *Man Against Crime* that was aired live on Friday evenings from the CBS studios atop Grand Central Station. "I had 10 minutes to get from the studios to the theatre. One night my taxi crashed and I staggered onstage in disheveled condition. Audiences seemed to like it well enough."

In 1952, Bellamy became president of Actors Equity—a further inducement to remain in Manhattan. His best remembered role as FDR in *Sunrise at Campobello* began in 1958 and resulted in his winning a Tony Award for best actor. "First night was quite something. It seemed that every New Dealer still living was there. Mrs. Roosevelt came backstage and was deeply moved. For the part, I had to train with weights to be able to wheel around. I keep up with those exercises even now and get up at 4:30 a.m.—even when filming—to have a half hour to do them properly."

Bellamy returned to Hollywood in 1960 to star in the film version of *Sunrise at Campobello*, but felt he was too old for the role. "Closeups are murder and I was just too old. Also, most of the cast had done the play with me and we were used to reaching the second balcony. I just wasn't as fresh with the part anymore." Bellamy stayed in Hollywood and, in 1964, replaced an ailing Wendell Corey in *The Eleventh Hour* television series. In 1966 he filmed both *The Professionals* and *Rosemary's Baby*, the latter a film, "I'm enormously proud of. I liked that little fellow Roman (Polanski). He'd wander around watching us film and never say cut. You'd hear a 'tee, hee, hee' when he was satisfied."

The year 1969 brought Bellamy another stint with a TV series—*The Survivors*. "More money was spent on scenes that never got on the air. I died in the pilot but that didn't stop them from calling me back. One $2 million episode shot on the Riviera was totally scrapped."

Bellamy remembers the Golden Years of Hollywood as if they were yesterday. He founded the famed Racquet Club with pal Charles Farrell and ran it for years on his own. "I guess they were good times because I was always working and the industry was thriving. Carole Lombard was a pal. Errol Flynn was close—he was part poet, part satyr. Sam Goldwyn—a great producer. I was playing Anna Sten's Polish bridegroom in *Wedding Night* (1935) and Sam started bellowing, 'Vy dooes hee talk like dat?'"

The afternoon rays are tilting across the lawn and Bellamy looks up from his reverie. His study with mementoes of a long career reflect his own inner peace. "I must have good genes," he says. "I can still put in a full day. There aren't many of us left ya' know. Memories. Memories. The ghosts of a lifetime almost overcome me at times."

The Film Career of George M. Cohan

Audrey Kupferberg

Originally appeared in vol. 4, no. 1 (Fall 1979)

The stage career of George M. Cohan had been carefully documented by biographers Ward Morehouse and John McCabe and in the movie of Cohan's life *Yankee Doodle Dandy*. Cohan's ventures into the film business provoke no more than a mention in any biographical work. The fact that so little has been said of Cohan's screen projects may imply that his films were second-rate or outright failures. Although the films in which he starred and others which he authored are not available for viewing or rarely shown, contemporary press notices treat the films as hits and praise Cohan's contributions. Why then did Cohan make so few films, and why is his motion picture career given so low a profile? The following is an analysis of the film career of George M. Cohan with background information on the Broadway stage career for which he is remembered.

George M. Cohan was born on July 4 (or July 3, according to the cynics), 1878, and by the mid-1880s he was an active member of the Four Cohans vaudeville act. As a teenager, he began writing material for other vaudevillians as well as for his family and himself. He wrote comedy routines, sketches and songs, and he performed his own variation on the popular clog dance. During the first decade of the twentieth century, Cohan rose to become "The Man Who Owns Broadway," as he so aptly titled his 1909 musical play.

As a member of a family of vaudeville troupers and a devoted showman in his own right, Cohan spent his free time in theaters enjoying and studying vaudeville acts and the legitimate shows of the day. Biographers comment on the number of hours Cohan spent at baseball games, too; however, nowhere in their writings do they mention his attending a motion picture theater. Perhaps he shared the attitude of many vaudevillians and stage actors of the time that movies were a low class way to make a living. And so it was not until 1916 that Cohan, at age 38, signed a contract with Artcraft to star in a series of films.

In 1916, Cohan was at the height of his popularity on Broadway. *Variety* headed a front page story, "Geo. Cohan For Mayor." The article went on to state, "As evidence everywhere, of the popularity of George M. Cohan, it was again proposed that Mr. Cohan should run for mayor of New York."[1]

The Films Beckon

Little wonder he had a series of offers to join a film industry which was tapping such stage talents as John Barrymore, Fannie Ward, Douglas Fairbanks, Julian Eltinge and DeWolf Hopper. Samuel Goldfish was among those most anxious to sign him up for a picture deal. Goldfish had been chairman of the board of directors of Famous Players-Lasky, the corporate product of two large producing concerns which had merged in July, 1916. Goldfish seemed dissatisfied with the restructuring brought about by the merger, and he left for a business trip to California in August. "Goldfish Resigns"[2] read the *Variety* story heading by mid-September. Goldfish sold his holdings in Famous Players-Lasky and formed his own company with W. W. Hodkinson as a releasing corporation. Soon *Variety* printed the following:

> Around Times Square it has been common report for the past fort-night that Samuel Goldfish was closing a deal with Cohan & Harris for the screening of their plays, which would be released through a new chain of exchanges to be established by W.W. Hodkinson, late president of Paramount.[3]

The same article mentioned that George K. Spoor of Essanay had sent a representative, Joe Harris, to the offices of Cohan & Harris with a check for $100,000 down payment on the rights to film George M. Cohan's plays.

In his recent book on Goldwyn, Arthur Marx chronicles Goldfish's efforts to bring Cohan into his newly formed organization.

> By October 18 [1916], he was already negotiating feverishly to go into business with that triple-threat Yankee Doodle Dandy of Broadway, George M. Cohan. Under the terms of the proposed deal, they would form a motion picture company for the purpose of converting all of Cohan's stage hits to the screen. Cohan would star in the roles he created on the stage, and Sam would produce.
>
> It looked like a formidable combination—Cohan's writing and performing genius, Goldfish's producing and business know-how. But the deal fell apart in November, when Cohan insisted that the new company be called George M. Cohan Film Corporation.

Having been a behind-the-scenes figure in two companies, Sam
was in no mood to accept another self-effacing position. When mega-
lomaniacal Cohan refused to share the credit with Goldfish, Sam
quietly bowed out and went looking for partners elsewhere.[4]

After a series of rumors and false starts, Cohan signed a contract with
Artcraft in early November, 1916, to star in four of his own stage successes.
Reportedly, Artcraft paid Cohan $150,000 upon the signing of the contract as
an advance on his share of the pictures' profits, with a guarantee of $400,000.[5]

In January, 1917, Artcraft announced that the first of the Cohan photoplays
would be *Broadway Jones*, a typical Cohan concoction which opened September
23, 1912, at the Cohan Theatre, starring George and his parents Nellie and Jerry
Cohan. The play ran 176 performances, even though the critic from *Theatre
Magazine* judged the plot "so simple that it is almost juvenile. But Mr. Cohan is
a true observer of men and conditions, and applies the little comic and pathetic
touches of life in a way which makes his completed fabric something distinctly
vital and real."[6]

Marguerite Snow was cast as Cohan's leading lady. She was a five-year veteran of films who had distinguished herself in the role of Countess Zudora in the
popular serial *The Million Dollar Mystery*. Three other experienced film actors,
Crawford Kent, Russell Bassett and Ida Darling, were placed in featured roles.
Joseph Kaufman was named director.

In February, Cohan and the cast of *Broadway Jones* traveled south to Jacksonville, Florida, where the exteriors of the film were shot. There, Cohan was
entertained by J.E.T. Bowden, mayor of Jacksonville, in the roof garden dining
room of the Hotel Mason. Cohan was presented by the mayor with a large portrait in oils of himself.[7]

Meanwhile, interior sets were being constructed at the Cohan studio on
West Fifty-Sixth Street in Manhattan, and at the Fort Lee studio, carpenters
were hammering together an exact replica of the Hotel Knickerbocker lobby
for a key scene in the film. Unfortunately, the set designers did not take into
account the amount of lights it would take to make the hotel set bright enough
for the cameras. *The New York Dramatic Mirror* reported:

> Work on the initial George M. Cohan, Artcraft production, *Broad-
> way Jones*, had to be suspended due to the fact that practically all the
> principals in the cast were temporarily blinded from the powerful
> lights used in the big Knickerbocker Hotel lobby set. The first to
> become afflicted was George M. Cohan, who had to be led from the
> studio and journeyed to Atlantic City to join his wife and children
> for a short rest. He is rapidly recovering and expects to be back at
> the studio in a few days. Marguerite Snow, who plays opposite the

star, Crawford Kent and Ida Darling were among those compelled
to leave the studio, but it is expected that they will be able to resume
work shortly.[8]

Despite the setback in production, the picture was completed during the first
week in March and released as a six-reel feature on March 28, 1917.

Broadway Jones tells the story of a young man who is dissatisfied with the
slow, conventional methods his Uncle Andrew employs at the Chu-Chu Chewing Gum factory in Jonesville. Broadway travels to New York to see for the
first time the street after which he was nicknamed and there teams up with an
advertising man, Robert Wallace. Wallace introduces Broadway to Manhattan
nightlife, and Broadway decides to marry a wealthy widow, Mrs. Gerard, to get
hold of her fortune. Uncle Andrew falls ill, and his secretary Josie[9] journeys to
New York to bring Broadway home to Jonesville. Broadway and Josie fall in
love, but the arrival of Mrs. Gerard scares Jones into returning home alone. As
Broadway starts to search for Josie, his valet hands him a telegram which he
is too distraught to open. Later, he returns forlorn to his hotel where he finds
Wallace and the president of the gum trust. Broadway opens the telegram to
learn that his uncle has died and left him heir to the gum factory. The gum
trust president offers to buy him out for one million dollars, but Broadway
refuses. He returns to Jonesville to find a crowd of workers ready to wreck the
factory. Broadway takes control of the situation, hires Wallace to set up a major advertising campaign by which sales increase and the workers are pacified.
Then Mrs. Gerard arrives, and Broadway leaves her in the hands of his valet.
Josie and Broadway marry and visit the street after which he was named on
their honeymoon. There they are delighted to see a large neon sign advertising
Chu-Chu Chewing Gum.

The critics were pleased with the film and with Cohan in his first screen role.
Exhibitors Trade Review stated that the film "more than justifies the exuberant
prophesies of the members of the press agent brigade who worked so zealously
to herald the first film experiment made by the renowned American comedian
. . . The picture will also be welcomed by the friends and admirers of Director
Joe Kaufman as a lasting tribute to the skill and stagecraft of that gentleman. For
him, no less than the star, it marks a red letter day in screen history."[10]

The New York Dramatic Mirror critic wrote, "*Broadway Jones* is pure entertainment from start to finish and it starts from the first foot and finishes only
when the last reel is completely unwound . . . George M. Cohan proves the
breezy actor upon the screen that he is on the stage; he is overflowing with what,
in the lonesome latter days, we are want to term 'pep' . . . Cohan is essentially
rapid in his movements, but fortunately they do not appear too rapid on the
screen. All his engaging mannerisms, which are so great a part of his personality,

are apparent in the picture. He 'gets over' with the same *eclat* that has characterized his work in the legitimate."[11]

Variety critic "Jolo" admitted that opinions were mixed. He began his review, "Emerging from the 44th Street theatre Tuesday morning after the private showing of the screen adaptation of *Broadway Jones*, with George M. Cohan, the 'wise' film folks were divided in their opinions of the initial Cohan filming, but all were agreed that it was certain to draw like the proverbial porous plaster. *Variety*'s reviewer desires to cast his lot with the ayes. Not only that, but he wishes to go on record as making the unqualified assertion that the filmed *Broadway Jones*, with George Cohan, is one of the best—one of the very best—photoplay features ever produced."[12]

The Photo-Play Journal concurred with the attitude of the others. "George Cohan in his motion picture version of *Broadway Jones* deserves a hearty, unanimous reception from all fans. It is the occasion of the advent of a new screen star of the first magnitude."[13]

Cohan's stage shows were praised for the fast-paced, slangy dialog of the characters. It was this witty style of speech which often contributed to the success of plays that had less than substantial plots. According to *Exhibitors Trade Review*, "Prior to the showing of the attraction, fears were expressed by many film experts that the true Cohan flavor might be lost in its new environment, owing to the lack of the inimitable George's terse, trenchant sayings as delivered orally. These fears would in a measure have been realized had not the sub-titles possessed the real Cohanesque punch, and were evidently edited by the star himself."[14]

Other critics also commented on the fine use of subtitles. According to *The New York Dramatic Mirror*, "Exceptionally fine are the subtitles, which are in the Cohanesque style, to the point, colloquial, and quite often genuinely funny."[15] *Motography* added, ". . . the star's inimitable personality registers with smashing effect without the voice, which is largely made possible by subtitles that have the spontaneity of conversational repartee and the true Cohan touch of humor. . . ."[16]

The major critics were enthusiastic about Cohan, and it seems he should have been on his way to a full and long career in films. One of the few complaints wielded against the entertainer was that his pale blue eyes sometimes failed to register under the lights; however, the critic was quick to add that the condition was temporary and in no way impaired the star's performance. A grim boost to ticket sales came when America entered the War in April, 1917. Cohan's flag waving proved a good means of marketing the debut film performance of America's own Yankee Doodle Patriot. And it was in that month that Cohan published the song that was to become a World War I standard, "Over There."

Two weeks after the release of *Broadway Jones*, Cohan told an interviewer, "I like movies, I think they're great. I learned a lot of interesting things from my first Artcraft picture, *Broadway Jones*. I would like to produce a picture myself in order to handle the big crowds in the outdoor scenes. That must be great!"[17] In this statement may lay the key to Cohan's staying clear of the film industry throughout most of his career. Cohan liked being boss. He wrote, directed and starred in his plays; he was used to making the decisions. The structure of film-making in a major studio such as Artcraft may have focused on the star or direc-tor, but the members of the cast and crew worked as a team. Teams were only useful to Cohan in baseball games, and, even then, Cohan was usually captain. His desire to run the whole show was evident throughout his career, especially in his hesitancy to play the part of Nat Miller in Eugene O'Neill's drama *Ah, Wilderness*, in his arguments with Paramount over script changes in *The Phan-tom President* and in his refusal to cooperate with the song composing team of Rodgers and Hart in the musical stage presentation *I'd Rather Be Right*.

Although his debut film performance was receiving critical praise, Cohan still saw himself as an outsider in the moving picture business. "The pictures were made for fellows like Douglas Fairbanks," he remarked. "It's an outdoor game and Doug is an outdoor fellow—a typical American."[18] Whether an out-door or an indoor game, Cohan had to play. His contract bound him to con-tinue his work before the cameras, and *Seven Keys to Baldpate* was announced as Cohan's second film.

Seven Keys to Baldpate was an excellent choice for his second screen effort. It had been a big success when it opened in the Astor Theatre in New York City on September 22, 1913, with Wallace Eddinger in the lead role. Cohan had based the mystery farce upon a story by Earl Derr Biggers. The play was filled with satirical jabs against political corruption, fast-paced comedy dialog, absurd but interesting characters and lightweight suspense which kept it running for 320 performances.

Shooting began in early June under the direction of Hugh Ford at the Fifty-Sixth Street studio in New York City. In the cast were Anna Q. Nilsson who had previously been starred in the *Who's Guilty* serial, Elda Furry (Mrs. DeWolf Hopper and later known as Hedda Hopper), Corrine Uzzell and Joseph Smiley. Walter E. Greene, president of Artcraft, stated the reason for rushing into a second Cohan feature so soon after the release of the first:

> Although we had not intended to start the second Cohan-Artcraft
> picture until a later date, the many requests from exhibitors for this
> production in the near future, as a result of the sensational success
> of his first film, *Broadway Jones*, have prompted Mr. Cohan and
> Artcraft to stage this subject immediately. Few stars of the stage have
> ever registered such an immediate hit among patrons of the screen as
> the popular actor-author-producer evinced in his first film offering.[19]

And it may have been that Cohan was eager to fulfill the demands of his contract as soon as possible in order to get back into stage work.

To satisfy the demands of the Artcraft people to keep in the public eye, Cohan took advantage of his Yankee Doodle Dandy image to present an American ambulance to the Red Cross in Russia as a gift from Hiram Abrams. All publicity for the patriotic offering was coupled with press notices on the production of *Seven Keys to Baldpate.*

The second Cohan feature was not released until early September, 1917; however, as early as July 14, critic Pete Schmid was acclaiming the film as meaning "more to the motion picture world than probably any production that has been released this season."[20] Schmid lists the reasons for his bold statement as being "the greatly desired character and personality of George M. Cohan to filmland" and "a new type of story . . . a farce of the most humorous variety and yet it is deeply mysterious and thrilling." Admittedly, the play has a humorous and absorbing plot, but this writer finds it difficult to recognize the "deeply mysterious and thrilling" content of the play. Perhaps those qualities are the result of Mr. Cohan's electric performance: they do not come from reading the script.

The play relates the twenty-four hour adventure of Billy Magee, a successful author of action novels written for popular consumption. Magee bets his publisher, Bentley, that he is able to complete a novel in twenty-four hours, and then, under Bentley's orders, he goes to the Baldpate Inn, a resort hotel deserted on account of its seasonal appeal. There he will have the quiet needed to concentrate on his writing. Throughout the night, strange events occur, all of which fall contrary to his belief that he is the only person to have a key to the Baldpate Inn. Crooked politicians, a newspaper woman and her aunt, a hermit with a distrust for mankind in general, a corrupt police official are among those who enter with keys of their own. $200,000 is stolen from the safe, removed from the inn, returned to the inn and then thrown into the fire. People are tied up, shot and chased all during the night into the morning. And there is even time for Magee to fall in love with the newspaper woman whose name—in the true Cohan tradition—is Mary. At the end of the story, it becomes evident that the events are set up actually by Bentley to prove to Magee the plausibility of his popular action novels. Magee has chronicled the events into a new book, and he wins the wager. The only event not staged by Bentley was Billy and Mary falling in love. So Billy wins the bet and the girl.

Reviews are not clear as to the extent the plot of the stage play was changed for the screen. One of the critics refers to the Cohan role as "George Washington Magee." The name change is quite likely as a way to appeal to a public actively involved in fighting the Great War.

The role of Magee was a natural for Cohan, and it is curious that he did not star in the play which he produced and directed for the Broadway stage in 1913. He cast Wallace Eddinger, an accomplished farceur, in the lead; however, as fate would have it, Eddinger and Cohan were involved in an automobile accident a few days prior to the opening.

Eddinger was too badly hurt to go on, so Cohan played the part of Magee on opening night. It was a part of which Cohan was particularly fond, and he played it again in May, 1935, at the National Theatre, New York City, in a Players Club revival.

If the critics were enthusiastic about Cohan's film debut, they were gushing over his second feature. *Motography* critic George W. Graves wrote,

> The thousands of admirers of the inimitable comedian all over the land will receive his second screen production with keener delight than the first . . .
>
> The star is freer and more natural in his second play. He seems to have become more sure of himself and of the camera's results . . .
>
> A star whose drawing power is not to be doubted for a moment, a play that is as full of 'pep' . . . hilarious fun from start to finish![21]

The remarks of the writer for *The Photo-Play Journal* are focused on the motion picture's superiority over the legitimate play, as proven by *Seven Keys to Baldpate.*

> What the increased latitude afforded by the camera didn't do to improve this play is not worth mentioning. A wonderful melodramatic, mystery farce has been changed into a super-wonderful one the minute the theme was removed from the limited confines of Stageland . . .
>
> In the role of George Washington Magee, . . . Mr. Cohan is right at home and he surpasses the excellent work he did in making his debut as an interpreter of the silent drama. *Seven Keys to Baldpate* is one of the choice salads of the present-day cinema menu which will cure mental indigestion and whet the appetite for optimism.[22]

At one point in the same review, the critic goes so far as to state that as good as the stage play was, "the screen version positively renders the erudite reviewer speechless when struggling desperately to find words to adequately describe it."

The New York Dramatic Mirror review credited all the actors and director for making *Seven Keys to Baldpate* "an ideal motion picture tale" and "an excellent production, in all departments."[23] Concurring with George W. Graves, this critic comments, "Cohan is far better in this picture than he was in his preceding production." Such statements indicate that Cohan's first performance may not have been as polished as the initial reviews implied. Having personally seen neither of the films, it would be over-stepping due bounds to conjecture. The sole complaint of these reviewers comes in the *Mirror* and concerns subtitles: "The one slip-up in the production is that the producers overlook an opportunity to increase the humor by using more lines from the play as titles. There are a number, but the picture could stand more."

Artcraft took a full-page advertisement in *The New York Dramatic Mirror* of September 1, 1917 (p. 2) which further played upon the patriotic conscience of the American public—especially, in this case, the exhibitor. The copy read, "George M. Cohan is a national character—a man every loyal American goes to see—regardless of the play—it's always good." Again, the patriotism which was linked to the American entry into the War was selling Cohan to the public. Frankly, this writer feels that the star and his feature probably would have been popular if there had been no patriotic image tie-in. Looking back from today's standards, the tactics of promoting Cohan through his "Grand Old Flag" image seems questionable—even for moving picture press agentry; however, in view of the patriotic spirit which was so prevalent in 1917, the method of advertising is understandable.

Hit-The-Trail Holliday was the next Cohan stage play to be picturized. It had had a long and successful run at the Astor Theatre in 1915 and 1916, starring Cohan's brother-in-law, Fred Niblo. The project was announced in mid-March, 1918, a time when all of America was singing the Cohan song "Over There." The song had become the most celebrated music of the War and had added to the popularity of the flag-toting song and dance man. To appeal to the current fervor of the populace, Cohan updated the story of *Hit-The-Trail Holliday*, a comedy spoof of Billy Sunday's fight for prohibition, to include many references to the War. To assure a high quality film adaptation, Artcraft hired Anita Loos, perhaps the wittiest scenario writer of the silent film period, and her husband John Emerson to write the script. Marshall Neilan, a prestige director who had completed a series of Mary Pickford movies, was chosen to direct. Alfred Green, formerly a Selig director, was named Neilan's assistant so that he might become acquainted with the Lasky lighting techniques. As before, shooting took place in the Fifty-Sixth Street studio in New York City. If ever the time was right for a George M. Cohan film, this was the time. For now, even more than before, Cohan stood high in the opinion of the public as a living symbol of American patriotism. By combining the American cause with the question of prohibitionism—a problem being talked about by many at the time, Cohan seemed to be making a surefire box office hit.

According to the plot of the play, a bartender of great renown named Holliday decides to stop serving hard drinks and links himself with a small-town temperance group. He talks a number of the townspeople into accepting prohibition at a large meeting and decides to travel to other towns to save those who are tempted by "booze." Holliday learns of a hotel keeper, Burr Jason, who has come up with a drink to take the place of whiskey. He boosts the drink to fame and fortune and then marries the hotel keeper's daughter Edith. Together, they preach the prohibitionist creed—even on their honeymoon.

The New York Dramatic Mirror implied the extent to which the play was modified to appeal to the public spirit:

> *Hit-The-Trail Holliday* had been brought up to date for the picturegoers. It boasts pro-Germans and an American flag and the first stanza of the 'Star-Spangled Banner.' These things were not found in the original work, but then, as a play, Mr. Holliday existed before the United States was at war, and Mr. Cohan, always up to the minute and with a decided hankering for the Stars and Stripes anyway, has brought them along to hit Mr. Holliday's trail of pro-hibs.
>
> This extensive use of the flag and Fourth of July fireworks has added to the original story, but in no way interferes with the forceful plea for trailhitters for prohibition. Some of the subtitles are decidedly amusing. The personality of Mr. Cohan dominates throughout the picture and he puts his accustomed 'pep' into his characterization. As a whole, *Hit-The-Trail Holliday* provides excellent screen entertainment.[24]

Variety's "Jolo" remarked that "The Star registered excellently, and is supported by an admirable company of players."[25] Margaret Clayton played the part of Edith Jason. She had worked in pictures for six years for various companies including Essanay and Paralta in such films as *Prince of Graustark*, *The Great Divide*, and *Inside the Lines*. Russell Bassett, who had appeared with Cohan in his first film, played Burr Jason and Pat O'Malley, a well-known silent screen actor, enacted the role of Kent B. Wurst (a prohibitionist from the sound of the name!). And, at an early stage in his film career, Richard Barthelmess took the part of Bobby Jason.

As to *Variety*'s reaction to the use of the national anthem, "Jolo" mentioned "the interpolation of 'The Star Spangled Banner,' necessitating the rising during its rendition by the orchestra."[26]

None of the reviews treat *Hit-The-Trail Holliday* with as much enthusiasm as they did his previous two efforts. The major focuses of the reviews are on the additions to the play to make the story appeal to war-conscious Americans and one particular scene which was shot in the New York City subway system. Since few films at the time had been shot in the subway, the press agents played up the situation as a good production news release:

An attempt was made to photograph some subway scenes, but such a large crowd gathered at the Fiftieth Street station to see Cohan that it was impossible to work. Arrangements have now been made with the Interborough Company to take these scenes at two o'clock in the morning some day next week.[27]

"Jolo" was quite taken by the subway scene:

. . . there were a number of human touches such as a trip uptown on the subway, the stopping at the vending machine for a piece of gum, which strikes home to New Yorkers, if not, to picture patrons in other communities.[28]

Second Thoughts about Films

In June, 1918, Artcraft bought a full-page advertisement in *Exhibitors Trade Review* to promote George M. Cohan Productions, Artcraft Pictures. The advertisement speaks of the Series of 1918–1919—Three New Artcraft Pictures and continues:

George M. Cohan's new Artcraft Productions will be based upon his most famous stage successes and will contain the same quality and the same popular appeal that has made *Hit-The-Trail Holliday* such a money-maker for the exhibitor.

The new George M. Cohan Artcraft pictures will be released at intervals of seventeen weeks.[29]

The advertisement ends with a listing of his three completed films with the phrase, "Now booking."

This advertisement suggests that Cohan was going to continue to star in filmed versions of his own plays. Five months later, the Screen Gossip column of *Picture-Play Magazine* announced:

George M. Cohan has been reengaged by Paramount-Artcraft to do at least three more feature pictures. It is rumored along the New York Rialto that the three productions in which the 'Yankee Doodle Boy' will be featured are *Little Johnny Jones, The Yankee Prince,* and *Forty-Five Minutes from Broadway,* all of which are nationally famous and have already shown their box-office appeal.[30]

Cohan never appeared in any further filmizations of his works. In fact, he did not make another film until 1932. Was it because he disliked filmmaking, or was it because the film audiences failed to show the enthusiasm for the entertainer that the Broadway stage audiences continued to show? Although the majority of critics liked Cohan's film performances, *Photoplay Magazine*'s Shadow Stage columnist has a different, perhaps more candid, view of Cohan's film career to date:

> Why, for instance, does that master of almost everything, George M. Cohan, fail to get across on the screen? When he made *Broadway Jones*, we were all delighted—he had transferred his snap, speed, and Americanism to celluloid, and he needed only a play or two to fully arrive. *Seven Keys to Baldpate* was a good surprise melodrama, yet, as an embodiment of Cohan, it didn't even come up to *Broadway Jones*. And *Hit-The-Trail Holliday*, save as a Bevo advertisement, was quite inefficient.[31]

In summing up Cohan's silent film career (it is the only mention of his Artcraft work in the book!), biographer John McCabe writes:

> Cohan made three movies of his plays, *Broadway Jones*, *Seven Keys to Baldpate* and *Hit-The-Trail Holliday*, principally in a New York studio and all within seventy days. The experience did not impress him. The usual cinematic procedure of shooting the story out of sequence frustrated him and he said, 'I am stage-minded, not motion picture minded.'[32]

It is clear that McCabe has been negligent in his research; however, the Cohan quote is interesting. Cohan avoided films for the first fifteen years of the industry's development. Then, once becoming involved, he left the business after only two years and three pictures. During his motion picture career, Cohan kept close to the stage. With his partner, Sam H. Harris, Cohan produced seven stage shows, authored *The Cohan Review of 1918* starring Nora Bayes and Charles Winninger, and appeared in *Out There* in April 1918 to benefit the Red Cross. Before embarking upon a career in motion pictures, Cohan had written a sketch for the Friars Frolic of 1918 called *The Moving Picture Studio*. Whether it was a satire, this writer does not know. Two years after that, having personally been a part of the industry, Cohan included several biting references to the film business in his play *A Prince There Was*, which opened on December 24, 1918, at the Cohan Theatre with Cohan in the leading role.

Cohan seems to be taking revenge upon the moving picture industry in this play. The plot deals with Charles Martin, a wealthy idler. He meets Comfort, a little orphan girl, who helps him to regain his business and personal ambitions and introduces him to the woman with whom he falls in love. Cohan satirical pokes against film people and the industry throughout the play. One of the humorous characters in the play is a $5.00-a-day film actor named Short who is "all the time bragging about some swell place where he eats. I think he calls it the Autocrat Restaurant."[33] Also in the play is this conversation between Carruthers, a publisher, and Bland, Charles Martin's butler:

> Carruthers: Did you enjoy California, Bland?
>
> Bland: Oh, it's a delightful country, sir.
>
> Carruthers: Very hospitable people.
>
> Bland: Oh, yes, sir. I'd no idea that moving picture people were so nice.
>
> Carruthers: Didn't you meet anybody but moving picture people?
>
> Bland: We did on the way out and coming back, but not in California. [34]

In Act Two, the following conversation takes place in the parlor of a boarding house:

> Miss Vincent: Is Caruso in moving pictures?
>
> Short: Yes.
>
> Miss Prouty: How can he sing in moving pictures?
>
> Short: He can't, that's the trouble. It makes me sore as a pig when these grand opera stars and bum two dollar actors try to horn in on our game. Pictures is pictures, and any time a picture fan lays down his ten cents he wants his money's worth.[35]

This conversation may be a key to Cohan's attitude towards moving pictures. He is equating himself with Caruso—both of whom were tops in their respective fields of entertainment. And Cohan's bitter attitude towards the film audience is revealed here, too. He seems to be scorning anybody who feels he can judge that great George M. for the cost of a ten-cent ticket. Probably Cohan's glad to be out of films and back on the home territory of the boards of the Cohan Theatre.

It is important to mention that in the summer of 1919, Cohan became involved in the Actors' Strike, an event which was to leave its mark on the entertainer for the rest of his life. Cohan sided with the managers and made enemies of the majority of actors on and around his Broadway territory. He was made the focus of the actors' hatred and even was deposed as leader of the Friars. Never at any time after the strike did Cohan win back the appeal he had held up to mid-1919.

Later Film Career

At the end of August, 1919, *The Miracle Man*, directed by George Loane Tucker and featuring Lon Chaney in the role of the fake cripple, The Frog, opened as a Paramount-Artcraft film. Cohan had very little to do with this motion picture, and according to *The New York Times* review:

> At George M. Cohan's Theatre last evening there was shown for the first time in this city an uncommonly interesting photoplay, based on Frank L. Packard's story "The Miracle Man."[36] The program and announcements described it as a screen version of Cohan's own dramatization of that story, but that is either for purposes of courtesy or advertisement. As a matter of fact, the motion picture is derived directly from the book, and proves to be between four and five times as well made as the somewhat weak-kneed play which Mr. Cohan derived from the same source. It is far more interesting, more varied, more ingenious, more dramatic.[37]

Whether the beating that Cohan received in this review was the result of his stand in the Actors' Strike is a question. It is true that Cohan's stage version was a flop. The Artcraft film is quite interesting and filled with fine suspenseful scenes. The action is fast-paced, filled with emotion, and the drama is in no way "weak-kneed." Chances are the reviewer was giving an honest appraisal of the Cohan contribution—that is, the lack of it.

Forty-Five Minutes from Broadway was the next Cohan piece to be picturized. Arthur S. Kane produced the film which was released through First National in September, 1920. Charles Ray starred in what had been a noteworthy musical on Broadway in 1912, with Cohan in the featured spot. Joseph De-Grasse directed the film version.

The photoplay tells the story of Kid Burns, an ex-pugilist from the East Side of New York City. Kid gets a telegram from his friend Tom Bennett informing him he has inherited a fortune from his relative named Castleton in New Rochelle. He travels to New Rochelle and there meets Daniel Cronin who sold bad mining stocks to his benefactor. Cronin is guardian of Mary, the housemaid, and it is to Mary Cronin wishes Castleton had left his money. Meanwhile, Bennett arrives and tells Kid that he is in love with an ex-chorus girl named Flora Dora Dean. She turns up shortly with her mother, whom Kid believes is an adventuress. Meanwhile, Kid falls in love with Mary. Kid finds a will in the pocket of one of Castleton's dinner suits which leaves his entire estate to Mary, and Kid tells Mary of the discovery. That night, he and Mary happen upon Cronin and Mrs. Dean as they are attempting to rob the safe. Bennett, saddened by the truth that his loved one and her mother are crooks, sends them from the house. Kid and

Mary leave for New York City. On the way, Kid tells her he wishes she were poor again so he could ask her to marry him. To show where the girl's priorities are, Mary tears up the will.

The film was popular with critics and film audiences. According to one review, "Much of the slangy humor and snappy appeal for which the original was noted is preserved."[38]

When *Forty-Five Minutes from Broadway* opened at the Strand in Manhattan, the orchestra accompanied the film with musical selections from the original musical, including such Cohan standards as "So Long, Mary" and "Mary's A Grand Old Name." The critic for *Picture-Play Magazine* was less pleased than the other reviewers:

> In Ray's first ingredient production, one looks in vain for the usual Ray characterization, for the warmth and appeal of the [Julien] Josephson stories. George M. Cohan's erstwhile comedy with music, *Forty-Five Minutes from Broadway*, was no more appropriate for this star than it would be for Charles Chaplin.
>
> I believe that there are some persons who liked Ray in the Cohan piece . . . I can't enjoy Ray as Kid Burns any more than I could enjoy Chaplin as Macbeth.[39]

Another Cohan play was made into a film by Paramount. *A Prince There Was*, based on the 1918 stage play described previously in this paper, was released in early 1922, although it opened in New York City in November, 1921.[40] The script stayed close to the plot of the stage play with the additional plot twist that the girl with whom Charles Martin falls in love is actually the daughter of a man who was ruined by Martin's stockbroker. The need for this complication is questionable, and the story in general did not impress the critics. The *Variety* staffer, "Fred," was particularly put off by the film:

> If there is anyone anywhere that isn't able [to] tell the answer of *A Prince There Was* after the first few scenes are flashed on the screen then that person is ready to become an inmate of an asylum for the blind. As a play *A Prince There Was* was a hit while George M. Cohan played the title role; as a picture it becomes a very ordinary program feature, even though Thomas Meighan is starred in it. The fact that the production was turned out as a Paramount picture makes it all the more lamentable. By titling it might have been a picture worthwhile, but the titles are the most trite and matter of fact that have been screened in a feature intended for the better houses in some time.
>
> On the whole, the picture is far from being up to Paramount standard for production.[41]

By 1921, George M. Cohan had turned forty-three years of age. This is not particularly the age for a person to pass his prime in a career—unless the career is singing soprano in a boys' choir. But Cohan had been around for nearly forty years as a professional entertainer. His roots and influences lay in turn-of-the-century techniques and attitudes. His thoughts were cosmopolitan, in the sense of being Broadway oriented but quaint in that he never developed the fiber of post-war Jazz Age culture. He was caught in a bind: his plays tended not to appeal to New Yorkers because they were too naive for the new breed of Broadway sophisticates, and his plays tended not to appeal to smalltowners and middle Americans because they had too many allusions to the New York theater scene.

To briefly summarize Cohan's involvement with motion pictures between 1921 and 1932, when he next appeared in a movie, the following is a list of Cohan stage shows which were filmed: *The Lure of Jade* (1921), *Get-Rich-Quick Wallingford* (1921), *Little Johnny Jones* (1923), *The Meanest Man in the World* (1923), *George Washington, Jr.* (1924), *Seven Keys To Baldpate* (1925), *The Song and Dance Man* (1928), *Fast Company* (1929), *Little Johnny Jones* (1929) and *Seven Keys to Baldpate* (1929). The remaking of such titles as *Seven Keys to Baldpate* and *Little Johnny Jones* suggests that there were a few Cohan plays which assured good box office time and again. Cohan had very little to do with the making of any of these films, so it is needless to go into detail on any of them. Two features of the early sound period made use of Cohan songs. "Give My Regards to Broadway" cropped up in *The Broadway Melody* (1929), and "Over There" was sung in *The Cock-Eyed World* (1929). Besides collecting a royalty, Cohan bore no responsibility for their inclusion.

Biographer Ward Morehouse, who was a friend of Cohan, mentions that the entertainer signed with United Artists in 1928 "to write direct and produce—but not to act. His first picture was to be an original story with songs and to be written for Al Jolson. . . ."[42] Before Cohan began the project, he decided against returning to the film business and backed out of the contract.

One of the films listed above, *The Song and Dance Man*, may be worth discussion, if for no other reason than a reference print of reels three through seven exists at the Library of Congress. This film is an example of what *Variety's* "Fred" meant when he said the titles could have saved *A Prince There Was*. In *The Song and Dance Man*, the titles make the picture worth seeing. Herbert Brenon directed the film which stars Tom Moore and charming Bessie Love. Outstanding in this picture about Hap Farrell, a vaudevillian of limited talent whose girlfriend goes on to become a star and marry her producer's best pal, are the clever uses of intra-theatrical devices, slangy dialog and old vaudeville jokes which always spiced up the Cohan stage plays. Will the reader who has no patience for vaudeville one-liners and the like excuse the indulgence of reprinting a few of the more humorous titles from the film?

- When the cop asks the landlady (who looks like a madam in a bordello) how she can appear so prosperous when she runs a boarding house inhabited by unemployed actors, she answers, "Say, what is this, the trial scene from *Madame X*?"
- As the producers and Hap Farrell gather together to discuss putting the Bessie Love character into the show, the landlady says, "The Mystery Quartet will now sing 'Old Black Joe.'"
- Cop: I'd like to get a smile out of you before I go.
  Landlady: But you did. I laughed out loud when I first saw you.
- (After opening night) Cop: I waved to you from the orchestra. Didn't you see me?
  Landlady: I did notice a draft, at that.
- Stage director to Hap Farrell after his very poor audition: Say, boy, you're from Swift's—the original ham what am!
- Discussing the success of the first night of *The Girl from the Bronx*, the producer says, "At the second curtain, ticket speculators began crying for joy."

These are the Broadway-oriented jokes on which Cohan built his successful career, and, whether they work out of context or not, they manage to give *The Song and Dance Man* a boost of energy.

In the summer of 1932, Cohan signed a contract with Paramount to star in *The Phantom President*, a musical comedy in which he would make his sound film debut. Morehouse best describes the situation surrounding the production of the film:

> In 1932, Cohan again signed with Hollywood. This time he actually went through with it. He went to the Coast, stayed for a time, made one talking picture (*The Phantom President*), and returned to New York quite unhappy about the entire experience. He kept his sense of humor about it.
>
> I spent several hours with him at his new home, 993 Fifth Avenue, when he had been back only a few days. Hollywood was on his mind, he wanted to talk about it, and he cut loose: 'If you want the truth, kid, I can only say that my Hollywood experience was the most miserable I have ever had in my life, I don't see how I lived through it. Another half hour and I would have gone crazy. I wouldn't go back there again for Rockefeller's money.
>
> . . . Those fellows didn't know anything about me. Lot of them had never heard of me and didn't care about being told. On the level, kid, Hollywood to me represents the most amazing exhibition of incompetence and ego that you can find anywhere in the civilized world. From all I could make out the only people with any sense are

the technical boys and the camera men. Those camera men saved my
life. When I left I thanked them for a million laughs. I didn't say
goodbye to any of the executives. Couldn't find them. They were
away on weekends' . . . [43]

The Morehouse report checks out with the stories appearing at the time in
Variety. According to one of the Inside Stuff—Pictures column, Cohan drove
up to the studio entrance on the first day, only to be turned away by an assistant
director who informed him the parking lot he was approaching was meant for
use only by "big and important stars."[44] The next day, he was refused entrance
by a doorman because he didn't have a pass. Later in the shooting schedule,
Cohan learned that the dialog he had been asked to write had been changed and
that as a stage person he had no understanding of how a film should be written.
Furthermore, Cohan insisted the film be completed by September 1; however,
Cohan balked when presented with the reality of night work. To complicate
matters, Cohan's wife Agnes was hospitalized for more than two weeks during
the shooting with kidney trouble.

Another factor of the production rubbed Cohan against his grain. Richard
Rodgers and Lorenz Hart were hired to write the score, something which Cohan
had been told he would compose in part. Rodgers and Hart had become prominent over the past several years, and Cohan considered them upstarts. Again, this
situation is another example of Cohan, the auteur, wanting to appear only in his
own creations. To take further control away from the entertainer, Paramount
went so far as to take Rodgers and Hart off the Jolson picture they were preparing at the time (*The New Yorker*, later titled *Hallelujah, I'm a Bum!*) in order to
have them supervise the recording of their numbers in *The Phantom President*.[45]

Ironically, while the belittling of Cohan continued at Paramount, West
Coast groups were giving him testimonial dinners to pay tribute to the grand
old man of songwriting. One such dinner was given at the Ambassador Hotel in
Los Angeles, and another at the Cocoanut Grove which was attended by 1,500
people, including Al Jolson who sang for the guests. *Variety* noted that the guest
of honor had to leave early to get up in time to comply with an early shooting
schedule.[46]

Cohan's disgust over the filming became most evident when, prior to the
New York City opening at the Paramount Theater, he refused to make personal
appearances for the two-week run of the film. "It was said that Cohan could have
written his own ticket for the Par[amount] date."[47]

The New Yorker, in reviewing *The Phantom President*, found Cohan's performance "lively and agreeable" but thought little of the film: "If most of the first
half of *The Phantom President* had been clipped and cut to nothing, this latest
outgrowth of *Of Thee I Sing* might have been pretty good fun."[48]

The New York Times was impressed with both the film and its star, "notwithstanding the acrimony that burst forth intermittently between George M. Cohan and Paramount Studio officials during the filming. . .".[49] The review continues by calling the film "a crackerjack show" and "a vehicle admirably suited to Mr. Cohan who . . . has the opportunity to sing, dance, and be as blithe as he has been in many of his stage shows."

Perhaps the candid review of *Variety*'s "Sid" best sums up the work of Cohan in this movie:

> For Cohan it suffices to say that this is his first picture [sic] and maybe his last. For pictures such as these, light and frothy, he brings nothing to the screen which it hasn't already at hand and other than the pomp and circumstance which the publicity can whip up around a traditional stage name his value here will mostly be provocatively sentimental as regards the old timers.
>
> Allowing that it may be heresy in the era of those who remember, it nevertheless appears that this picture will do much to definitely establish that Cohan belongs to another generation. Love interest is not for him, and the embarrassment caused thereby may have done much to impede an otherwise carefree and, for the audience, an enjoyable performance.[50]

The review highly praises Jimmy Durante's comical contributions and regards Claudette Colbert's presence as "wasted in another inconsequential role."

The reviewers were pleased with the Rodgers and Hart score, but it is interesting that no attention was paid to director Norman Taurog.

The New York City run did big business. Between $72,000 and $75,000 was taken in during the first week, despite the Jewish high holy days which occurred on Friday and Saturday of that week. Other cities did poor business with the film. Buffalo, Detroit and Kansas City did poor business. In cities such as Baltimore, the film appealed to a limited crowd which brought good business to a small house.[51] In Boston, business "sagged badly during last days."[52]

Cohan did not return to films. Over the years, the list of Cohan plays made into films lengthened to include the following: *The Miracle Man* (1932), *Gambling* (1934), *Seven Keys to Baldpate* (1935), *The Song and Dance Man* (1936),[53] *Times Square Playboy* (1936), *Cowboy Quarterback* (1939), *Ladies Must Live* (1940), *Little Nellie Kelly* (1940), *The Meanest Man in The World* (1942) and, again, *Seven Keys to Baldpate* (1947). Cohan did not take an active part in any of these productions, with the exception of *Gambling*, which he may have supervised.[54]

Yankee Doodle Dandy has done more to keep the memory of George M. Cohan alive than any of his plays or films, any history book or statue. The script was checked carefully by Cohan, and he designed the scenario to leave out details of his life such as his first marriage to Ethel Levey which ended in divorce, his nightmarish involvement in the Actors' Strike of 1919 and many sides of his career which he chose to forget—including all of his film projects. His daughter Georgette commented, "That's the kind of a life daddy would have liked to have lived."[55]

Cohan saw the film in a screening room just as it was completed, and later in his home in Monroe, New York, according to both his biographers. Cohan, the critics and audiences were happy with the film. James Cagney seemed to be everyone's ideal Yankee Doodle Dandy. The film opened in late October, 1942, at the Hollywood Theater in Manhattan. Cohan was very ill, but he convinced his nurse to accompany him on a last tour of the theater district. He and the nurse stopped in at the Hollywood Theater and watched part of *Yankee Doodle Dandy* without being noticed. Soon after, on November 4, 1942, Cohan died.

Cohan never really liked working in moving pictures. Whether it was an anti-film attitude which evolved from his boyhood as a vaudevillian or whether it was the lack of auteurist control he was able to have over a project, the fact remains that he often ran fast from film contracts. It is ironic that such a legend of the American theater has been recorded through *Yankee Doodle Dandy* in the memories of the current generation via a medium which he shunned in the latter part of his life. Cohan was a leading contributor to the vaudeville and musical comedy heritages. He is a very small part of the American film heritage, but his contributions are sound, and his film works should be made available for further analysis.

Notes

1. *Variety* June 16, 1916, p. 1.
2. Ibid. September 15, 1916, p. 22.
3. *Variety* November 3, 1916, p. 21.
4. Marx, Arthur, *Goldwyn*, W.W. Norton & Company, Inc., New York, 1976, p. 71.
5. *Variety* November 10, 1916, p. 22.
6. McCabe, John; *George M. Cohan: The Man Who Owned Broadway,* Doubleday & Company. Inc., Garden City, New York, 1973, p. 120.
7. *Motography* February 24, 1917, p. 408.
8. *The New York Dramatic Mirror* February 24, 1917, p. 31.
9. Cohan's sister Josie was unable to join her family in the cast of the Broadway stage version in 1912, so Cohan named the love interest in her honor.
10. *Exhibitors Trade Review* March 31, 1917, p. 1180.

11. *The New York Dramatic Mirror* March 31, 1917, p. 26.

12. *Variety* March 23, 1917, p. 22.

13. *The Photo-Play Journal* April, 1917. p. 33.

14. *Exhibitors Trade Review* March 31, 1917, p. 1180.

15. *The New York Dramatic Mirror* March 31, 1917, p. 26.

16. *Motography* April 7, 1917, p. 743.

17. *The New York Dramatic Mirror* May 10, 1917, p. 31.

18. Ibid.

19. *The New York Dramatic Mirror* June 16, 1917, p. 31.

20. Ibid. July 14, 1917, p. 18.

21. *Motography* September 22, 1917, p. 630.

22. *The Photo-Play Journal* September, 1977, p. 30.

23. *The New York Dramatic Mirror* September 8, 1917, p. 18.

24. Ibid. June 22, 1918, p. 888.

25. *Variety* June 14, 1918, p. 29.

26. Ibid.

27. *The New York Dramatic Mirror* April 13, 1918 page number not noted.

28. *Variety* June 14, 1918, p. 29.

29. *Exhibitors Trade Review* June 29, 1918 unnumbered advertising section page.

30. *Picture-Play Magazine* December, 1918. p. 293.

31. *Photoplay Magazine* November, 1918, p. 106.

32. McCabe, p. 136.

33. Line spoken by Comfort in *A Prince There Was* by George M. Cohan, p. 22 of script.

34. Ibid. pp. 11–12.

35. Ibid. p. 29.

36. The Packard story on which *The Miracle Man* is based is actually titled "None So Blind."

37. *The New York Times* August 27, 1919, p. 9.

38. *Exhibitors Trade Review* September 11, 1920, p. 1619.

39. *Picture-Play Magazine* December, 1920, p. 52.

40. *The American Film Institute Catalog: Feature Films* 1921–30, p. 618.

41. *Variety* November 18, 1921, p. 43.

42. Morehouse, Ward; *George M. Cohan, Prince of the American Theater*, J.B. Lippincott Company, Philadelphia, New York, 1943, p. 180.

43. Morehouse, pp. 185–6.

44. *Variety* September 27, 1932, p. 6.

45. Ibid. August 23, 1932, p. 3.

46. *Variety* August 30, 1932, p. 3.

47. Ibid. September 27, 1932, p. 3.

48. *The New Yorker* October 8, 1932, p. 61.

49. *The New York Times* October 1, 1932 page number not noted.

50. *Variety* October 4, 1932, p. 15.

51. Ibid. October 11, 1932 under Picture Grosses.

52. *Variety* October 18, 1932 under Picture Grosses.

53. Bosley Crowther, (*The New York Times*, March 12, 1936, p. 18) found the plot "about as contemporaneous as a Pat Rooney buck and wing, or a Keith-Albee painted perspective of the little Trianon."

54. McCabe, p. 229.

55. Morehouse, p. 229.

Boris Karloff

AN AFFECTIONATE MEMOIR OF
THE GENTLEMAN OF TERROR

DeWitt Bodeen

Originally appeared in vol. 7, no. 2 (March/April 1983)

Boris Karloff's first screen appearance is listed in most of his filmographies as a Douglas Fairbanks feature comedy *His Majesty, the American* (1919), for which he worked as a $5-a-day extra in 1919. He once admitted, however, that the first time he appeared before the camera was as an extra in a Frank Borzage film at Universal, and records indicate that he may have appeared as early as 1916 as an extra in Lois Weber's *The Dumb Girl of Portici*, starring Anna Pavlova, also released by Universal. Heaven knows how many other film appearances he may have made, but it is generally acknowledged that his first important role was in 1920 when he played with Blanche Sweet as Jules Borney, a villainous French-Canadian trapper, in *The Deadlier Sex*, released by Pathé.

He continued playing other supporting parts—heavies and downright villains—throughout the silent era. He was a murderous Indian in Maurice Tourneur's *The Last of the Mohicans* (1920), and the following year he was to be seen as the arch villain Ahmed Khan in a moving version of Kipling's *Without Benefit of Clergy*. Throughout the twenties his name appears on cast sheets at Hollywood film studios, and several times he managed to get parts in plays being performed in Los Angeles. On one occasion he managed to snare the role of Ned Galloway, a convict trusty forced to do murder, in Martin Flavin's play, *The Criminal Code*. So outstanding was he that when Howard Hawks directed a film version of that play in 1931, Karloff was chosen to play the same role before the camera.

He had made his first talkie in 1929 at Fox in *Behind That Curtain* playing an Oriental—not the lead role—but as support to Warner Baxter and Lois Moran. It was not until his twentieth appearance in a talking feature that he made a real bid for stardom in a non-talking role, playing Frankenstein's Monster in *Frankenstein*. Originally, Bela Lugosi had been cast in the part, but he turned it down because the Monster was mute. When James Whale took over the production as director, he espied Karloff in the Universal Studio commissary, and persuaded him to test for the role. Karloff got the part, and it made him a star.

Lon Chaney had befriended him at one time, and had advised him to look for a role that was truly unusual. "Find something no one else can or will do—and they'll begin to take notice of you. Hollywood is full of competent actors. What the screen needs is individuality." Karloff remembered Chaney's words, and with the help of makeup man, Jack Pierce, he made the Monster both unforgettable and entirely sympathetic.

For *Frankenstein* he held a nonexclusive contract at Universal, and he made such films as *Scarface* for Caddo/Howard Hughes and the talkie remake of *The Miracle Man* at Paramount, before Universal realized that his name meant money at the box office, and he was starred with his name above the title—KARLOFF in *The Old Dark House*, in which he does not really have a starring role, but plays the brooding, dangerous menace named Morgan. It was the second time he worked for director James Whale, who believed in him as an actor.

The man who became world-famous as Boris Karloff was born in Dulwich, a suburb of London, on November 23, 1887. He was the youngest son of a very large family, with one sister and seven older brothers. His real name was William Henry Pratt, and it was not until he entered the theatre as an actor that he changed his name, choosing "Karloff," which had been his mother's family name, and "Boris" because it seemed to go with the surname. He had always been fascinated by the theatre since he played his first role, the Demon King in *Cinderella*, a Christmas pantomime. His family discouraged his acting ambition, and pressured him to study for the consular service. He was completely disinterested in a diplomatic career, and his first term reports revealed that he attended more plays than classes. "I was becoming a disgrace to the family name," he once said. "In those days, black sheep in England went to Canada or Australia." He flipped a coin, and it was Canada for him. He sailed from Liverpool to Ontario in May, 1909, with the idea of learning farming, but he didn't stick with that for long. As Boris Karloff, actor, he journeyed west to Kamloops in British Columbia, where he joined the Ray Brandon Players. When that troupe was forced to disband in Saskatchewan because a cyclone struck the town, he was able to join the Harry St. Clair Players. With them during a run of 53 consecutive weeks in Minot, North Dakota, he played 106 parts; he was a quick study, and played leads in such favorites of the day as *Way Down East, Paid in Full, East Lynne,* and *Charley's Aunt.* He learned his craft of acting by acting, and eventually joined Billie Bennett's road company of *The Virginian,* which took him as far west as Los Angeles, where he managed not only to get further stock engagements, but he was not above unloading and loading trucks. What he liked best was film work, and he picked up extra work, which gradually led to bits and finally, in 1920, with *The Deadlier Sex,* actual supporting parts, usually heavies. In 1923 he married a dancer, Helene Vivian Soule, but that marriage lasted only five years. Shortly after the advent of talkies, his career quickened, and he married a second time after he had appeared on the stage in *The Criminal Code*. She was Dorothy Stine, a children's librarian, and by her he fathered a daughter—his only child—named Sara Jane.

Meanwhile, his career as a film star was booming, and not only at Universal, which held him by contract. For Universal he starred in *The Mummy*, of which the *Los Angeles Times* critic said that it beggared description, adding that "It is one of the most unusual talkies ever produced." Universal, however, refused to up his salary, so he left Hollywood to make *The Ghoul* in England for Gaumont-British. Cedric Hardwicke was prominently cast; it was Ralph Richardson's first film credit; and it proved to be one of Karloff's best roles.

Returning to Hollywood in 1934, he made *The Lost Patrol* for John Ford at RKO Radio, and it still stands as one of Ford's most effective pictures. In freelancing, he also appeared that year for United Artists as the anti-Semitic Baron Ledrantz in the lavish production of *The House of Rothschild*, which starred George Arliss. Realizing the gold mine they had let slip away from them, Universal retaliated by offering a new and more favorable contract, and Karloff's first top billing over Bela Lugosi in a picturization of Edgar Allan Poe's *The Black Cat*. The real bait, however, was the chance to work for a third time with director James Whale as the star of *The Bride of Frankenstein*, an ingenuous screenplay with a prologue involving Mary Shelley, Lord Byron, and Percy Shelley showing how Mary re-created the Monster, who had presumably been burned in the mill fire that closed the original film of *Frankenstein*. Considering that that was far from the finale Mary Shelley used in her novel, it is nonetheless effective on the screen, and Karloff's interpretation of the Monster had great pathos, while Elsa Lanchester—as the bride who is created for him and comes to life in an electrifying thunderstorm—is wonderfully effective. It is the best and most effectively realized of the *Frankenstein* pictures.

There was one more, however, in the series in which Karloff was revived as the Monster, *Son of Frankenstein* (1939). Universal not only had Karloff in his original role, but made use importantly of Basil Rathbone, Bela Lugosi, and Lionel Atwill. One of the best features Karloff made, however, was on a loan-out to Columbia for *The Black Room*, in which he played twin brothers—one good, the other evil. It is all Victorian Gothic, handsomely made on a small program picture budget, and far more worthy of Karloff's presence than others in his film list.

He made an effective period horror picture, *Tower of London*, in which he played Mord, the royal executioner. It dealt with historical facts somewhat in a Grand Guignol way, but this was set in the time of Richard III, the murder of the little princes in the Tower, and the drowning of Clarence in a huge wine vat. Extravagance suited the story, for much of it was a bloodbath.

Karloff hesitated when he was approached about making his Broadway debut in Joseph Kesselring's murderous comedy, *Arsenic and Old Lace*, but he realized then that the role of the homicidal brother, Jonathan Brewster, was not a starring part. The two old aunts, he conceded, "were the stars of the show. My part was simply mustard on a plate of good roast beef." *Arsenic and Old Lace* had its Broadway opening at the Fulton Theatre on January 10, 1941, and was an instant hit, running for more than 1400 performances. It made a fortune for its producers, Lindsay and Crouse. For the first time also, Karloff was in the money, for he was not only commanding a weekly salary of $2,000, but at the suggestion of his producers, he had invested $6,000 in the production, and subsequently gained that sum back with enormous profits over the years.

I first met Karloff at this time and found him a charming man, almost shy, certainly gentle. I met him through Judith Evelyn, a very good friend of mine, who was enjoying, like him, her first appearance on Broadway as the star of *Angel Street*. Those were the years of World War II, and theatre audiences relaxed in a play like *Arsenic and Old Lace* where murder was treated lightly with good humor, and they loved the tight suspense of a Victorian melodrama like *Angel Street* (called *Gaslight* on the screen), wherein a greedy husband tries to drive his wife mad.

The theatre frequently became home to Karloff, and after two distinguished failures *(The Linden Tree* and *The Shop at Sly Corner)*, he again enjoyed real success with the 1950 revival of J. M. Barrie's *Peter Pan*, opposite Jean Arthur as Peter, and with music and lyrics by Leonard Bernstein. Karloff played Mr. Darling, father of the children, as well as Captain Hook, the villainous Pirate King. I remember that children, attending matinees, crowded backstage, where Karloff willingly signed autographs and let the children try on the hook he wore on one hand if they could respond in the affirmative to his query, "Did you clap for Tinker Bell?" which, of course, they all admitted freely.

Val Lewton starred Karloff in three features—the last three Lewton made for RKO—*The Body Snatcher* (1945); *Isle of the Dead* (1945); and a genuine masterpiece of terror, *Bedlam* (1946). I was then a contract writer at RKO, and had written three films for Val—*Cat People, Seventh Victim,* and *Curse of the Cat People*. I renewed my acquaintance with Karloff when Val reintroduced me to him, and I was often on the sets of his pictures for he was a kindhearted, well-spoken gentleman with a lovely sense of humor.

It was pity that only *The Body Snatcher* was a genuine critical and artstic moneymaker. RKO went through some executive changes and *Bedlam*, the last of the Lewton films, and one of my own favorites, was sloughed off in its initial release by the front office and not acknowledged as the masterpiece it was—and is now accredited to be.

Karloff made a final appearance on Broadway as the sympathetic Bishop Cauchon in Jean Anouilh's *The Lark,* adapted by Lillian Hellman and starring Julie Harris as Joan of Arc. He regarded it as the "first solid, successful, serious acting part" he had done on Broadway.

In 1946, while he was acting on Val Lewton productions he was divorced from his second wife, and he then married Evelyn Hope Helmar, who had once been a story assistant to David O. Selznick. He worked a great deal in television, and came to prefer it to playing in movies. He nevertheless made a great number of pictures, including one for Cecil B. DeMille, *Unconquered,* in which he played with Gary Cooper and Paulette Goddard, as Chief Guyasuta, a treacherous Indian rebel. In 1959 he returned with his wife to live for good in London, saying "I'm home at last." He did return to America, however, for additional film roles, but London remained "home" for him. He died of a respiratory ailment at the King Edward Hospital in Midhurst, Sussex, in early February of 1969. He was then 81 years old.

Robert Redford

A LESSON IN "TAKING CHARGE"

John C. Tibbetts

Originally appeared in vol. 6, no. 1 (January/February 1982)

It shouldn't have come as a surprise to anyone when Robert Redford turned to directing in *Ordinary People*. The film garnered several Academy Awards, including Best Picture and Best Director. Redford's directorial debut can hold its own with many other noteworthy debuts in the history of American film—Welles with *Citizen Kane* and Lawrence Kasdan with *Body Heat* are only two examples of many that immediately come to mind. One has only to recall the wonderful sequences in *Ordinary People* involving the young boy (Timothy Hutton) and the psychiatrist (Judd Hirsch) to appreciate Redford's incisive and confident directorial style. As an actor, Redford was able to bring a sympathetic attitude to his handling of other actors; available reports from on the set confirm his relaxed approach with such pros as Hirsch, Donald Sutherland, and Mary Tyler Moore.

Redford's directing ambitions should come as no surprise because Redford as a man and as an actor has always demonstrated a fierce independence of mind. This is a man who has consistently shown that he is unwilling to fall into stereotypes and molds; at the same time, he has always sought control over his own lifestyle and his work in films. A brief survey of his career proves the point. He was born in Santa Monica, California in 1937. His early years were filled with a wide variety of pursuits—sports, painting and sketching, and a taste for adventure. His earliest recollections were of the shame of Hollywood—the artificial sets and backdrops that seemed to him so false when juxtaposed against the real locales of the area. Things in the movies were not real, the youthful Redford noted; how could he take that world very seriously? There were years spent on the streets—racing hotrods and street fights were part and parcel of his daily life. After graduating in 1955 he did not choose to remain on those "mean streets"; rather, his wanderlust took him outdoors for skiing, hiking, and even a stint working in the oil fields. He lived by his wits for over a year in Europe, committing violent images to canvas, filching meals from the Parisian vegetable markets.

In a word, he lived and painted as he chose, free of the dictates of universities and art schools. All in all, it must have been one of those periods we all seek in our youth—those "palmy days" where living is lean, meals are scarce, yet where the blood is active and ambitions are still to be tested and proven.

Back in America, he married Lola Jean Van Wagenen (now an activist for Consumer Action Now) and made his first forays into the strange yet fascinating world of acting. After experience in two Broadway plays, *Tall Story* and *The Highest Tree*, he left for California for his first motion picture *War Hunt* (1962). Small roles were soon succeeded by major parts, and with *Inside Daisy Clover* and *The Chase* (1962 and 1966, respectively) he came into critical prominence.

His film roles have consistently delineated a personality that is both sensitive and almost brusquely independent. As Private Roy Loomis in *War Hunt* he was an observer of the horrors of the Korean conflict. As Wade Lewis, in *Daisy Clover*, his portrayal of the homosexual actor was applauded for its freedom from stereotypes and postures. He was a distinctly nonconformist personality in *The Chase* (as Bubber Reeves, an escaped convict), *Downhill Racer* (as David Chappellet, a loner), *Little Fauss and Big Halsy* (as Big Halsy, a brash scoundrel), *Jeremiah Johnson* (as a solitary trapper thwarted in his desire to raise a family in the wilderness), *The Sting* (as Johnny Hooker, a green con artist learning the ropes), and *Waldo Pepper* (as a barnstorming pilot adrift in a world of violence and terrible beauty). Time and again he has turned down roles that seemed to offer only stereotypes. Periodically, he has left Hollywood, retreating to his home in Utah or to travels in Europe. Only worthwhile projects appealed to him—films about "specifically, intrinsically American guys, with their roots solidly in the American scene or tradition." Today, at the height of his success, he often speaks of being interested primarily in directing films about distinctly non-Hollywood kinds of subjects: "My goal is to retire from acting and produce and direct documentaries on the Indians and mountain men of the great American West."

These were not years spent in obtaining only a knowledge of the actor's craft; to the contrary, Redford was exposed to many of the finest film directors in America. For example, he worked under Robert Mulligan for *Daisy Clover*, for Arthur Penn in *The Chase*, for Jack Clayton in *The Great Gatsby*, for Michael Ritchie in *Downhill Racer* and *The Candidate*, for Abraham Polonsky in *Tell Them Willie Boy Is Here*, and for George Roy Hill in *Butch Cassidy and the Sundance Kid*, *The Sting*, and *The Great Waldo Pepper*. All of them, particularly Polonsky and Penn, have long been noted for their abilities to infuse a personal vision into their work. In what must be one of the toughest professions in the world, Redford learned that somewhere in the welter and complexity of film directing was a place for the individualist, the man dedicated to pursuing his own personal aims against almost impossible obstacles.

In turning to directing, Redford has followed in the footsteps of a long and honorable line of actors-turned-director. There are too many examples to mention, but a few may serve to emphasize the parallel. Erich von Stroheim and D. W. Griffith were both actors before they turned to the director's megaphone. Others from the silent period included William Wellman and Albert Parker (both of whom began as actors for Douglas Fairbanks before 1920). These men are known to us today primarily as directors; but others apportioned their duties more equally between acting and directing. There was Donald Crisp who directed Buster Keaton in *The Navigator* and made one of the first two-strip Technicolor films in 1929, called *The Viking*. One of the only women in the past to make the jump was Ida Lupino. At the same time she was appearing in films like Nicholas Ray's *On Dangerous Ground* (1952), she was also directing—*The Bigamist*, *Hard, Fast and Beautiful*, and *Outrage*. Since then, she has directed many television dramas (more recently, Lee Grant has duplicated this pattern). Certainly one of the most impressive debuts as director in recent years was Charles Laughton's production of *The Night of the Hunter* in 1955. More recently Jerry Lewis left the tutorship of Frank Tashlin and struck out on his own as "the complete filmmaker" with such notable comedies as *The Bellboy*, *The Errand Boy*, and *The Nutty Professor*. Today, it is almost commonplace to discover top stars essaying their own directing ventures—witness Burt Reynolds (*Gator* and *Sharky's Machine*), Clint Eastwood (*The Eiger Sanction*, *The Outlaw Josey Wales*, and *Play Misty for Me*), and Paul Newman (*Rachel, Rachel*, *Sometimes a Great Notion*, and *The Effect of Gamma Rays. . . .*).

And so it goes. I wonder if the obvious motives of Redford and the others have not something to do with that ever-present need to control a performance. Long ago, such diverse commentators as Vachel Lindsay, Vsevelod Pudovkin, Luigi Pirandello, and Walter Benjamin (not to mention a recent view expressed by Jerry Mander) noted that the actor in films is deprived of this essential need. The medium of the motion picture, wrote Pirandello, places the actor in a kind of exile, deprived on screen of his weight, substance, and voice. Pudovkin seemed to echo this when he wrote in 1929 that the actor loses his ability to command a performance. Instead, the real controller of a film performance is the director who, by virtue of his opportunities to edit and place the camera, makes the decisions necessary to shape the total work. As a consequence, the actor often works in a series of discrete fragments of film, with little sense of the totality of the finished product as formed by the cutter and the director.

An actor does not need to be aware of these theoretical principles to feel this loss of control. The obvious answer to the problem is to assume a mastery of the filmmaking process. And perhaps it is the inherent individualism of a Robert Redford that transcends a relative lack of experience at the director's helm. That is what really counts, after all. It was at the time that he appeared (and co-produced)

All the President's Men that Redford seriously began to consider directing. "I always wanted to do something completely on my own," Redford said just after completing the shooting of *Ordinary People*. Even in his choice of casting, he exhibited a certain maverick sensibility. "A lot of people thought I should be committed for the chemistry of that casting, but I believed in it." (Incidentally, rather than taking his usual multimillion acting fee for that picture, he took only a director's minimum of $53,066.) Significantly, he sees this sense of control as an escape from the high visibility he has always been uncomfortable with as an actor. ("Not so many people are paying attention to you," he said in a recent *People* interview.)

Thus, as Robert Redford considers more the possibilities of directing and reconsiders further the hazards of film acting, his individualism finds opportunities in many other areas—such as community development (his 2,300-acre Sundance project), politics (a commissioner in the Wasatch Mountains of Utah), and farming (he breeds quarter horses and grows alfalfa, corn, barley, and wheat). It's all part of his lessons in control—and responsibility. The complete filmmaker is also part and parcel of the complete man.

Mickey Rooney

William Hare

Originally appeared in vol. 1, no. 5 (May/June 1977)

To secure the ever elusive brass ring of film stardom involves surmounting astronomical odds. The act of achieving stardom as a youngster and retaining it
for the better part of two generations would register a computer figure of one
in billions.

The fact that an indefatigable bundle of unceasing talent named Mickey
Rooney has been able to remain a sustaining influence in motion pictures from
precocious childhood status during the Great Depression and continue as a celebrated notable in the post-Watergate era is probably the foremost example of
his versatile talent and explosive creative energy that was in evidence from early
boyhood to the present.

Currently Rooney is appearing with Gene Hackman and Candice Bergen in
the Stanley Kramer adventure thriller *The Domino Principle* while a Walt Disney
Production *Pete's Dragon* with Helen Reddy is being readied for release. He is
also starring in a new television series, *A Year at the Top*, for producer Norman
Lear while, between films and television work, Rooney also manages to squeeze
in stage appearances having recently completed stints in Las Vegas and Dallas.

The multi-faceted entertainer launched his show business career practically
from the crib. Born Joe Yule Jr. in New York City, he was appearing on stage in
his parents' vaudeville act at the age of two. He made his film bow in 1926 at
the tender age of four, appearing in short comedies under the moniker Mickey
McGuire.

In 1932 the youthful dynamo made his MGM debut in *Broadway to Hollywood*, appearing as Mickey Rooney and holding down more than his share of
attention amidst a stellar cast which included Frank Morgan, fellow child star
Jackie Cooper, Alice Brady, Jimmy Durante, Una Merkel, and Nelson Eddy.

Although MGM was destined to be the studio where Rooney would enjoy
his greatest measure of film fame, the picture that sprang him to stardom was
made at Warner Brothers, the 1935 Shakespearean classic *A Midsummer Night's
Dream*. Warners spent considerable money on the lavish production and im-

68

ported celebrated German director Max Reinhardt to tackle the assignment. In addition to Rooney, other performing notables were James Cagney, Dick Powell, Olivia de Havilland, Anita Louise, and Joe E. Brown.

It is difficult to conceive of any part being more appropriately adaptable to young Rooney's talents than that of Puck, an elfin spirit of dazzling grace, evoking the imagination of filmgoers as, in the words of a writer of the period, " . . . a juvenile Tarzan with an even weirder cry and a much more vivid imagination."

The moguls at MGM must have been favorably impressed by Rooney's performance since that same year he was signed to a contract. The studio had big things in store for the youthful performer with the storehouse of energy and a teaming with Spencer Tracy served to benefit both actors. In 1937 Rooney performed with Tracy in *Captains Courageous*, portraying the son of sea captain Lionel Barrymore. In one of the film's memorable scenes, Rooney lends some of his clothes to Freddie Bartholomew, the spoiled only son of a millionaire, who tells him, "This is a dirty rotten little boat, and these are the worst clothes I ever saw."

A pattern was established in *Captains Courageous* which was repeated successfully in other Rooney films. He typified the unaffected, unfettered All-American boy, an image that contrasted dramatically with that of the priggish Bartholomew. *Captains Courageous* was hailed by critics. Howard Barnes of the *New York Herald Tribune* rated it as belonging with ". . . the screen's few masterpieces" while *Variety* acclaimed it ". . . one of the best pictures of the sea ever made."

Spencer Tracy won an Academy Award for best performance by an actor in *Captains Courageous*, which was directed by Victor Fleming, who two years later would cop an Oscar of his own for *Gone with the Wind*.

High echelon executives at MGM spotted both box office and artistic magic in the Tracy-Rooney tandem. They wasted no time in following up on the success of *Captains Courageous* with *Boys Town* the following year, a film which proved to be one of the biggest winners in the studio's proud history. The story provided Rooney with lots of dramatic latitude and the determined teenager played his role to the hilt, portraying a bullying boy gone bad who ultimately mends his ways. Aiding him along the path to moral rectitude was Tracy, who enacted the role of the legendary real life personality, Father Flanagan.

Boy's Town resulted in two Oscars for the Tracy-Rooney team. Tracy secured his second Academy Award in a row for best actor, the only time in Academy history this was accomplished, while young Rooney secured a special Oscar.

The following year (1939) found Rooney leading the film industry's top ten among all performers, highlighted by his teaming with Judy Garland in the effervescent, non-stop musical entertainment vehicle, *Babes in Arms*, directed by the imaginative Busby Berkeley. Rooney's prestigious position at the top of the rung becomes all the more significant in that many film experts have selected 1939 as the finest in the history of the industry, a fact reported on the recent television special "Life Goes to the Movies."

The assertive young actor was nominated for an Oscar for the best performance by an actor for his role in *Babes in Arms*. Robert Donat took the honor for his masterful performance in *Goodbye, Mr. Chips*, while the other nominees, along with Rooney, were Clark Gable for *Gone with the Wind*, Laurence Olivier from *Wuthering Heights*, and James Stewart for *Mr. Smith Goes to Washington*, an ample manifestation of the keenness of that year's competition.

Never one to rest on his laurels, Rooney remained busy in the early forties, repeating his number one position in Hollywood's top ten both in 1940 and 1941. Rooney also found a young actress to complement his energetic All-American boy image, the tremendously talented Judy Garland, whose wholesome sweetness blended perfectly with Mickey's likable aggressiveness. MGM used the Rooney-Garland team to create some more charismatic magic under the watchful directorial eye of Busby Berkeley in *Strike Up the Band*, a 1940 blockbuster which used the same success formula of appealing youngsters and dynamic musical entertainment as employed in *Babes in Arms* the preceding year.

Amidst all the aforementioned Rooney activity was the creation of a series which will live interminably in the annals of filmdom both for its solid entertainment value and its consistent box office wallop.

In 1937 George Seitz directed *A Family Affair* based on a modestly successful Broadway play. It was the story of a small town judge and his family, with Lionel Barrymore cast as the judge, Spring Byington as his wife, and Mickey Rooney as one of the children. MGM had affixed a "B" label to the film and sent it on its way to distributors, never realizing what a blockbuster it had on its hands until those same distributors sent back urgent messages to supply them with more of the same kind of product. Eager to please, the studio launched the *Andy Hardy* series, which extended to thirteen profitable pre–World War II vehicles with Rooney emerging early as the series' dominant figure while Lewis Stone and Fay Holden replaced Barrymore and Byington beginning in the second episode.

The first thirteen Andy Hardy films encompassed a period between 1937 and 1944, the year that Rooney went into the Army. Judy Garland performed in three of the features, while springboards to stardom were attained through the popular series for actresses Lana Turner, Kathryn Grayson, Donna Reed, and Esther Williams.

In seeking to determine why the Andy Hardy films attained such great success one would have to begin with the magnetic personality of Rooney. In a period of worldwide turbulence in which America was still in the throes of a depression and warclouds were simultaneously rising as the country pushed closer to global conflict, the youthful, confident Rooney afforded moviegoers an opportunity to escape from domestic and international uncertainties of the times. The energetic confidence that Mickey Rooney displayed, and the sweetness that Judy Garland expressed, invested film audiences with both escape from their problems and some badly needed optimism to keep on plugging like an indefatigable Andy Hardy. Before Rooney flung his duffel bag over his shoulder to become a member of Uncle Sam's Army in 1944, he turned in what many deem to be his finest performance as an actor in *The Human Comedy*, which was said to be MGM studio boss Louis B. Mayer's favorite film. The 1943 epic was an optimistic affirmation about the goodness in man as exemplified in a small town World War II setting. Rooney received an Academy Award nomination in the best actor sweepstakes, while screenwriter William Saroyan copped an Oscar.

Rooney returned from military duty to star in another Andy Hardy film, *Love Laughs at Andy Hardy*, a 1946 release, which would be the last of the series until twelve years later, when he would appear in *Andy Hardy Comes Home.*

The following year Rooney performed in *Summer Holiday*, a MGM Technicolor musical directed by Rouben Mamoulian, in which he was flanked by an all-star cast which included Walter Huston, Agnes Moorhead, Marilyn Maxwell, Gloria DeHaven, Frank Morgan, and "Butch" Jenkins. The film was a musical adaptation of Eugene O'Neill's play, *Ah Wilderness.*

Retaining his dynamic flair for action, Rooney turned in an adroit performance of a young racecar driver who gets the bighead, then develops humility in the 1949 film, *The Big Wheel*, in which he starred opposite standout veteran character performer Thomas Mitchell. The perky Rooney performance was bolstered by excellent racecar action footage.

As the Rooney career moved into the fifties the diligent performer starred in his own television series entitled both *The Mickey Rooney Show* and *Hey Mulligan* in 1954.

In 1956 Rooney was once again accorded an Academy Award nomination, this time in the best supporting actor classification for his performance in the RKO war film, *The Bold and the Brave* with Wendell Corey and Don Taylor. Despite the movie's war theme, it was interlaced with many comedy sequences, which gave Rooney an opportunity to excel in one of his favorite entertainment settings. The most hilarious sequence of the film involved a "crap game" in which the Rooney comedic instinct rose to soaring heights.

Since Rooney received an Oscar nomination largely for his comedy work in *The Bold and the Brave*, it remained for the versatile star to tackle something totally different, which he did in 1957 when he performed in the title role of *Baby Face Nelson* with Carolyn Jones and Cedric Hardwicke.

Rooney, the actor who had proven he could be both charming and irrepressible in the *Andy Hardy* series, and who had demonstrated a flair for comedy and sustained dramatic action in scores of vehicles, had an opportunity to demonstrate great ferocity in his razor sharp portrayal of one of crimedom's fiercest figures.

Furnishing standout direction in the action-packed crime drama was Don Siegel, who more recently directed Clint Eastwood in *Dirty Harry* and John Wayne in *The Shootist.*

Remaining busy in the sixties, Rooney starred in his second television series, *Mickey,* in 1964, while also performing in films such as *Breakfast at Tiffany's, Requiem for a Heavyweight, It's a Mad, Mad, Mad, Mad World,* and *Skidoo* to name a few.

The Rooney bandwagon is presently riding on all cylinders as the performer maintains a rigorous schedule that extends to various phases of the arts. In *The Domino Principle,* his heavier dramatic spy surfaces as he portrays a con man with a devious mission in the spy intrigue adventure. *Pete's Dragon,* in which he stars with Helen Reddy, gives the Rooney comedy flair ample working room. The Walt Disney Production finds Rooney cast in the role of a heavily imbibing lighthouse keeper who is the only person able to see the dragon in the film.

On the television front Rooney will star in the new Norman Lear comedy series *A Year at the Top,* the story of a group of vaudevillians who sell their souls to the devil for the opportunity to appear for one year as a star rock and roll group. Additionally, Rooney is seeking to close a syndicated television series in which he will provide advice to people seeking to better their lives, a format on the order of an Ann Landers newspaper column, which is presently in the formative stage.

With legitimate stage appearances in Las Vegas and Dallas just recently having been completed, Rooney will be visiting Hawaii this summer to do a play.

In summarizing Rooney's career one must think of a never-ending series of encores in which the energetic performer continually surprises us with new and unique ways to spellbind audiences. Ever looking forward, never looking back, the sun truly never sets on Mickey Rooney.

Perhaps the most appropriate phrase one could invoke concerning the Rooney career is that which the great Al Jolson used at his performing peak:

"You ain't seen nothin' yet!"

Kidflicks

THE WESTERN FILMS OF FRED THOMSON

Bruce M. Firestone

Originally appeared in vol. 6, no. 2 (1982)

Although the fledgling American film industry was churning out western movies even before the turn of the century, only two real western stars had emerged by the end of World War I. They were Max Aronson, who had decided that America wasn't quite ready for a Jewish cowboy, and so he dubbed himself Broncho Billy; and William S. Hart, who overcame a late start in movies (he was 44 when he made his first film) to stake out a major portion of the market with his unique blend of austere realism and gushing sentiment.

But it wasn't long before the genre had proved itself too lucrative not to attract stiff and often fierce competition. The studies launched campaigns to find new and younger sagebrush heroes, and soon there were more western stars in Hollywood than there were western states in the union: Ken Maynard, Hoot Gibson, Harry Carey, Jack Hoxie, Tim McCoy, Buck Jones, and many, many more. Best known in this galaxy of new stars was, of course, Tom Mix, who had been making westerns since the early teens, but who didn't really come into his own until the early twenties when he moved to Fox Studios. Next best known was probably Fred Thomson, who film historian William Everson calls "the closest rival to Mix," and who, according to Ernest Courneau, "ranked among the top five cowboy stars of the silent screen."

Who's Fred Thomson? That's a good question. I first got interested in Thomson's career in 1972. I'd been asked to write a chapter on the western genre for a film textbook, and I'd run across several references to Thomson (like Everson's and Courneau's) while I was researching the essay. But these remarks were generally in passing, and there was very little of substance available to back them up. If you look Thomson up in Leslie Halliwell's *The Filmgoer's Companion*, or Paul Rotha's *The Film Till Now*, or any number of other film histories and encyclopedias, you won't even find his name mentioned. George Fenin and William Everson do devote a few pages of their book *The Western: From Silents to Sound* to Thomson, but their treatment is superficial and not even entirely accurate. If you try to obtain some of Thomson's films, you'll find out that of the thirty he made between 1921 and 1928, only two are known to survive—*Thundering Hoofs* and a non-western called *A Chapter in Her Life*.

It was about this time as I was struggling to put together a brief sketch of Thomson for my chapter, that I first met Frances Marion, Fred Thomson's wife during his Hollywood years. Ms. Marion had just recently completed a book about her long career as a screenwriter (called *Off with Their Heads*), and she had agreed to come and talk to my film class about writing for the screen. Her achievement in film was impressive. She had worked her way into the booming film industry in the teens, and by the early twenties was already both writing and directing, most often for her good friend Mary Pickford. Between 1915 and 1953 Ms. Marion wrote over 130 screenplays, including *Stella Dallas* (1925), *The Scarlet Letter* (1926), *Bringing Up Father* (1928), *Dinner at Eight* (1933), and two Academy Award Winners—*The Big House* (1930) and *The Champ* (1932).

Frances Marion didn't speak very much about Fred Thomson (her third husband), but with the help of her book and some other published information I was able to piece together an outline of the nine years they were together. In 1917, Ms. Marion had gone with Mary Pickford to visit American troops preparing to depart for Europe, and she met Thomson, who was serving as a chaplain in the armed forces. (At the time he was in a regimental hospital recovering from injuries suffered "in action" during an inter-service football game.) Apparently they hit it off right away, and when the war was over they got together again and soon were married.

The decision to marry must have been a difficult one for Thomson, who had been ordained a Presbyterian minister in 1913 before entering the service. Marrying the twice-divorced screenwriter meant giving up the ministry. But he went ahead with it, and while they were honeymooning in Europe Thomson came up with the idea of making a new kind of western film for children; one which would advocate clean, wholesome living, and which would—somewhat preposterously—star a horse instead of a man. Ms. Marion explains his conversion from pulpit to saddle in her memoirs:

> As a Boy Scout Master, Fred had seen them flock to the theatres whenever Broncho Billy, Tom Mix, or William S. Hart appeared on the screen. These men were heroes for youth to emulate . . . [But] gunplay was more in evidence than was healthy for youngsters to see, and Fred wondered if daring adventure stories such as Doug Fairbanks made could be converted into westerns. I agreed that it was an interesting idea, and feasible. But I must say that I was taken

aback by his suggestion that a horse and not a man should be starred in these pictures.

Hoot Gibson was also somewhat taken aback when the Thomsons arrived in California with Silver King, a giant Arabian stallion they'd bought on the East Coast. "Man, you going to make cowboy pictures with that horse?" Gibson asked. "Nobody every saw a big horse like that on the range. Screwy idea . . ."

The man who ended up backing this "screwy idea" was a Boston financier named Joseph Kennedy, who was in the process of masterminding F.B.O. (Federated Booking Offices—a motion picture studio in the late '20s) into a major power, and, not incidentally, accumulating a fortune for himself. Kennedy talked Thomson into co-starring with his stallion, something no one else, including Frances Marion, had been able to do, and within a year F.B.O. was churning out low budget western adventures that caught on quickly. In a very short time Fred Thomson was a top box office draw, as was his horse Silver King, who ranked higher than even Lillian Gish in a 1925 farm magazine popularity poll. In 1926 the Thomsons built a $625,000 mansion (including a luxurious stable for Silver King) in Beverly Hills, and by 1927 Fred Thomson was making a reported $100,000 per film.

The following year, in the winter of 1928, Thomson died. As Ms. Marion describes it in *Off with Their Heads*:

> A week before Christmas we fell into the true Santa Claus spirit: almost all the houses in Beverly Hills had lighted Christmas trees on their lawns. . . . In order to plan where we could put the outdoor tree, we walked through the garden and onto the front lawn that spread over five acres of our hilltop. Below us sparkled the lights of Beverly Hills. The main Los Angeles boulevard that stretched to the sea looked like a ladder of stars lying supine on the ground, while searchlights, playing upon the backdrop of the night sky, proclaimed the temporal fame of some fledgling actor or actress. As [Fred] put his arm around me and we walked . . . I noticed that he limped a little, A year before, doing one of his stunts, Fred had broken his leg, and I asked if it was troubling him. "No, I stepped on a rusty nail and it bothers me a little. Nothing to worry about."

A week later, on Christmas Day, 1928, Fred Thomson died of tetanus.

It's difficult to say exactly how close Thomson adhered to his original intention of making wholesome movies for the nation's youth, because so few of his films have survived. But from the one surviving western, *Thundering Hoofs*, and on the basis of plot summaries published in exhibitor's journals and *The American Film Institute Catalog of Motion Pictures Produced in the U.S. (1921–1930)*, it appears that Thomson strayed little from his self-imposed ethic. If there is a consistent pattern running through all twenty-five westerns, it is that they sought to entertain and to provide instructive models at the same time. As Frederick Elkin has pointed out, the typical western formula has much to offer children. It presents a simple unambiguous world in which there is no difficulty in forming allegiances; it provides a vicarious outlet for aggressive feelings; it allows the child to identify with a hero figure whose moral victories can be shared and seen as a way of earning love and admiration; and it all occurs against a backdrop of wide open spaces which spells out *freedom* in a world of too many "dos" and "don'ts."

All these elements are present in Thomson's westerns, and no doubt account for much of their appeal. But Thomson went beyond the standard features of the genre in his effort to attract and influence children. For one thing, he often included children in the storyline, or least included subplots which involved children. In *The Tough Guy*, for instance, Fred prevents Buddy, an orphan boy, from being trampled by a runaway horse and then helps him escape from the orphanage. In *A Regular Scout*, made in 1926, Fred rescues a boy from danger, and then later, when he's been framed for a crime he hasn't committed, it's a Boy Scout troop (along with Silver King) that rescues him. In *The Bandit's Baby*, a 1925 film, the character Fred plays (Tom Bailey) is charged with robbery and murder, yet the sheriff rather inexplicably grants him amnesty for a day so he can ride in a rodeo and judge, of all things, a baby contest. The baby that wins the prize turns out, of course, to have a beautiful sister, and by the end of the film Tom proposes. The title sequence goes like this:

> Tom: "Gosh, Esther, I don't want to get hitched up, but I'll do anything to get that baby."
>
> Esther: "All right, Tom, I'll do anything to get that horse."

Another prominent feature in the Thomson formula was, of course, Silver King, who often played an active role in Thomson's films. Silver King and Fred would frequently rescue each other from difficult situations, each time eschewing violence in favor of athletic virtuosity. Thomson did his best to avoid bloodshed in his films by relying instead on stunts and elaborate action sequences to excite his viewers. When Fred and Silver King stumble upon a stage hold-up in progress in *Thundering Hoofs*, they team up to subdue the desperadoes without hurting anything but their dignity. Fred lassos all three of them with one throw, loops the rope over the branch of a tree, and then Silver King pulls the rope until the hapless culprits are suspended twenty feet in the air. Later Silver King unties the rope from the horn of the saddle and lets them plummet back to earth— shaken up a bit, but no worse for wear.

This gentle breed of law enforcement was common in Thomson's films, with Silver King often handling matters entirely on his own. In fact there's little that Thomson's wonder horse could not do. In *Thundering Hoofs*, the hero rides off on another horse leaving Silver King behind to take care of Fred's ailing father. Shortly afterward we see the father succumb to what seems to be a heart attack, and then, after a slow fade, the next scene shows Silver King patting the soil over a neatly dug grave with a cross planted at its head and, to cap it off, a jar containing freshly picked flowers. We are left to draw the inevitable conclusion that Silver King, kneeling now at graveside, has handled the funeral arrangements on his own.

The stunt work in Thomson's films was by no means confined only to Silver King. Thomson himself was quite an athlete. He had played football and baseball in college, and the year he graduated he'd won the National Track and Field Competition. He went on to win it again in 1911, and again—this time breaking Jim Thorpe's World record—in 1913. And, in the 1918 Inter-Allied Athletic Games it was chaplain Fred Thomson who took first place—among all allied forces—in, of all things, the hand grenade throwing event. Like his contemporary Tom Mix, Thomson relied heavily on good stunt work to keep the film action moving. There were few men in the business—including professional stuntmen—who could outdo him. Even Douglas Fairbanks, who was a close friend and who could swing from chandeliers with the best, admired Thomson's stunt work. Like Fairbanks, Thomson would rarely use a door when there was a window to be vaulted through; rarely climb down stairs when a light fixture was handy for swinging. But perhaps most important to Thomson about these action sequences was his belief that the outdoor life of physical activity was itself wholesome and worth pursuing. He told Grace Hilton in a 1924 interview that a primary purpose of his movies was to show boys "the benefits of living clean athletic lives." He went on to say that the moral standards of young men in college at the time were considerably higher than ten years earlier, and that he believed it directly due to the then current interest in athletics.

Fred Thomson was not the first western star to direct his films at a youthful audience; nor was he the first to blend horsemanship with homily. Broncho Billy, William S. Hart, Tom Mix, and numerous others had all done this to one extent or another. But in the short time Fred Thomson was active making western films, he developed a distinctive style and approach which made him one of the most popular western stars of the silent era. His sudden death in 1928, and the disappearance, through loss or destruction, of virtually all of his films, have turned Thomson into one of the least-known cowboys in the history of American movies. For what he was, and for what he tried to do, he deserves greater recognition.

Cornel Wilde

THE COMPLETE FILMMAKER AND MAN OF ACTION

Gene Sheppard

Originally appeared in vol. 6, no. 6 (November/December 1982)

Cornel Wilde flourished in Hollywood films, but his rightful home seemed to be Mount Olympus. With a classic face and a perfect physique, he seemed the reincarnation of Apollo, the Greek god of manly youth and beauty.

Cornel Wilde was one of the few swashbucklers who came to films both as an accomplished swordsman and with a sound acting background. This six-foot, one-inch physical specimen with dark eyes and hair combined with smoldering handsomeness and a powerful, athletic body seemed preordained to be cast in the classic matinee, leading man mold. Yet, Cornel Wilde possessed a brilliant mind, and courage, sensitivity, and integrity that would make him a symbol of controversy for four decades. He was the Hollywood super-star who fought for superior roles to satisfy his innate creativity and who went on to produce and direct some of his own films.

Born to Hungarian-Czech parents in New York City on October 13, 1915, as Cornelius Louis Wilde, Cornel spent a good part of his early life traveling with his father in Europe. While there, he acquired a fluency in six languages that would later be an asset to his film career. The family finally settled permanently in New York City and upon completing a four-year pre-med course, Cornel won a scholarship to Columbia University's College of Physicians and Surgeons in 1935. In 1936, he was a leading member of the U.S. Olympic fencing team but abandoned medicine and the Olympics when he was bitten by the acting bug and embarked on a career in the theatre. He was featured in a series of Broadway plays and eloped with an aspiring actress, Patricia Knight, in 1937.

Fresh from their brilliant triumphs in *Gone with the Wind* and *Wuthering Heights* in 1939, "America's most famous lovers," Vivien Leigh and Laurence Olivier embarked on the over-ambitious theatrical production of *Romeo and Juliet*. Cornel Wilde was summoned to Hollywood as a fencing instructor for

Olivier and the featured role of Tybalt in the play. Cornel received a total of eighteen scars from dueling with Olivier, but miraculously these injuries did not mar his perfect features. The Broadway production closed after thirty-six performances in 1940, but Cornel had secured a Warner Brothers contract due to his participation in the ill-fated play.[1]

His first film role was in *The Lady with Red Hair* (WB, 1940) starring Miriam Hopkins, followed by a part in Raoul Walsh's *High Sierra* (WB, 1941) with Humphrey Bogart and Ida Lupino.[2] Warner Bros. starred him as a boxer in *Knockout* (1941) with Arthur Kennedy and Anthony Quinn, and this tight-knit film was lauded as a solid entry for Cornel. Because of his disgust with these three roles, Cornel tends to ignore his role in *Kisses for Breakfast* (WB, 1941) with Dennis Morgan and Jane Wyatt. He feared that he was being groomed at Warner Bros. as a gangster-type character heavy with no chance of exercising his acting ability.

His agent arranged for a screen test with Twentieth Century-Fox, which impressed Darryl F. Zanuck and Hollywood's powerful sage, Louella Parsons. This prompted Parsons to write in her next column that she had seen nothing better since Paul Muni came to Hollywood. Cornel says, "I was insecure enough to carry that newspaper clipping in my wallet for years."[3]

Zanuck cast his new contractee with Lynn Bari and Anthony Quinn in *The Perfect Snob* (Fox, 1941), a delightful farce that received good reviews. Appearing with Carole (the Ping Girl) Landis in *Manila Calling* (Fox, 1941), this patriotic film gave Cornel the opportunity to emote dramatically as a doomed civilian caught in the Axis thrust.

Cornel received his biggest role to that date with the Nunnally Johnson production, *Life Begins at 8:30* (Fox, 1941). Directed by Irving Pichel, Cornel portrayed the romantic lead as the boyfriend of Ida Lupino and his performance was applauded by critic Bosley Crowther in *The New York Times.* Sonja Henie, the skating queen at Fox, took her final whirl around the ice in *Wintertime* (Fox, 1943), and she selected handsome Cornel as her love interest. Together, they effectively ushered out Miss Henie's illustrious career with charm and affection.

Cornel felt that it was time for his career to shift into high gear with sensitive, high-voltage performances. To gain recognition from his studio and the public, he had to outshine the front ranks of Fox's formidable male stars— Tyrone Power, Henry Fonda, Richard Greene, Dana Andrews, John Payne, Don Ameche, Victor Mature, and Cesar Romero.

Rumors abounded that Harry Cohn, the president of Columbia Pictures, was planning a biographical film of the life of classical music composer Frederic Chopin. Cornel pleaded for three months to set up a screen test to play the title role. Cornel believed in the screen role and felt it was his chance to demonstrate his superior acting ability.[4] He was frustrated because everyone felt he was "too healthy looking" to portray the short, effeminate, aristocratic, and consumptive composer. Using his ingenuity while fencing at the YMCA with director Charles Vidor, Cornel persuaded the director to arrange a screen test. After four screen tests, Columbia boss Harry Cohn was convinced and persuaded Fox's Zanuck to loan Cornel to Columbia. Cornel Wilde won the coveted role!

The laughters laughed and the scoffers scoffed, but Cornel worked diligently preparing for the difficult role. Although the soundtrack music was provided by Jose Iturbi, Cornel learned to play a dozen intricate piano passages and his hands were shown playing the piano throughout the movie. Cornel says, "I asked the wardrobe people to make my shoulders narrower. The makeup was paler. I did not use robust, athletic movements."[5]

A Song To Remember was released in January, 1945, to thunderous applause and critical plaudits. *Newsweek* proclaimed, "The film's best performance is that of a relative newcomer, Cornel Wilde as the troubled, inspired Pole." The Technicolor film was an overwhelming success, earning six Oscar nominations and more money than any other film with classical music. Cornel received an Oscar nomination as Best Actor in 1945 and became an overnight matinee idol. It created a Chopin boom and encouraged other films about serious composers.[6]

Cornel's contract at Fox was revised in 1945 for a loanout to Columbia for one picture a year through 1948. To capitalize on his fencing talents, Columbia cast Cornel in *A Thousand and One Nights* (1945), co-starring Evelyn Keyes, Adele Jergens, and Phil Silvers. Cornel was never more acrobatic and athletic than as Aladdin. In vivid Technicolor, Cornel wore sexy fantasy costumes, and his acting was excellent.

Back at Fox, Cornel starred with Gene Tierney and Jeanne Crain in *Leave Her to Heaven* (1945), the Ben Ames Williams' best seller of murder, madness, and accidental suicide. Superbly directed by John M. Stahl and an Oscar winner, this dramatic tour de force was a distinct triumph. Cornel says, "It was a sumptuously made example of what Hollywood could do in that era of the 1940s. Beautiful, good cutting, off-beat characters. That was one I really liked."[7] Cornel and Gene Tierney honed their characters to classic perfection and were praised by critics and public.

In 1946, Cornel, as the son of Robin Hood in *The Bandit of Sherwood Forest*, elected to interpret his swashbuckling role in a manner that would not compare with Douglas Fairbanks (1920) or Errol Flynn (1938). Choosing to be wholesome, boyish, and guileless, Cornel created a charming performance with pleasing robustness, demonstrated unparalleled fencing expertise, and capered athletically with ease and conviction. In stunning color, Cornel was an endearing swashbuckler and the film initially grossed over three million dollars in the United States alone, making it Columbia's most successful adventure film.

Cornel's charm, physical appearance, and French accent were frosting on the cake in *Centennial Summer* (1946), Fox's answer to MGM's *Meet Me in St. Louis*. The film was a turn of the century family affair, featuring Jerome Kern's last musical score, Linda Darnell and Jeanne Crain as pretty sisters, and Cornel in sexy costumes that purportedly left female audiences gasping. Directed and produced by Otto Preminger, the film is still as entertaining today as it was in 1946.

In 1947, Cornel's salary was three thousand dollars per week and his fan mail volume was larger than any other Fox star according to James Robert Parish's *The Swashbucklers*. With his emergence as a super-star, a long-buried feature suddenly appeared in theatres. In 1940, twenty-five-year-old Cornel had played some brief scenes in an abortive, untitled film. This incomplete film spliced with unrelated scenes and "specialty" acts, was released as *Stairway for a Star*, "Cornel Wilde's latest film." The potpourri feature drew audiences to theatres, but they left puzzled over how Cornel had regressed so remarkably in age and physical appearance. Released by Stairway for a Star Corp., producer Jack Krieger successfully pulled a lucrative stunt without Cornel's knowledge.

Cornel Wilde and Maureen O'Hara were teamed for *The Homestretch* (Fox, 1948), an exciting racetrack yarn. But all *The New York Times* could say was: "Cornel Wilde is handsome and manly, both in dinner jacket and bathing trunks." Cornel and Maureen O'Hara made a striking couple and, with her fiery nature and his calm demeanor, they balanced each other's temperaments to perfection.

Forever Amber, the "hottest" novel since *Gone with the Wind*, languished from 1944–1947 awaiting filming. Countless difficulties arose regarding filming Kathleen Windsor's sexy bestseller of Amber St. Claire, who bedded some twenty males while searching for her beloved Bruce Carlton (Cornel Wilde). The role of Amber was not easily cast. Initially, Amber was played by Zanuck protégé Peggy Cummins, but the studio allegedly lost $500,000 when the production was halted because Miss Cummins was inadequate in age and ability. Director Otto Preminger and Cornel Wilde wanted MGM's Lana Turner,[8] but, although Preminger had been promised complete authority, Zanuck insisted Amber would be played by a Fox star.[9] Finally, Linda Darnell was awarded the role and shooting resumed.

Produced by William Perlberg with a screenplay by Ring Lardner, Jr., and Philip Dunne, the color film was beautiful in scope, costume, and scenery. Over six million dollars were spent on the sumptuous production with swashbuckling scenes, the Black Plague of 1665, the Great Fire of London in 1666, the court of King Charles II, and countless costumes for Cornel, Linda Darnell, and the large cast. Cornel was effective as Bruce Carlton due to his physical dominance and fencing expertise. Although it was panned by the critics and condemned by the

Catholic Church, the film earned a fortune! Now, some viewers think it tedious and overlong; others regard it as a classic.

For a badly needed change of pace, Cornel jumped to Columbia and *It Had to Be You* (1947) with Ginger Rogers. This comedy of mixed identities was a joyful romp for both stars.

Having been suspended by Fox several times for refusing roles, Cornel condescended to film *The Walls of Jericho* (1948), the Lamar Trotti production with Kirk Douglas and Linda Darnell. Cornel's final contract role at his home lot was *Road House* (1948) with Ida Lupino and Richard Widmark. Described as "muscularly attractive," Cornel used brute force and torture in this hard-hitting story of a psychopath and a prison parolee.

With Cornel's contract up for renewal in 1948, he opted to freelance and, to assuage his wife's acting compulsion, he starred with her in Columbia's *Shockproof* (1949), a film notable only for Douglas Sirk's direction. Cornel traveled to Switzerland for *Four Days Leave* (Film Classics, 1949) and, returning to the United States, he starred with Jeff Chandler in *Two Flags West* (Fox, 1950).

In 1952 Cecil B. DeMille selected Cornel Wilde for the important role of "the outstanding aerial daredevil, the debonair king of the air, the great Sebastian" for Paramount's *The Greatest Show on Earth* starring Cornel, Betty Hutton, Charlton Heston, James Stewart, Dorothy Lamour, Gloria Grahame, and members of the Ringling Brothers and Barnum & Bailey Circus. Expert gymnast Cornel had to climb a rope hand over hand properly, perform acrobatic trapeze stunts on the high wire with no stunt man, speak with a French accent, and emote dramatically and romantically with effervescent Betty Hutton. Although he suffered from acrophobia, he turned in a solid classic performance that prompted *Newsweek* to declare, "Wilde played what could have been a garden variety of rake with considerable charm and plausibility."

The Greatest Show on Earth won Oscars for Best Picture and Best Screenplay of 1952, and Cecil B. DeMille received the Irving Thalberg Award for eminence in the film profession. The movie grossed over fourteen million dollars in U.S. and Canadian rentals alone and continues to be one of the all-time box office champions. DeMille said, "I stopped making pictures for critics. I make pictures for people."[10]

Allegedly, Cornel's marriage to star-struck Patricia Knight had been an unhappy union since their elopement in 1937 because she expected Cornel to be her stepping-stone to stardom. On August 30, 1951, the Wilde marriage was officially dissolved, and Cornel married actress Jean Wallace on September 4, 1951. Perhaps his unhappy home life combined with his frustration in demanding sensitive, substantial roles from Fox had contributed to his brief decline in popularity from 1948 to 1951.

At Sword's Point was actually lensed in 1949 by RKO to take advantage of MGM's *The Three Musketeers* (1948) and because Cornel was disappointed that he was not paired with Lana Turner in that epic.[11] Due to difficulties with temperamental RKO boss Howard Hughes, the swashbuckler film was delayed in reaching the screen until April 1952. Based on Alexandre Dumas' *Twenty Years After* and directed by Lewis Allen, Cornel, as the son of D'Artagnan, and Maureen O'Hara as his fencing partner, exhibited their most energetic swordplay to date. Cornel was the cooperative and compassionate man that had been his trademark in earlier years and, in one sequence, he worked for six straight hours with his arms suspended by chains. The joint effort of cast and crew made this a memorable adventure film.

Like a chameleon with a variety of colors, Cornel pursued each of his next film projects to suit his own personal interpretations with the formation of his own "Theodora Productions." The prestige of Theodora enabled him to star, direct, produce, and finance choice assignments from the studios.

From 1952 to 1963 he starred in nineteen successful films that proved his super-stardom was intact. *California Conquest* (1952) with Teresa Wright was an adventure western; *Operation Secret* (1952) was a World War II spy thriller; *Treasure of the Golden Condor* (1953) proved he could have easily replaced Fox rival Tyrone Power in this *Son of Fury* remake; *Main Street to Broadway* (1953) was a favor to director Tay Garnett; and *Saadia* (1954) paired Cornel with sultry Rita Gam in French Morocco. In 1954 he matched wits with June Allyson, Lauren Bacall, and Arlene Dahl in *Woman's World* and appeared in *Passion* with Yvonne De Carlo. He went on to score brilliantly in *The Big Combo* (1955), comforted Jean Wallace in *Storm Fear* (1955), and fenced for Anne Francis in *The Scarlet Coat* (1955). Sexy Jane Russell excited his *Hot Blood* in 1956 and then Cornel and Jean Wallace searched for the *Star of India* (1956). In 1957 Donna Reed took him *Beyond Mombasa*; lovely Debra Paget soothed him in *Omar Khayyam* (1957), and Jean Wallace forced him on *The Devil's Hairpin* (1957). In 1958 he made love to Jean Wallace and Abbe Lane in *Maracaibo*. Victoria Shaw showed him the *Edge of Eternity* in 1959; and, in 1962 he was the great emperor in *Constantine and the Cross* with Christine Kaufmann.

In 1963, Cornel produced, directed, and starred with his wife in *Sword of Lancelot*, his best film in over a decade. Audiences discovered he was still filmdom's most proficient sword wielder and, as a director, he was equally effective. In the colorful, action-filled epic, audiences had never seen a Lancelot as muscular as Cornel and a Guinevere as lovely as Jean Wallace. Artistically and financially, the film provided a boost to Cornel's career.

Cornel traveled to Africa in 1966 to produce, direct, and star in *The Naked Prey*, the classic epic of survival that assaulted the senses with audiovisual depictions of intense heat, exhaustion, brutality, and starvation. Cornel portrayed

"Man," stripped of his clothes and material possessions, pursued through African bush for miles wearing a tattered loincloth without food or water, and fighting for his life against almost impossible odds while retaining the dignity of his manhood and the innate spirit of humanity. Nominated for two Oscars, it is a raw and sensitive study of survival and remains one of his most important films.

Beach Red (1967) was hailed by *The New York Times* as Cornel's "best picture to date." It was a sincere, ambitious anti-war film with unrelenting realism. After the initial spurt of interest, the daily box office receipts were low. Cornel protests that it was an out-and-out anti-war film but the releasing company stressed its gore and nudity and failed to advertise its profound message.[12] Even today, the movie is gaining acceptance as a relatively unrecognized classic with its timely condemnation of war.

No Blade of Grass (1970), Cornel's seventh directorial job, was a futuristic depiction of the effects of pollution.[13] Financially troubled MGM could not promote this prescient, specialized feature adequately, and it received little critical or public attention. But, there are talks of a planned re-release because of the public's increased concern over environmental and conservational problems that are very real today.[14] The California Environmental Health Association did present Cornel Wilde an award for bringing these devastating problems to the attention of the public.

Although he was often underrated by his peers and critics in the past, Cornel's film portrayals, as viewed today, show strong sensitive characterizations and an adventurous courage that reveal him as a formidable multi-talented Hollywood legend. In the past few years, Cornel has received countless awards for his contributions to the arts as an actor, director, producer, and writer. He is always enthusiastic about multi-faceted ideas, fresh scripts, and a quest for beauty and perfection in life.[15] He continues to work in such films as *The Comic* (1969), *The Gargoyles* (1972), *Shark's Treasure* (1975), *The Horseman* (1978), and *The 5th Musketeer* (1979).

Cornel and Jean Wallace have been happily married for over thirty years and divide their time between their Beverly Hills home and travel abroad.

Today, Cornel Wilde will fight for creative, sensitive screen roles, although he has been willing to accept inferior roles to make money which can later be invested in superior projects that meet his high artistic standards. He has beat the studio system on his own terms.

Notes

1. Edwards, Anne. *Vivien Leigh*, Simon and Schuster, New York, 1977, pp. 116–120.

2. Michael, Paul. *The Great American Movie Book*, Prentice-Hall, Inc. Englewood Cliffs, New Jersey, 1980, pp. 84, 105, 119, 154, 260. The former managing editor of

Show Business lists *High Sierra, A Song to Remember, Leave Her to Heaven, Forever Amber,* and *The Greatest Show on Earth* among the best-loved films of the sound era.

3. Cornel Wilde interview with the author.

4. Ibid.

5. Ibid.

6. Thomas, Bob. *King Cohn,* G. P. Putnam's Sons, New York, 1967, pp. 163–165.

7. Cornel Wilde interview.

8. Ibid.

9. Morella, Joe and Epstein, Edward Z. *Lana: The Public and Private Lives of Miss Turner,* Citadel Press, New York, 1971, pp. 83–84.

10. Edmonds, I. G. and Minura, Reiko. *Paramount Pictures,* A.S. Barnes and Company, Inc., San Diego, California, 1980, pp. 240, 250.

11. Cornel Wilde interview.

12. Ibid.

13. Eames, John Douglas. *The MGM Story,* Crown Publishers, Inc., New York, 1979, p. 357.

14. Cornel Wilde interview.

15. Ibid.

Part II

ACTRESSES

Dear Beulah

REFLECTIONS ON THE LONG AND
DISTINGUISHED CAREER OF BEULAH BONDI

Frank A. Aversano

Originally appeared in vol. 3, no. 4 (March/April 1979) and no. 5 (May/June 1979)

Because the transition from illusion to reality is often disappointing, my feelings of anticipation were blended with a generous amount of uncertainty and trepidation as I rang the doorbell of Beulah Bondi's home atop Whitley Terrace in Hollywood. I have known Miss Bondi for forty years. Our relationship began when I was about six years old in the dark confines of my neighborhood theatre. Those of my generation who grew up in the thirties and forties all had their neighborhood theatres. Mine was in the Bronx, New York, and was aptly called the Pilgrim. It is difficult to comprehend fully, even now with the advantage of hindsight and education, what attracted me to one particular actress. Whatever the reasons were, they are no longer important. Quite simply, I fell in love with Beulah Bondi—a secret I kept to myself for forty years and then shared with her. I saw all of her latest films and eagerly awaited her next one.

It is now four decades later. I had just seen *Make Way for Tomorrow* for about the one hundredth time. Overwhelmed, as I always am by her performance, and faced with the ultimate reality of life, I decided to write to Miss Bondi and tell her about this one-sided relationship.

As the doorbell rang, I glanced to my right. Beulah Bondi was framed in the window of her kitchen and was moving about preparing the lunch she had invited me to share. As she stood in the open doorway extending her hand and smiling, I was struck by two things: her diminutive size and the radiance and warm expression of her eyes. She said quite simply, "We really need no introductions, for we have known each other a long time." Immediately, I knew she understood.

As she showed me about her lovely home, I adjusted to the reality of it. I delighted in all that took place. From her porch, I had a commanding view of

Hollywood below. ("The view has changed considerably since I first moved here in the mid-forties.") She showed me part of her collection of elephant statuary. I saw that her home was filled with mementos of her travels. I was to learn later that she was an avid traveler and still is. As we sat drinking sherry, I was completely at ease. Occasionally, I had to remind myself that I was actually there talking to her. However, the reminders became less frequent as her warmth, sincerity, and infectious smile made me realize she was genuinely pleased to see me. She told me that one phrase in my letter had particularly impressed her—that I knew Beulah Bondi the actress and I wanted to know Beulah Bondi the person.

I learned that her house had once been the home of James Hilton, then Joseph Schildkraut, and finally Rosalind Russell. She had originally rented it and then decided to buy it. She lived alone except for the couple she knew for many years who lived in the apartment attached to the house and took care of general maintenance and repairs.

She had recently received an honorary degree from Valparaiso University, her alma mater.

I was genuinely disappointed when she told me that she had turned down the role of Felicity in the Broadway production of *The Shadow Box* because she thought the language offensive. (Ironically, the language was "cleaned up" considerably before the play was finally presented and won the Pulitzer Prize in 1977.)

We talked of current films. She expressed a genuine concern for the decline in the standards of many of today's films exhibited by the coarseness of language, the gratuitous nudity, and the lack of characterization in the roles as well as the acting.

However, she was thrilled and delighted by *Madame Rosa*. She had seen it twice and was deeply impressed by the brilliant acting of Simone Signoret. Several nights later, we went to see it again. It is difficult to fully communicate the feelings I had as I sat next to Beulah Bondi watching a carefully etched performance. She had told me that there was one scene in the film which she believed no American actress would be willing to play. The scene she meant depicts the aging, overweight, and now dying Madame Rosa sitting looking into the mirror. Stuck in the frame of the mirror is a snapshot of her in her younger and more radiant days. It is a deeply moving moment, brilliantly played. Later when we were sitting in the Japanese restaurant in Gower Gulch drinking green tea from "cunning little cups," I asked her about the scene. She said quite simply, "I don't believe any American actress would be willing to allow herself to be seen in such a contrasting way."

As I watched and listened, I found myself noticing little movements and gestures that I had seen before. Once when she took off her glasses and put them on the table, I was suddenly transported to watching her in *Penny Serenade*. There was that same gesture as she had removed her glasses after reading the letter from Irene Dunne in which she told of the death of her adopted daughter. Another time she turned her head slightly, and I saw only a glimpse of Mrs. Webb in *Our Town* as she talked to her daughter Emily. I found myself doing this constantly in the remaining week.

The following Sunday, after brunch at the Scandia, we settled down in the comfortable surroundings of her living room. I was curious to hear about how she had first become interested in acting. As we spoke, and several other times during the meetings we shared, I remember one phrase that she repeated with variations. I asked how she had come to choose the theatre. She answered, "Well, I don't think I ever really chose the theatre any more than I perhaps have chosen the way of my life." On another occasion, when I suggested that she had been fortunate in being selected for a variety of roles in different plays, she responded, "so many things in my life have come about . . . they're not accidental. I really have come to believe that there is a direction in a way of being in the right place at the right time." Being in the right place at the right time contributed signifi-cantly to her early career in the theatre. This fact and certain ironies and coin-cidences worked together in helping her to select acting as her life's expression.

Beginnings

Born in Chicago, Beulah Bondi (it was originally spelled Bondy, but this was changed when she realized that the "y" was the only letter in her name which went "below the line" on a marquee) moved to Valparaiso, Indiana. Her father was a realtor, and her mother was a woman who was interested in the arts with a particular talent for writing. It was her mother who indirectly encouraged her "acting" at the age of about four: "They had what was known at the time in the dramatic world as *Delsarte*. Delsarte was a sort of mime, an imitation, and as a little child back to my earliest recollections, Mother was perhaps showing off her child. I was standing before her and a friend just before I went to bed and Mother would be putting me through these . . . really they were gestures. She would suggest a word like sympathy and I would go into a posture denoting sympathy or happiness and my face would light up and I was expressing hap-piness. She would just say a word or two, and I would kneel down and go into a posture or a prayer or there was supplication or there was anger or there was jealousy . . . I was inspired to go through these gestures . . ."

At the age of seven, she had her first real taste of theatre. A theatrical troupe came to Valparaiso. The child who was to play Little Lord Fauntleroy in a pro-duction of the same name was taken ill. Inquiries indicated that there was a child in the town who could play the role. Her mother explained the relationships of the characters in the play, invited them to the Bondi home, and Beulah came to know them "as my relationship to characters in a play rather than as strangers."

Her mother's fears that she would have difficulty in memorizing the seven pages of dialogue were quickly dissipated. She not only learned her part, but the entire play. "I was at complete ease. It seemed to be a natural bent for me."

At the age of ten, she won her first gold medal for a poetry recitation at the Deerfield Opera House: "And that was a very happy occasion. And I don't think I ever had any thought really of going into the theatre or becoming an actress. I think I just enjoyed it. I don't know whether it was ego or what it was, but I was at complete ease and I loved performing . . . at an early age." Although both her parents loved the theatre and often took her to performances, she was always discouraged from considering it as a career. Actors had a very poor reputation with those outside the profession, and it was only natural that her father never encouraged her.

Although there was no conscious rebellion on her part against her father's deterrent to the stage, Beulah was attracted by the magic of the theatre. Once, when she and her father were watching Grant Mitchell perform, she turned to him and said, "'You couldn't object to my being in a company with a gentleman like this,' and my father said with a very solemn face, 'Well, Beulah, he's playing a gentleman.'" This scene was repeated almost verbatim when Beulah and her parents were watching Louise Closser Hale. Trying to overcome his objections by referring to Miss Hale as a member of a company "with people as lovely as she is," again he responded, "Well she's playing a lady. We don't know what she's like as a person."

Both these performers, Grant Mitchell and Louise Closser Hale, were to be more than an impetus for her to plead her case for a dramatic career. Years later, when as a hopeful actress fresh from her stock experience, she would be in New York "making the rounds" with an armful of photographs. Emerging from the subway, she met a former director who offered her a part as a seventy-year-old in a new play he was doing. He "fought the battle for her" and the producer gave her the role at the director's suggestion. As she was being introduced to the other players, she learned that the second lead in the play was Louise Closser Hale. This was only part of the irony. After several rehearsals and out of town tryouts the play was recast. At one of the rehearsals, a gentleman came forward on the dimly lighted stage and introduced himself. "Miss Bondi, I saw your performance and I noticed the cast has been changed. I am going to play the lead now. My name is Grant Mitchell!" This was her first Broadway play.

On Stage

Although Miss Bondi accepted the admonitions and warnings from her father against considering the stage as anything more than an amateur experience, she still maintained the desire to pursue an acting career. Undoubtedly her father was aware of her intense desire to act. Her repeated attempts to wear down his resistance to the unsavory reputation of actors began to take their toll. This may have been a gradual erosion or simply an exasperated realization on his part that his daughter was going to have to prove to herself whether she could be a professional actress.

Beulah Bondi's "break" came in Chicago. Once again it was a series of unexpected events that produced it: "A friend of mine had married an owner of one of the theatres in Chicago and he had said to me, 'Beulah, I can understand your father's objection to your being an actor. You aren't really made of the stuff that actors are made of. I don't think you'd be happy with many of them that I have met. I can understand his objections.'" However, he suggested that she contact Maurice Brown who was opening a "beautiful art center—cultural" called the Chicago Little Theatre. Mr. Brown was looking for ten amateurs to fill out his company. Beulah's friend was certain that her parents could not object to this type of atmosphere. He proved to be right.

During her initial interview with Mr. Brown, in response to his question, "Why do you want to be an actor?" Beulah Bondi answered, "I don't know that I do, and I don't know that I can act, but I'll never know unless I have the chance." Mr. Brown accepted the candid quality of this response. He invited her to return in several days to audition. What he asked her to prepare in comparison to today's "cold reading" auditions seems a bit overwhelming. "I would like something from George Bernard Shaw, I would like something from Euripides, I'd like something in a dialect, I'd like a little comedy, and you can choose your material and come back in ten days for an audition." This formidable audition was only one of the obstacles she had to overcome. The company required a fee of four hundred fifty dollars. Since she was certain her father would not support her in this venture, she turned to a bachelor uncle. It was from him that she received the money—"Well, we'll say nothing about it and here is your four hundred fifty dollars, and when you become a great actress you can repay me."

Having passed the audition and paid the fee, Beulah was still faced with the task of convincing her father that she was not heading for destruction by joining the Maurice Brown group. It was a clever maneuver, skillfully planned, that won him over: "Following a beautiful Sunday program at the Little Theatre, they served tea, and I invited Mother and Father to come without telling them any of the things that had gone before and they met Mr. and Mrs. Brown and got the feeling of the whole Little Theatre and after the tea, when we went home, I said, 'Would you object if I became a part of that unit?' and my father said, 'I couldn't imagine anything lovelier.'"

Beulah Bondi spent two years with the Little Theatre where she had "wonderful training from nine thirty in the morning to one thirty a.m. because as amateurs we had our own special dancing and diction classes and then the amateurs had to put on a production of their own with costumes, scenery, and direction from a member of the senior company."

It was about this time that she was to encounter the second most important influence in her early acting career. This was the director Stuart Walker. When Stuart Walker was in Chicago, she met him through an introduction by Maurice Brown. Mr. Walker chose to ignore the "favorable letter" which Mr. Brown handed him and decided, "I'll judge for myself." He must have judged favorably, for he suggested that she keep in touch with him in New York. "I'd write a simple line. I'd say, 'Do you remember Beulah Bondi? I hear you're doing a play in New York, is there anything in it for Beulah Bondi?' I made my sentences brief and short."

Finally, she went to New York only to learn that Stuart Walker was with his company in Indianapolis, Indiana. After a play for a women's club in Gary, Indiana—"the turning point of my life"—she was invited to the State University to direct a one-act play. As she was passing through Indianapolis, her trunk was misplaced and had not yet arrived. It was then that she met Mr. Walker again, and he engaged her. "As you can see, everything in my life has fit so marvelously. I had no idea when I accepted the direction of a play in Indiana University, that I would meet Stuart Walker in Indianapolis. I was engaged there and I stayed about twelve weeks and that was my first year with him."

To say that Beulah Bondi's relationship with Stuart Walker was traumatic would be an understatement. "I loved creating the roles and I felt completely happy. As far as working and memorizing, his direction was fine. He was a very good director, a very fine director and I learned so much under his tutelage. But he really put, as I like to say, an elephant's hide on me so that I could meet any director, I could meet any producer, in New York or anyplace else, with a very calm interior and exterior. I don't think my heart ever missed a beat in meeting with a prospective employer."

This elephant's hide would be the result of confrontations that can best be described as brutal. Mr. Walker's rather unique direction resulted in her having to take a year off from the theatre. This decision has to be weighed against her genuine love of acting in order to fully understand the emotional impact Stuart Walker had upon her. This incident may best sum up his approach to actors and acting. "Well, the reason I took a year off . . . I just want to say one thing that he said to me about the second or third week I was with him . . . I was supposed to laugh. The rippling laughter of a society woman. And I had never laughed out loud in my life. Dress rehearsal came and I had not laughed. I'd say, 'I laugh here,' and 'I'm offstage on the balcony and you will hear this rippling laughter.' Dress rehearsal came and I said, 'I laugh here,' and he said, 'Aren't you going to?' and I said, 'No, but I will,' and he said, 'Take stage center and cast sit down.'

He was out in the audience and I heard these seats that were down clicking with a bang and a bang and a bang and finally he said, 'Bondi, you think you're an actress, and that you're going to be an actress? You haven't brains enough to balance on the head of a pin. And if you were my kid, I'd choke the guts out of you. That's what I think of you as an actress.' That was my beginning with Mr. Walker."

Although her relationship with Walker was emotionally upsetting, it did nothing to deter her ultimate acting ambitions. She is deeply indebted to him for his help which became invaluable as she moved through stock companies on her way to New York.

First Successes

She was developing into a fine character actress—polishing and honing those minute details of gestures, voice, walk, and mannerisms that would develop her portrayals into well turned characterizations. It is this attention to detail that gives all her performances that mark of individuality which is the trademark of Beulah Bondi. Her performances were gaining recognition from both audiences and critics. She was building up a following. She rarely failed to achieve the perfection she sought for each character she played. This article from the *Boston Herald*, dated October 17, 1926, asked,

> "Wouldn't you like to play an ingénue role, just once?" a friend asked Miss Bondi the other day. "No, indeed," was her reply. "The ingénue field is all littered up as it is, without me adding to the confusion. I don't like simpering goo-goo parts. I like a role with a little ironic bite in it, a role a little drab and bitter. There are so few young women playing old lady roles that I consider it excellent tactics to continue along my present route. Perhaps when I do get crinkled and some-what withered I shall about-face and try to become gay and impudent with a ribbon in my hair."

Although success in New York did not come immediately, and there were times when both her spirits and finances were low, she still exercised a wisdom in choosing roles that were offered to her:

> I would go into an office and be offered a role, but I knew the quality of the office, the quality of the men was such that I'd never work for them. And I would say, "Thank you very much," and they'd say, "Take the script with you." It would cost my fifty cents to send the script back—and I would say, "I'm sorry, but I don't think I'm right

for the part." So, I don't think I ever, as they say, "sold my birthright." I came very close to being tempted when finances got low and Father said, "Don't you think it's time to come home?" and I'd say, "No, I'm going to stay," and I'd hang up the receiver and be called to an office for an engagement for ten weeks at a hundred dollars a week.

In 1927, she appeared in *Saturday's Children* as Mrs. Gorlick. Her selection is another one of those strange turns of events which are characteristic of her career. Two years before, she had been doing stock in Denver, portraying the chairwoman in *Outward Bound*. At that time Guthrie McClintic was in town with a comedy. He visited the company in which Beulah was appearing, and was so taken by her performance that when he started to cast *Saturday's Children*, he immediately thought of her for the role of the boarding house keeper. While he was trying to recall her name and locate her, he was interrupted by Maxwell Anderson, who rushed into his office and said that he must have Beulah Bondi for the part of Mrs. Gorlick. Anderson had recently seen her in *One of the Family*, and was impressed by her characterization.

In Hollywood

On January 10, 1929, she performed at the Playhouse in *Street Scene* by Elmer Rice. It was her performance as Emma Jones that brought her to Hollywood. Samuel Goldwyn bought the rights to the film version of the play. He auditioned several members of the cast and selected Beulah and about six others for the film. However, this was not to be a permanent change for her. She would return to the stage several times during her forty year career in films.

King Vidor was chosen to direct the Pulitzer Prize–winning play. Its debut at the Rivoli in 1931 was the occasion for a great deal of excitement. The theatre was filled long before the film began; many patrons sat on the steps of the balcony, and mounted policemen had difficulty in controlling the throng of disappointed people who remained outside the theatre. In his *New York Times* review, Mordaunt Hall is quick to comment—"It is a swiftly moving production, this shadow version of *Street Scene*, but one that in comparison with the play always seems to be more than slightly exaggerated."

As a film *Street Scene* has a stagebound quality. All of the action takes place in front of the tenement building; there are no interior scenes; and the violence, the murder of the wife and her lover by the suspecting husband, is performed offstage and vividly depicted by gunshots and screams.

However, setting aside any further considerations of the film, let us focus on Beulah Bondi's film debut. Her performance is a beautifully etched performance of a gossiping, meddling, troublemaking bigot. Resembling a Greek chorus character, Emma Jones dominates the expository portion of the film. Lips protruding, walking as if in pain, scratching, tugging at her perspiration soaked clothes, adjusting her slip strap, and inevitably and repeatedly punctuating her caustic comments and venomous innuendo regarding every aspect of the street, its inhabitants, her neighbors, and the weather by sweeping her hand up along the back of her neck and adjusting her hair—Beulah Bondi is a joy to behold.

Her lines are never simply spoken. They are spewed forth laden with invective. Even a simple greeting becomes a condemnation; and answer to a question a barbed insinuation—nothing and no one is spared. Possessing the only obvious unethnic name, her remarks are democratically bigoted. Her judgments are sweeping anathemas. Her complaints—real or imagined—are delivered with the tone of a martyr. She enlivens the screen and the film sags considerably when she is not on camera.

The Hollywood Years

Street Scene was the first of what would be fifty-two films with Beulah Bondi. However, it set the standard for her performances which would never come to be judged by the length of time she appeared on screen. Beulah Bondi's performance as Emma Jones can best be called consummate. In her first film, she established her standard of excellence. In none of her films would she fall below it.

Undoubtedly Samuel Goldwyn and Irving Thalberg were also impressed. They offered her the inevitable seven-year contract. This was done at a party following the filming of *Street Scene*. It must have come as a bit of a surprise to Samuel Goldwyn that she did not jump at the opportunity to sign with MGM. Instead, she asked to read the contract completely. Goldwyn's reaction of surprise at this unusual request was followed by one of consternation. Beulah Bondi decided not to sign: "I had a choice, but I didn't want to. I didn't know anything about the ERA at that time, but I think that my freedom of choice and what I wanted to do . . . I knew there was something within me . . . that was fearless. But I won't say that because I'm sure many times when I'd finish a play or a picture, as every actor does, I'd think, 'I'll never get another role.' But I was evidently fearless enough to stay free and be able to choose."

However, considering her previous dealing with Goldwyn, it is safe to say that her refusal may not have come as a total surprise. When she was informed that she was to go to Hollywood to appear in *Street Scene*, Beulah Bondi refused to sign a contract because it did not specifically state that she would play the role of Emma Jones in the film. In addition, the contract did not provide for expenses which would be incurred in bringing her maid with her. No amount of assurances that it was understood that both of these matters were obviously implied would convince her to sign. It was only after the contract was redrawn and specifically detailed as to her role and necessary expenses that she agreed. This determination to make her presence felt is characteristic of her both on and off the screen.

Her refusal to sign with MGM might have been detrimental to her career in Hollywood. Having refused the protective custody of a major studio and as a fledgling actress, Beulah Bondi might have found herself in the difficult position of trying to get roles. Although she might have had some afterthoughts, she was certain at the time that she was doing what she considered best for her! "I don't know whether Mr. Goldwyn or Mr. Thalberg thought that perhaps they hadn't given me a fair contract or that they could. They were quite famous for getting good actors at very small salaries and really you're caught and for a long time, not able to choose. But, it's quite true that many of those people became great stars. So, maybe I wasn't wise after all. But I've had a very happy life and no contentions, so it was worth it."

As her film career proves, her fears were unfounded. She would have little difficulty in obtaining roles. In fact, she worked for every major studio in Hollywood and its finest directors—Frank Capra, John Ford, Leo McCarey, George Stevens, William Wellman, and King Vidor.

The manner in which she obtained roles in future films was varied. She told me that she made very few tests. Her roles were often the result of meeting with the directors or obtained by her agent—Myron Selznick.

Sam Goldwyn offered her a role in *Arrowsmith*. When she went to his office to sign her contract, she met John Ford. She discounted the stories that he was difficult to work with. "Never . . . at that time he was very charming." However, she did relate one amusing incident: "I said, 'Mr. Ford, may I ask who the leads are?' He said, 'Yes, Ronald Colman, and, um . . . ' He snapped his fingers and looked off into the distance and said, 'Hayes? Is there a woman by the name of Hayes out from New York?' And then I realized why, when I had left New York, Natasha Rambova said to me, 'Don't lose your sense of humor.' And I looked at Mr. Ford, almost with sympathy, and I said, 'Yes, Helen Hayes, a New York star.'"

However, her next meeting with Ford would not end on such a pleasant note. She had been told that she was the only one who had been considered for the part of Ma Joad in *The Grapes of Wrath*. She had two tests with John Ford—one a very pathetic scene and the other was a very angry scene. They had been two very good scenes, so good that the crew members responded with applause when she was finished. Ford said, "Well, I can't ask for anything better than that."

"By the time I'd finished, the gentleman who'd made the test with me, who was under contract to 20th Century, turned to me and said, 'Miss Bondi, it may not mean anything to you because I'm just an extra here testing with people but of the five women that they have considered and tried out—no one can compare with you.' And I knew then that there had been prevarication. He had told me that I was the only one they were considering . . . that no one else had tried out and I knew that anything based on a lie . . . I knew instantly that I would not play the role."

It is difficult to minimize her disappointment considering the preparations she had made for playing the role. "I had gone up to Bakersfield and I lived with the Okies incognito for two days. I visited five different camps as an unknown. I was an Okie. I lived with them for two days to get the feeling of the role. So, I was a gainer in a way. Naturally, I should have loved to play the part but Jane Darwell was under contract and she got the role and I was happy for her, but I can't say it was a tremendous disappointment because it was such an experience meeting those poor, bewildered, downtrodden Okies . . . I visited five different camps and they were all different where no one knew me until the very last camp, one woman looked at me and said, 'I've seen you someplace before.' I turned to the man who was going to be the critic on the picture and I said, 'I think we should leave.'"

The disappointment felt by Beulah Bondi fans is in no way intended to minimize the brilliant performance by Jane Darwell. She justifiably merited the Academy Award she won for her performance as Ma Joad. The only regret comes in having been deprived of another Beulah Bondi film characterization.

For the next five years, she divided her time between Broadway and Hollywood. In New York she was appearing in *Distant Drums* (1932); *The Late Christopher Bean* (1932); *Mother Lode* (1934). In Hollywood, she was enhancing the concept of character actress in such films as *Stranger's Return* (1933-MGM); *Finishing School* (1934-RKO); *Ready for Love* (1934-Paramount); *Bad Boy* (1935-Fox); *The Good Fairy* (1935-Universal); *The Gorgeous Hussy* (1936-MGM); *The Trail of the Lonesome Pine* (1936-Paramount); and *Maid of Salem* (1937-Paramount).

In all those years, the lure of stardom was never attractive. In the *Detroit News*, dated February 14, 1937, under the title "Beulah Takes Anti-Stardom Stand," reviewer Harold Heffernan quotes her as saying: "Give me a good supporting role, and that's all I ask. I never want to be a star again. The life of a star with few exceptions is brief. It's like a merry-go-round—only suddenly the music stops playing. Supporting players, unless they are typed, go on forever."

The word "again" indirectly makes reference to the one film of which she must be considered the star—*Make Way for Tomorrow*.

Between her work in *Make Way for Tomorrow* in 1937 and her return to Broadway in 1950, Beulah Bondi made some thirty films. In all of them her individuality shines through. Her performances never ran to stereotypes, such as "the grandmother," "the old woman," etc. Rather she explored the characters completely. Even if her film appearances were sometimes brief, her performances were lasting. This was achieved in her approach to her craft: "It's partly my observation and my true love of people. I think I was born without prejudice. I see something that is interesting, and, of course, the world is really a wonderful place to observe and remember and put those things. It's like a post office box. A great place in which you can file things. Voices, imperfections, tempo. I don't think any two people have the same tempo, I don't think any two people have the same tone. It's like a magnificent orchestration. You have to use your imagination and observation, many times, of people on the street."

This attention to detail was particularly evident in such memorable performances in films like *Make Way for Tomorrow* (1937); *Of Human Hearts* (1938); *On Borrowed Time* (1939); *Mr. Smith Goes to Washington* (1939); *Our Town* (1940); *Penny Serenade* (1941); *Shepherd of the Hills* (1941); *One Foot in Heaven* (1941); *It's a Wonderful Life* (1946); and *The Black Book* (1949).

In several films she worked with Lionel Barrymore, and it is her relationship with him that offers us a valuable insight into the character of this woman.

She worked with him in 1933 (her third film) in *Stranger's Return*, directed by King Vidor. They were both cast in elderly roles, and she was playing his sister. At that time he was very ill and suffering from arthritis. His knees were swollen; he was on drugs, and he had to be wheeled around the set by a man-servant. However, she is quick to note, "He always knew his lines." During one scene, he suddenly turned on her and told her quite positively and explicitly that he felt she was not "giving him what he wanted." She offered little resistance or objection until he was finished. Then she responded to his question, Well, have you anything to say?

"Mr. Barrymore, don't ever yell at me. Don't ever speak to me in those terms because I'm here as a cooperative actress. I will do anything you want me to and if I didn't stress one word that you wanted me to, all you have to do is request it."

Although he was irascible and short-tempered, she could sense that he was in pain. He muttered some apology and was wheeled off the set.

Working with him again in that same year for director Sam Wood in *The Late Christopher Bean*, Beulah made her presence even more emphatically felt: "We had this amusing thing happen because there were two children in one scene. Lionel was on my right and my "daughter" was on my left. There was a laugh on one particular line, but just as I would be talking his left hand would come across my face as I would come to this good laugh line. Sam Wood said, 'Well, that first take was alright.' Wood suggested taking another for protection. I had my plan and we started the scene just as before, and while I was talking,

I put my hand very definitely on his wrist so that it couldn't move. When we finished the scene, Sam said, 'That's a good one. Now we'll take just one more.' Lionel didn't say anything and on the next take, my hand went over his wrist. When we finished it, Lionel looked at me and with a big smile said, 'I'll be good.'"

Six years later they worked together again in *On Borrowed Time*, and she notes that he was completely changed. "I had always called him Mr. Barrymore, but he was now Lionel." He looked and acted like a different person, and he had abandoned his use of drugs. In 1952 they appeared together for the last time in *Lone Star*.

In her acting career, Beulah was secure and confident enough never to yield to any pressure either from actors or directors. In 1954, director William Wellman was made acutely aware of this on the first day of shooting. The film was *Track of the Cat*. Wellman always had a reputation of being a "man's director," and voicing his criticism in language that Beulah has always found offensive. Wellman's first comments on her acting, although they may have been justified, were expressed in adjectives that Beulah Bondi accepts from no one. She immediately made him know that she would take his direction; but she would not listen to it expressed in vulgarisms. Wellman apologized. Throughout the remainder of the filming, he increased his admiration for Beulah Bondi as both an actress and individual.

She continued to be active in films in the fifties and sixties, and it was *Track of the Cat* that offered her a truly challenging role:

'It was a very difficult role. The woman was complex. I tried to go back and think what her beginning was in the early days. The woman was within herself. She held onto the Bible—it was the only straw that she had left for any faith or any relief in anything. Her children were disappointing, her husband was a drunken sot. She had to avoid turning into something that was brutal. She still had love for her children and a certain concern for them and their danger. But she was warped, very warped."

Although there are some weaknesses in the film because it never fully sustains the dramatic conflict within the snowbound mountain family, Beulah's performance is truly the finest element of the film. Bosley Crowther, in his *New York Times* review of December 2, 1954, synthesizes it best: "Miss Bondi as the pinch-lipped mother takes command and browbeats her brood of frightened weaklings by the very force of her hard, demanding will. Then a feeling of tragic frustration seeps out of the Cinemascope screen, and the shadow of an O'Neill character flickers on the fringe."

Beulah returned to the Broadway stage in 1953, when she was reunited with Victor Moore in *On Borrowed Time*. She also recreated her role of the Grandmother in the television production of the play in 1957. She appeared in several other television dramas including the *Dirty Sally* series, featuring her friend Jeanette Nolan and several appearances on the *GE Television Theatre* and others including *The Waltons*. Sitting on her fireplace mantel is the Emmy she received for her performance in *The Waltons* for the episode entitled "The Pony Cart."

Make Way for Tomorrow is one of those rare films that loses none of its impact forty years later. The flawless blend of script, acting, and direction is a product of the genuine feeling that went into it. It is a tale rare for its time in Hollywood—a story of an aging couple who have grown apart both from each other and from their children.

"When I saw the script, of course I wanted to do it," Miss Bondi told me as we relaxed in her home. "I felt it was quite a challenge. I think that Lucy Cooper was perhaps the oldest character I had played. I supposed her to be in her late seventies or early eighties. I thought it was a challenge, but I loved the story. When Leo McCarey got the script he changed its name from *The Years Are So Long* to *Make Way for Tomorrow*."

The cast is uniformly excellent. Victor Moore plays Beulah's husband, Bark Cooper, the displaced head of his family. Separated from his wife Lucy, he is shuffled from child to child, refusing to accept the inevitable reality that he can no longer work. He clings desperately to the belief that he can be reunited with Lucy and find work. Standing outside an employment agency, he inquires of someone if there are any listings for bookkeepers. "Were you a bookkeeper?" the man asks. "I am a bookkeeper," is his emphatic reply.

As George Cooper, the oldest and favorite child of his mother, Thomas Mitchell captures perfectly the plight of a son torn between the obligations he feels for his parents and the responsibilities he has to his wife (Fay Bainter) and daughter (Barbara Read).

The other children are portrayed with equal conviction. Minna Gombell, Elizabeth Risdon, and Frank Mayer deliver performances that mirror the problems faced by countless children whose parents are unable to provide for themselves. Their attitudes range from complete indifference, reflected in the daughter who lives in California whom we never meet, to ineffectiveness as seen when Minna Gombell attempts to convince her husband Porter Hall that they should take care of her mother.

Vina Delmar's screenplay, based on both the novel by Josephine Lawrence and the play by Helen and Nolan Leary, is written to present the "case" for both parents and children equally. It is undoubtedly that our sympathies are with the parents who are separated and only wish to remain together. However, we are also aware of the disruption they cause in their new households. Grandma Cooper shares her granddaughter's bedroom, the decor of which is dominated by a huge oil painting of Grandpa Cooper. Her squeaking rocking chair is a permanent fixture in the modern setting of a New York apartment.

Fay Bainter teaches bridge to formally dressed students. Grandma sends George's shirt to a laundry because she noticed it was cheaper and also because she noticed that "your shirts are not looking as crisp as they used to," thus leaving him without one. Fay Bainter resists Grandma's attempts to help with the sandwiches by telling her that they will be prepared by the delicatessen, and that they will be "fancy"; to which Grandma responds, "How fancy can a sandwich be?" When it becomes obvious that her presence and squeaking rocker is an intrusion on the bridge class, Fay Bainter has to resort to deception to get her out of the house by asking her to chaperone Rhoda, her daughter, to the movies. When she returns, Grandma proceeds to recount the plot of the film to a group of patient but embarrassed listeners.

Perhaps Bondi's most memorable scene is the famous "telephone" episode. Those who have seen *Make Way for Tomorrow* would be hard pressed to find a scene more delicately directed and touchingly played than Lucy's talk on the telephone with her husband Bark. Having returned from the movies with her granddaughter, Lucy is told that Bark has called earlier and would call again. In the midst of a room filled with students anxious to proceed with their bridge game, she answers the phone. McCarey has Beulah framed against a background of these unintentional listeners:

> *(Mother takes the phone eagerly and ANITA goes back to her table. Mother is of the old school of telephone talker—the shout school. Just a trifle louder and she would need no phone at all.)*
>
> Hello—is that you, Bark? This is Lucy, Bark. How are you? . . . I say, how are you? . . . Oh, that's good.
> *(The bridge players fold up their cards and sit deathly still with hostility on their faces at this interruption.)*
>
> I was worried about you. Why didn't you write? . . . But you ought to write. You know I worry . . . Oh, I'm fine . . .
> *(ANITA's despair is seen to be complete and GEORGE seethes inwardly.)*
>
> Yes, they're very good to me. They've got some friends in tonight, playing cards. Oh, lovely people. Bark . . . *(moving closer to the phone)* How is Cora? How are the children? Really? How is Bill? Well, how are you? You know what I mean, how is everything . . . Oh, oh of course. Three months isn't long. Bark . . . Bark, it's getting cool now. Don't forget your coat when you go out. And if it rains, don't go out at all . . . I'm as happy as a lark. Of course, I miss you, Bark. That's the only trouble . . . I know you do, but don't forget what I said. We'll soon be together for always . . . Don't you worry Bark. Only please take care of yourself.
> *(The hostility on the faces of the players, who are known seen watching, has changed to one of frank interest.)*

Well, Bark, it's good to hear your voice. It must have cost a lot to call me . . . Well, that's a lot. You could buy a good warm scarf for that . . . Alright, Bark. Good night Bark. Good night my—my dear. *(She hangs up the receiver slowly. When she turns back to the living room her eyes are misty with unshed tears. She gives them her company smile, despite the lump in her throat.)*

I think I'll go to bed now, if you'll all excuse me. Good night, everybody.

(The hostility has completely left the faces of the people at the tables. They are now soft—not a person in the room has missed the pathos of the old lady's situation. The men rise—and there is a respectful chorus of "Good night, Mrs. Cooper.")

The film captures the tragic sense of inadequacy on the part of both children and parents in this conflict of the generation gap—one that is being played in countless families today as it was when the film was first released. The film touches close to home for many, and perhaps, that is what accounted for the negative reaction on the part of many viewers who claimed the film was depressing. Perhaps it touched too close.

Beulah Bondi also has a favorite scene. "Of course, my favorite scene was where she saves Tommy Mitchell. Before he can really send her to the home, she's already helping him." The scene takes place after Lucy has seen the envelope from the Idylwild Home and realizes that her son has the painful duty of telling her she must go. She senses the difficulty he is having, and before he can say anything, she suggests to him that she is not really happy living with him, and that it might be some time before she can be reunited with his father. Therefore, she would like to go to the Idylwild Home. For those who have seen it, there can be no doubt as to why it is her favorite scene.

The entire film is a series of carefully orchestrated scenes dealing with the tragic separation of the old couple, building to the inevitable climax. Having outworn their welcome and posed problems that none of their children can handle, the Coopers accept the reality (although not admitting it to each other) that they will be separated and never see each other again. Grandma is going to the home, and Grandpa is going to California to live with his daughter, "because the winters are so severe in the East."

They are reunited for one last day when they relive their honeymoon in New York eventually returning to the hotel where they had stayed fifty years before. Here, among strangers, they find more sympathy and warmth than they found with their own children. Lucy and Bark have a drink at the bar, "two old-fashioneds for two old fashioned people," are warmly attended by the director of the hotel. They dine, dance, and reaffirm their love. Each is willing to take full blame for the fact that they have been reduced to their present situation. "You can't sow ashes and reap wheat."

The last scene is especially memorable. The scene is the train station. Bark has just kissed Lucy good-bye and promised he would get a job and send for her. Lucy reassures him that she knows he will. As he boards the train, he pauses. He senses the reality of the situation; he pauses, turns, and faces her again:

> In case it should happen that I don't see you again, it's been very nice knowing you, Miss Breckenridge.
>
> She responds:
>
> And in case I don't see you *(cough)* for a while—I want to tell you that it's been lovely. Every bit of it. The whole fifty years. I would sooner have been your wife, Bark, than to have been anybody else on earth. I was always mighty proud of you.
>
> They wave to each other as Bark appears at the window of the train.
>
> All abo—oard!
>
> *(Suddenly the train gives a lurch—and it is serious now. There is time for one quick wave. She doesn't quite get to throw the last kiss—for the train is gone. She stands with her back turned, her eyes straining into the distance; she stands so for a few moments. There is the soft, low howl of the train whistle coming from the distance; the train is out of sight now. MOTHER turns, squares her shoulders and walks, alone and lonesome down the platform toward her future. SLOW FADEOUT)*

Beulah, as usual, did her preparation thoroughly. McCarey was pleased with the filming and very encouraging in his discussions with her. "Leo, well, he loved the picture, and I think he felt he had a very good cast, and it was all very pleasant. I think we were very sorry when it ended."

The Bondi touch, the perfecting of the character, the attention to all details is evidenced in her own comment: "I had to really hang on to that characterization. I didn't do too much socializing. The shooting was long and I enjoyed every bit of it. It was a character that I had to keep inside myself and really not go too far away from it at any time. I know I dreamt and slept with her. The calls were at five in the morning, so I'd get plenty of rest, but it was such an interesting character for me to study."

Although the film was spared the usual Hollywood mandate of the happy ending, Beulah did have one suggestion: "Because the picture was so touching and so sad, I said well, of course, Grandma doesn't really have to go into the home, and instead of taking the train they could both have gone out by bus and they could have stayed together in California for a happy ending."

The film did not receive a single Academy Award nomination, a tragic over-sight. However, the irony is that Leo McCarey did win the Academy Award that year as best director for *The Awful Truth*.

Today Beulah Bondi lives her quiet but active life, as she always has, in a Hollywood that bears little resemblance to the city she first came to in 1932. No final comment can be made on the career of this gracious woman, for she is not ready to end her career. She still is offered scripts which she reads and rejects as she searches for a part that is "right for her." Those of us who appreciate the fine art of acting can only hope that the right script will come along soon.

No one anecdote or story or comment can sum up a career. However, there is a single incident that comes close to epitomizing Beulah Bondi as an actress. Once, when she had finished filming a scene for Anatole Litvak, he asked her to do it again. He offered no criticism, simply that he would like her to do it again. This happened seven times—the same scene. After each take she turned to him for some criticism or comment. Perhaps he had a suggestion—something that she was doing wrong. He made no reply other than that he wanted her to do it again. Finally, after seven takes, and a bit exasperated, she turned to him and told him that she didn't mind doing the scene, but could he please offer some comment. Anatole Litvak spoke for millions, when he said, quite simply:

"I just love to watch you act."

Surviving Mother Hollywood

DIANA SERRA CARY ("BABY PEGGY") SPEAKS OUT

Betty Dodds

Originally appeared in vol. 6, no.1 (January/February 1982)

The year is 1945, and the jukebox in a Hollywood cafe is playing the old vaude-ville theme, "Baby Face." Suddenly, an attractive brunette in her mid-twenties leaps up from the table where she is seated with a friend and runs out sobbing. She flees down the street, crying hysterically, as though pursued by some name-less, inescapable terror. Her companion pursues for several blocks and finally overtakes the fugitive comrade—now clinging to a nearby telephone pole, screaming uncontrollably.

What caused this young woman to feel helpless, to become so overwhelmed and terrified? Reflecting on this question some 34 years later, the victim of this episode told me, "It was something I just couldn't handle—when that song started to play. It was a reminder that I couldn't escape that child and the pres-sure of PERFORM, PERFORM, PERFORM . . . 'You've got to come through for us just one more time.'" Her dark brown expressive eyes become more in-tense as she continues, "I didn't know then what it was, but I was dealing with a very serious trauma. Until then, I dealt with it on a day-to-day basis and tried to build a new image, but I was like a person who keeps on their feet when they're sick."

This reply came from Diana Serra Cary, author of two books about Holly-wood, and a respected film historian. She was formerly known as "Baby Peggy," one of the youngest child stars in Hollywood history. Her traumatic experience was a partial consequence of that early career. Baby Peggy was discovered in 1920 at the tender age of 19 months, seated on a property man's stool, while visiting "Poverty Row's" Century studios. Pioneer film director, Fred Fishback, soon became impressed with her natural talent, personality, and ability to take directions. Possessing an irresistible comic appeal, she appeared in over 150 two-reeler comedies by the age of three. Most of these were well-costumed and highly sophisticated satires of classic fairy tales or modern melodramas, where she lampooned famous films and popular movie idols.

Diana recounts vividly, how, as Baby Peggy, she was exposed to dangerous work situations like working all day in a bathtub of sour whipped cream (to simulate soap suds), being nearly drowned in a ten-foot surf, and being thrown from a speeding pickup truck, together with a terrified goat to which she had been wired. Since these experiences were about average for a movie child, most directors barred mothers from the set. She recalls being concerned about her mother and memorizing everything on two levels. She remembers "going through it and then thinking about how I was going to tell my mother an edited version, so she wouldn't be upset about the things that happened on the set. She always lived in that structured version of what it must have been."

With a salary that soared to $10,000 a week, earnings any adult might envy, Baby Peggy made a fortune almost overnight. And like so many of her contemporaries, it was spent or squandered even more rapidly by her parents and others. On one occasion, her grandfather who was her business manager, absconded with everything . . . including the family crystal, linens, and silver, and eloped with a Texas oil heiress he met on the veranda of the Hollywood Hotel. Needless to say, he was immediately excluded from the family's evening prayers.

Recalling these incidents in her early teens, Peggy didn't show bitterness because her parents were so distressed and she didn't want to pour salt on their wounds. Pretending as though it didn't make any difference, in interviews she would always say that the money had been lost in the crash. "I did it to save their face and my folks believed it. Lies proliferate lies, and as a result, it became *their* story and the truth to them. Even the best of parents can become spendthrifts under pressure and then spend the rest of their life with heavy guilt feelings."

Then there was the adulation and fame. Film producer Sol Lesser had learned much about building the child star's public image through the famous child star Jackie Coogan. During the time he filmed *Captain January* at Laguna Beach in 1923 and starred Baby Peggy, Lesser launched his most ambitious child star promotion yet. In addition to performing as the Democratic National Convention's adorable mascot in 1924, there were the "in-person" appearances, autographs, look-alike contests, Baby Peggy dolls (worth about $1,000 today as collector's items), toys, dresses, books, etc. A leading New York jewelry firm, wanting a piece of the publicity, photographed her with a million dollars' worth of jewels. She received a wristwatch valued at $1,250 in appreciation from them on her fifth birthday. Diana relates today that "Often the child who is brought into show business without precedent in his family can become absolutely addicted to fame and adulation. It's like a hard drug. When it's taken away, the child panics—and has real withdrawal symptoms."

Almost overnight, at the age of six, Baby Peggy was no longer considered a "hot commodity" by the volatile movie industry. After the loss of two front teeth, she felt as though she had fallen victim to some disfiguring and terminal disease. This was further complicated by the pressures of letting the family down as the breadwinner. At this point, she was put on the comeback road via vaudeville, and it was at her first matinee performance in Fort Worth that Peggy heard the song "Baby Face," which triggered her near mental breakdown seventeen years later. During that period, she was haunted by the recurring nightmare of being forced to go on before an audience without a script; her family desperate in the wings, begging her to come through for them "one more time." In later years, she would wake up in a cold sweat, relieved to find it had only been a dream. But the first time she was only seven and was wide awake . . . the nightmare was inescapably real.

At sixteen, Baby Peggy found herself—together with Jackie Coogan, Marie Osborne, Philippe de Lacy, and the original members of Our Gang—listed in the professional obituaries which ranked them as Hollywood's youngest has-beens. Many problems were encountered during those painfully adolescent years. It not only required making the passage from child to adult, but fighting for survival on several levels at once. Not ever knowing a normal childhood made social relationships with average teenagers extremely difficult. Diana says, "We could not make small talk with people our own age and it was not easy for me to find a world where I belonged." She recounts also trying to cope with an overriding sense of failure and guilt and not being able to free herself from a lifelong pattern of wanting to make her parents happy by giving them money. "I felt committed to making a comeback in order to have their love." Additionally, there was the quest to find a new self-image to replace the prosperous one that had been outgrown. This has its effects on the parents as well. "Parents who are accustomed to seeing themselves as happy owners of a 'Golden Egg' become devastated when that child tries to break the shell," Diana philosophizes. "The child star is going to have to be the one who does it, or it isn't going to get done. And usually if the pieces aren't picked up by that person, they really never get it all together psychologically because it's a broken part of themselves. . .it's gone."

The opening scene of this story seemed to provide the catalyst for Peggy to break that shell and emerge. With the realization that she was facing a serious mental breakdown, she knew it was time to get out of Hollywood. Moving to Santa Barbara, Peggy discovered solace in religion, talked out her problems and fears with a professional over a two-year period, and tried to build a life of her own. This even entailed a change of name from Peggy Montgomery to Diana Serra; the new surname being a result of her work as a public relations writer for the canonization cause of Father Junipero Serra.

In Santa Barbara Diana met an artist and art historian, Robert Cary. Being a mature and understanding man, he became instrumental in her search for identity. In 1954 they married and moved to Mexico where they shared a deep interest in Mexican history. It was there Diana shed the Baby Peggy image and found peace in a completely different environment.

Diana also began to fulfill the ambition she had from a very early age—to become a writer. She began writing Western stories at the age of seven and novels and poetry in her early teens. Regarding her writing, Diana comments, "It was a very natural way for me to go. I enjoyed acting on the stage but didn't like the life that went with it. The life of a writer always appealed to me . . . it's something you can do alone. You don't have to bring in the cameraman, the script writer, the director, and a whole cast of thousands . . . you can have privacy, if you wish." She was about 30 when she began being published regularly as a freelance writer in a diverse spectrum of publications such as *Reader's Digest, Esquire, The Saturday Evening Post,* and *American Heritage,* having now authored some 350 articles.

During the time she was working in the theatrical profession, she mentally recorded events on the set and backstage as a historian would see them, and determined at that early age to tell the story of what it was like to be a child star. Feeling a sense of obligation to her fans for opportunities provided in the early days, Diana says that she "had a very philosophical attitude toward leaving something here beside an ephemeral image on the screen." This dream was realized in her book, *Hollywood's Children: An Inside Account of the Child Star Era* (Houghton Mifflin, 1979). Taking six years for completion, the unique account not only tells of her own experiences and those of contemporaries such as Jackie Coogan, Shirley Temple, Mickey Rooney, Judy Garland, and Deanna Durbin, but it also gives the reader an intimate history of child stars from little red-haired Lotta Crabtree of the California Gold Rush era through the Second World War.

In addition to feeling that this information was an integral part of history and a very singular situation, Diana strongly felt a deep personal commitment to tell her story to provide deeper understanding of the grave psychological risks inherent in the child star experience. While over the years psychologists and sociologists had written volumes about the dangerous influence movies exerted on the youngsters who frequented them, nothing had been written about the crippling effects that an entire childhood spent working in films could have upon a person. *Hollywood's Children* became the first work to shed light on these little known facts and provided raw material for a pioneer movement just begun by a group of child psychologists in San Diego, California. Designated as the "Performing Children's Research Project," Doctors Malvin Galper and Michael Mantell hope to open the door to provide counseling services for today's child stars and their parents in an attempt to discover their strengths, and help them cope with their singular problems.

If Diana and the Performing Children's Research Project are successful, no future child star will ever have to run away from a theme song or other reminder of an unhappy childhood. Perhaps it can be different for them and their parents, thanks to this caring and sympathetic woman who was once adored as "Baby Peggy," now playing her grandest role.

Charlotte Henry's Adventures in Wonderland

THE BRIEF BUT MEMORABLE CAREER OF A HOLLYWOOD "ALICE"

Michael Thomas Lord

Originally appeared in vol. 7, nos. 5 and 6 (November/December 1983)

At the age of seven I first saw Paramount's film version of *Alice in Wonderland*. Included in the notable cast were Gary Cooper, W. C. Fields, and Cary Grant; but to my eyes it was love at first sight with "Alice," played by nineteen-year-old Charlotte Henry. Thus began my fascination with the actress who rose to stardom in 1933 playing Lewis Carroll's celebrated heroine, who received one of the biggest publicity campaigns in movie history, and who, only a few years later, was totally ignored by Hollywood, and drifted into obscurity.

Charlotte Virginia Henry was born in Brooklyn, N.Y., March 3, 1914. While still a young child she moved with her parents to Manhattan and began modeling. In 1928 she decided to try her luck at acting, auditioned for and won the role of "Gladys" in Tom Barry's Broadway comedy *Courage*. The play, which starred Janet Beecher and Junior Durkin, was a huge success, running over three hundred performances. When the play closed a year later Charlotte convinced her mother they should go to Hollywood. Once there she began landing small roles in various pictures. Warner Bros. filmed *Courage* in 1930 with Charlotte recreating her stage role. 1931 saw her back on Broadway for a brief run in a play called *Hobo* and a return to California for more film appearances—the role of "Mary Jane" in *Huckleberry Finn*; small parts in John Ford's *Arrowsmith*; Frank Capra's *Forbidden*; and *Rasputin and the Empress* with the Barrymores. In 1932 she landed her first starring role in Tiffany's production of *Lena Rivers*. This was followed by another starring role, once again opposite Junior Durkin, in *Manhunt*. While each of these two films brought her some recognition from critics and filmgoers, both were low budget programmers. By the middle of 1933 with ten films to her credit, she was still just another featured player, lucky to be working, but without the much needed backing of a major studio to establish her with the public.

About this time Paramount announced its wish to cast an unknown as "Alice" in its all star, high budget screen adaptation of *Alice in Wonderland*. Supposedly, over seven thousand girls from around the world applied for the role. Paramount even considered a young actress from England, Ida Lupino, but decided against her, thinking she was too sexy for the part. Charlotte was busy appearing at the Pasadena Playhouse in their production of *Growing Pains* when fellow cast members started talking about the search for "Alice." Intrigued at the possibility of playing the role, she went to Paramount's publicity department seeking an audition. Upon entering the office one of the men working on the "Alice" hype looked up and exclaimed, "There's Alice." She was immediately rushed to director Norman McLeod for a brief cold reading of the caterpillar scene. Two days later she was given a formal screen test in costume—the fifty-seventh girl to be given this chance. The next day Paramount had found its "Alice," and Charlotte had her first major studio contract.

Immediate press releases announced to the world that Charlotte Henry was Hollywood's newest star. Paramount did all it could to avoid mentioning Charlotte's previous films, wishing to promote her as an "unknown" suddenly finding fame. During the two months she worked on the film she was interviewed by writers for U.S., British, Italian, French, German, South American, and Japanese film magazines. When the picture was released on December 22, 1933, she began a nationwide tour with her mother, appearing at movie houses to help promote the film. On December 25th her picture appeared on the cover of *Time* magazine; by January 1st she was on the cover of *Movie Classic* and *Film Pictorial*. Without a doubt Paramount's publicity department had done its job well. The public was, by this time, quite familiar with the name Charlotte Henry.

The reviews for *Alice* were mixed, leaning toward the negative. The film was applauded for its technical achievements, but most critics found it to be a tedious ninety minutes, bogging down in its own inventiveness. One thing most reviewers agreed upon was Paramount's choice for "Alice." Howard Barnes, in his *N.Y Herald Tribune* review, wrote, "The *Alice in Wonderland* which has taken holiday tenancy of the Paramount . . . is distinguished by a beautiful performance of Alice, by Charlotte Henry . . . for Miss Henry in the role of Alice there can be nothing but praise." Argus in the *Literary Digest* put it quite simply, "A virtual newcomer, Charlotte Henry, gives the best performance."

Unfortunately Paramount was going through a very troubled time financially. *Alice* was expected to generate a substantial amount of money. When it became evident that the picture would be a financial failure, despite the high pressure publicity, the Queen of Hearts famous cry "off with their heads" probably echoed throughout the studio. Paramount decided to cash in on their young star's newfound fame by loaning her out. Even though numerous press reports announced Charlotte's next picture for Paramount as Mrs. *Wiggs of the Cabbage Patch* (made in 1934 with W. C. Fields, Zasu Pitts, and Pauline Lord), she spent the next year and a half working at other studios. During this period she appeared on stage with Will Rogers in Eugene O'Neill's *Ah Wilderness*, and made perhaps her two best films. For 20th Century she starred with George Arliss in *The Last Gentleman*, a successful comedy with Arliss in top form. While her reviews were good, it was hard for anyone in the cast to outshine the gifted Mr. Arliss. Over at the Hal Roach Studio she played "Bo-Peep" in one of the best features made by Laurel and Hardy, *Babes in Toyland*. Shown on television each Christmas as *March of the Wooden Soldiers*, this is virtually the only film that television audiences would know her for.

By the time Charlotte returned to Paramount a new regime was in charge. As she once stated in an interview, "No one knew Charlotte Henry. I was just a name on a payroll, from which I was promptly removed." Trying to change her "Alice" image which the major studios identified her with, she sought leading lady roles. At Monogram she starred with Norman Foster in *The Hoosier Schoolmaster*, a faithful adaptation of the Edward Eggleston book. The film is fine, and Charlotte quite good. One of the film critics for *Variety* predicted that "Charlotte Henry seems headed for better stuff." Unfortunately Monogram was part of Poverty Row, where, except for two films, Charlotte would remain for the rest of her career. The newly formed Republic Pictures gave her a contract for five films. With Charles Farrell she was starred in *Forbidden Heaven*. They were announced as Hollywood's newest love team, Republic hoping Mr. Farrell would repeat with Charlotte the success he had with Janet Gaynor. It was their only picture together. She was teamed with Eddie Quillan for two films, *A Gentleman from Louisiana*, and *The Mandarin Mystery*, both forgettable. A crime drama called *The Return of Jimmy Valentine* was well received but did little for her career; nor did an ambitious picture for Republic entitled *Hearts in Bondage*. This Civil War drama was directed by actor Lew Ayres, had excellent special effects, but was met with a cool critical reception, and prompted the critic for *Variety* to write, "Charlotte Henry deserves a better fate." When her Republic contract expired she freelanced about town. More "B" films at Monogram, a serial for Columbia opposite Frank Buck called *Jungle Menace*, and the role of Boris Karloff's daughter in *Charlie Chan at the Opera*. Considered one of the best entries in the Chan series, her role was little more than adornment. It did give her a chance to work with Karloff though, who, according to Charlotte was the nicest person she appeared with.

Charlotte Henry left Hollywood by 1938 to do some stage work. By the time she came back two years later her image had changed totally. Her hair was black, and she was a beautiful twenty-six-year-old woman. Back at Paramount the people she had worked with on "Alice" were stunned by the transformation. She was announced for leading roles in two pictures, *Flying Blind,* and *I Live on Danger.* In *I Live on Danger* her so-called leading role is billed sixteenth as "Nurse." As for *Flying Blind,* her name is nowhere to be found in the credits. Her final two films, *Bowery Blitzkrieg,* and *She's in the Army* gave her cause to retire. As she told Richard Lamparski for his *Whatever Became Of . . .* books, "I simply lost interest."

In twelve years Charlotte Henry made twenty-nine films, starring in most of them, but never becoming the star she could have been had *Alice in Wonderland* been a success. Looking at her films today, she was, as William K. Everson wrote in *The Films of Laurel and Hardy,* . . . "Winsome and charming . . . The nearest the talkies ever came to a Betty Bronson." Interestingly, *Time* magazine in its cover story wrote, "Whether, as she herself hopes, she will presently become a cinemactress celebrated in her own right or whether her career will parallel that of Betty Bronson, who five years ago made a success as 'Peter Pan' and now thankfully plays bit parts, will depend less on 'Alice' than on Charlotte Henry's subsequent performances." Hollywood never gave Charlotte another chance to shine.

I met Charlotte Henry in 1971 during a visit to San Diego, her home for many years. She was a beautiful, gracious, elegant woman. During our years of correspondence we very seldom discussed her days in Hollywood. For the most part her career in films was kept in the past, although she was quite proud to have been part of the movie industry during its golden age. It's hard to speculate what would have happened to Charlotte's career had Paramount continued to promote her and put her in good pictures; or for that matter, what would have happened had she not been cast as "Alice." Charlotte Henry died on April 11, 1980, having led a full and active life. And while she always retained a trace of disappointment about *Alice* and the effect it had on her career (she drove a car with the license plate ECILA), because of that role there will always be a place in film history for "The Wonderland Girl."

Siren Song

THE TRAGEDY OF BARBARA LA MARR

Jack Marston

Originally appeared in vol. 4, no. 1 (Fall 1979)

In the history of every human being who has endured disgrace, ruin, untimely death, or all these things at once, blame can usually be fixed on one causal element. Contrary to that formula, silent screen star Barbara La Marr, who did suffer all those disasters, was ambushed from several directions at the same time. First, somehow, sometime, she contracted tuberculosis, which was prime among many movers that sent her to the grave at twenty-nine. Medical lore tells us that TB thrives in abused, deconditioned bodies, and that rest and regular habits are essential to fight it. Barbara, on the other hand, followed a desperate, even suicidal, lifestyle that readily perpetuated the disease once she had it. Second, raised in small-town environments in which her childhood was monitored and managed by restrictive, though loving parents, she was slow to learn about life. Once she left the family, this lack of sophistication allowed errors of judgment and of behavior that eventually precipitated a moral collapse. Always a dreamer, seeing in life things that weren't there, or not seeing things that were, she failed to learn from experience, from copious reading, from stories that she, herself, wrote for the screen, and from roles that she played as an actress that echoed her own life. Third, she was endowed—burdened is a more likely word—with classic beauty: black hair framing a handsome face; a pair of kill 'em green eyes that always trapped people's attention; skin that never needed treatments or aids of any kind; and a form and figure that gave the boys plenty to think about. Fourth, her looks were a magnet for insincere, impulsive men who carelessly translated their infatuation into love, a mistake that generated considerable mutual suffering. These men were drawn to the appearance rather than to the mind and spirit that made up Barbara La Marr's warm and generous persona. It is with this last problem that we chiefly concern ourselves in this writing.

Barbara La Marr was born Reatha Watson in tiny North Yakima, Washington, in mid-1896. Most of her youth was passed in such small towns. Lacking vig-

116

orous social life as they usually do, these places can be poison to the spirit of an adolescent; they certainly were to Reatha Watson's. It didn't help, either, that her parents kept constant watch over a defiant daughter whose ripening beauty they measured with increasing trepidation as the years went by. Her dad, W. W. Watson, printer by trade, gypsy by inclination, moved his family from one western town to another, opting, finally, for the Imperial Valley in Southern California. Once there it didn't take young Reatha Watson long to track down the exciting life in Los Angeles. At sixteen she took work in a department store, signed up for dancing lessons, and began to associate with people whose sophistication appealed to her. Soon she was well known as a party-goer and habitué of night clubs.

On one occasion, deciding that Reatha's visits home were too infrequent, Mr. Watson dragged her before a judge and asked him to rule on sending his daughter back to the family. Adela Rogers St. Johns was a cub reporter then, and recorded the scene for us in one of a series of articles about Barbara that she wrote for the December, 1928 *Liberty*. She tells us that the judge, having studied the problem, looked over his glasses at the young girl and said, "You are too beautiful to live alone in a big city." With that he sent her back to hearth and home—to the life she didn't want. In the process, the judge gave her the nickname always associated with Barbara: The Too Beautiful Girl. From then on, with a title like that to attract readers, the newspapers chronicled young Reatha's comings and goings with more vigor than ever before.

Shortly after that, Reatha visited some friends in Yuma, Arizona. Through them she met a young cowboy, Jack Lytell, who, we can be sure, had never before seen the likes of Reatha Watson. Impetuously, he proposed marriage to her, virtually within minutes of meeting her. She refused all his overtures, but the determined Jack had alternate plans. Next day, apparently anticipating the action, he spied her driving along an isolated road. He stopped her, dragged her out of the car, and packed her off on his horse. He hid her in a ranch house and there maintained so strong a campaign to win her heart that she accepted him. Two days after they had met, they married. It's difficult to say for sure whether it was Lytell's brash manner and rustic ways that convinced the girl to choose a hasty marriage, or whether she fretted about returning to the cloistered life in Southern California; but it is common knowledge that many spiritually fettered young girls have eloped with insistent young men to escape parental supervision. Whatever the motive, she was happy with Lytell, Mrs. St. Johns tells us, and it may have been the only time in her life that she enjoyed such happiness, brief as it turned out to be. One rainy evening, while tending his range cattle, Jack caught a chill. Rather than go home to fight the ague, he stayed out, developed pneumonia as a result, and died within days. At eighteen, after a few months of marriage, Reatha Watson Lytell was a widow.

Back in Los Angeles, Reatha returned to the life she had known before the judge's ruling changed it. Her dad had moved to Burbank, a suburb of Los Angeles, thus facilitating her movements. She began to circulate with her old cronies, often frequenting Birdie Hughes's home, a hangout for the hippies of the day. During one such visit she met a young, suave lawyer named Lawrence Converse. Mrs. St. Johns happened to be there and witnessed that, in the classic way, Converse fell in love at first sight with the young widow, and that, with this love as a driving force, he called upon all his experience, his knowledge of poetry, and his sense of dramatic timing to ask her hand in marriage. Within hours, any and all resistance faded, and she accepted him. Precisely what her motive was we must leave open to argument; but, two days later, on June 2, 1914, she married Lawrence in her father's home.

No doubt it was the battling for the girl's hand and the calling to mind of so many romantic images that caused Lawrence to forget or to neglect a most important fact: namely, that he was already married and the father of three children. Within twenty-four hours, thanks to newspaper coverage of the wedding, the young man was in jail under a charge of bigamy. As a lawyer, he must have known that he would have to stand criminal charges. Nevertheless, apparently disregarding the possible consequences, he had to have Reatha if only for a short time. What could Reatha's unschooled mind have thought about a "love" that would drive the father of three children to bigamy?

Doctors who examined Lawrence shortly after told that he had a blood clot on his brain. This, they said, could very well explain his irrational behavior. Sad to report, Lawrence died soon after while undergoing an operation to remove the clot. If Reatha had been deeply shocked by the bigamous marriage, she was devastated at the news of the young man's death. Upon hearing of it she wandered off and was found days later sitting in a friend's house, mourning.

It was probably this entanglement that set up her somber outlook toward the opposite sex. In an article titled "Why I Adopted a Baby," written for the May, 1923 *Photoplay*, Barbara wrote, "Men—bah! I am sick of men. The admiration of men. The so-called love of men. Men's love is most unsatisfactory, the most disillusioning thing in life." What an odd situation! She could attract all the men she wanted—and then some—but she was never satisfied with them when she had them. This bizarre study in cause and effect handily sums up her entire love life, insofar as existing information permits any interpretation at all.

Phil Ainsworth, once a juvenile stage performer, was husband number three. One night in 1916 he saw Reatha, now an entertainer, dancing with her partner, Robert Carville, in a show at the Saddle Rock Cabaret. History repeats itself right before our very eyes; for, Phil fell in love with her, wouldn't stop telling her about it, and within two weeks, on October 13th, they wed. For various reasons the new husband was jealous of his bride and made the fact well known. Robert

Carville, for his part, was not only disappointed to lose Reatha's love, but he was also angry about losing her as a dancing partner—though he was quick to find another. There developed between the two men an animosity based on the tiniest provocations that alienated them both from Reatha's feelings, and that sealed the fate of this marriage: it lasted seven weeks.

During the time that they were together, Phil wrote forged checks to buy luxuries that he felt a pretty young girl like Reatha would want. These lessons in calligraphy eventually cost him two years as a guest of the state of California. Once ensconced behind bars, Phil filed a divorce suit—the only good thing to come of it.

One imagines that she might have learned to be more selective and observing, but apparently precious little rubbed off—unless, as we are often led to suspect, there was something that drove her into enjoying pleasures of the moment. By now there was a change in the pattern, though: while the essential ingredient, love at first sight remained the same, from here on in she was charmed by more experienced gentlemen.

Some eight months after she and Phil parted, Reatha met white-haired Ben Deely, a professional dancer, at a Los Angeles theatrical party. Twice her age, Deely knew that to win her attention he must work opposite to what the young swains were about—that is, to play "hard to get," or at least, "not interested." It worked. She fell hard for this approach, and for his good looks to boot, and before the party was over, she agreed to accompany him to New York City as his dancing partner.

Reatha Watson Lytell Converse Ainsworth Deely was to be disappointed again. Marriage did nothing to extinguish Deely's drinking and gambling habits, which eventually ruined his wife's affection for him. At this point she opted for a return to Southern California for yet another try at breaking into films.

The Hollywood Years

With a new name, Folly Lytell, she broke into the films well enough—having failed on previous occasions—though not as an actress or dancer, but as a scenario writer. In short order she earned $10,000 for her writings, based mostly on her own life. When literary glamour faded, though, and a lack of new ideas created problems, Folly turned to acting as a livelihood, pausing just long enough to take the name Barbara La Marr. Of course, the name changes were designed to cancel the notoriety that her romantic wanderings and entanglements had engendered.

By no standard was Barbara La Marr a great actress, but some writers—Mrs. St. Johns is one—claim that, given time, she would have become a polished screen player. Given time! However it may have been, our study shows that her acting ranges from barely acceptable to adequate; that what drew audiences to her films was a potent screen charisma; and that, in general, Barbara's appeal was to women who wanted to study their "worldly" heroine's way of solving problems. But Barbara La Marr at death was forgotten in the sense that she could no longer be a sounding board for coteries of fans. (It is interesting that beautiful Austrian actress Hedwig Keisler was re-named Hedy Lamarr by L. B. Mayer who, in doing so, remembered Barbara's beauty and honored her memory.) She left no noteworthy acting heritage; but even today her powerful screen presence is discussed by people who knew her and by some who didn't.

Barbara first appeared in a film titled *Harriet and the Piper* in 1920. The next year she made *The Nut* which featured Douglas Fairbanks who cast her. Also in 1921 was *Desperate Trails*, her only western.

Of her first three roles there is not much to say, bit parts that they were. Of the fourth, Milady de Winter in *The Three Musketeers*, 1921, there is much to learn. The minute this quintessential, real-life *femme fatale* appears on screen her immense capacity to draw attention is established, and we can readily understand why Fairbanks chose her to play the villainess: Milady's fatal, yet irresistible charm is as perfect and natural in Barbara La Marr as it is in the character that Dumas wrote into the pages of his novel. That this fledgling actress should have been chosen to play the part tells that this special quality transcended the lack of acting experience. At all events, this picture, more than any other, founded the stardom that eventually brought to La Marr fame, fortune, and coteries of fans not matched by any other star during the early twenties.

In September of 1921, just after *Musketeers* was finished, Deely and Barbara split, he to vaudeville and she to films.

Of *Arabian Love*, 1922, *Moving Picture World* noted that Barbara's characterization of the sheik's daughter was "unusually effective." We also learn from this venerable journal that Barbara's Annette de Mauban in *The Prisoner of Zenda*, 1922, was the work of an actress of "uncommon ability." Of the film the *N.Y. Times* wrote: ". . . if you've been seeing the average film, you'll think it great . . ."

She was able to lend her naturalness to roles in *Domestic Relations* and to *Poor Men's Wives*, both from 1922. She "vivified" the first, *Moving Picture World* tells us, and was "natural and convincing" in the second. On the other hand, *Quincy Adams Sawyer*, 1922, though it featured the singular talents of Lon Chaney, was a disaster, due mostly to inept titling. As for *The Brass Bottle*, 1923, a bottle-jinni affair, she plays only in the prologue as the Queen.

It was February, 1923, while promoting one of her films in Dallas, Texas, that she visited a foundling home. She saw what she termed a "small atom" that took her heart as it looked up from his crib and demanded, by means of his very presence, that she take him home with her. On the spot she filed adoption papers. This would be the "man" in her life, or to say it in her own words we'll quote from her *Photoplay* article: "The only thing I've found in the world that is at all satisfactory to love is a baby." Barbara named the boy Marvin Carville La Marr, today known as Don Gallery. At her death, Barbara entrusted him to her pal, Zasu Pitts, who, by agreement with the star, re-adopted the boy, giving him her family name.

Godfather to the baby was Paul Bern, a well-known producer and story editor around the studios. One of Hollywood's most interesting characters, Bern is best remembered as the man who killed himself two months after his marriage to Jean Harlow, in 1932. Years before he knew Jean, he had chased Barbara La Marr who knew that he had a deformity which rendered him impotent and therefore had always turned down his proposals. In response to one such refusal, he did 500 dollars damage to her home; but all this forgotten, and as godfather to Marvin, he provided nicely for the child both before and after Barbara's death.

Around the time that Bern became a fixture in Barbara's life, actor Jack Dougherty also came onto the scene. Described as a tall, red-headed Irishman who had a way with the ladies, he was a two-reel player when they found each other, but she fell hard for him and he for her. In short order Jack proposed. Coincidentally Barbara was apprised of some happy news: she discovered that when she and Deely married back in 1918, her divorce from Phil Ainsworth had not been final. California requires litigants to make application for the final divorce decree, having first waited a year. With this new turn of events, Barbara reckoned that she had never been legally married to Ben Deely; hence, it would not be necessary to divorce him. Thus, on May 9, 1923, she married Jack Dougherty. In this case we wonder whether Barbara married Jack not only because of her feelings for him, but also as a reaction against Ben. At any rate, the couple lived happily ever after—for a few months. The official separation is noted as July 17, 1924, but the marriage was in trouble long before.

It must have been in '23 or '24 that Barbara learned she suffered from tuberculosis, then an almost incurable disease. The TB and the maze of legal problems that gathered virtually with each passing day accelerated an already noticeable decline in her health and well-being. How she contracted tuberculosis is not known, but it and her legal troubles worked in tandem to ruin her, which is abundantly clear from existing evidence. She lived a "good" life, with the best of food and vats of booze to wash it down, a carload of cigarettes, late hours and early risings, topped by heavy dieting to meet picture schedules. So remarkable were these abuses that many thought she was on dope of one description or another. Everything considered, it is not the kind of life lived by people who look forward to many, happy, healthy years on earth.

All evidence suggests that Barbara's best film—her peak—was *The Eternal City*, made in 1923, just after marriage to Jack Dougherty. This rarity features cameo appearances by none other than Mussolini and by King Victor Emanuel.

In brief, the story: David Rossi, an Italian orphan, is cared for by Bruno, a tramp. Dr. Rosselli, a pacifist, adopts him and rears him together with Roma, his daughter. They grow up and pledge their love. Dr. Rosselli dies, and David and Bruno join the army after the war breaks out, and Roma becomes a famous sculptor with the financial aid of Baron Bonelli (Lionel Barrymore), the secret head of the Communist Party. David joins the fascists and becomes Mussolini's right-hand man. He meets Roma and denounces her as Bonelli's mistress; then he leads the Fascists against the Bolsheviks and kills Bonelli. Roma takes the blame for Bonelli's murder thereby convincing David that she had not betrayed him.

The January 24, 1924 *Variety* review notes that "if the picture gets anywhere, it will be due to some of the smashing bits of mob effects and to the assemblage of stars. The scenic features . . . are splendid and the acting is fine."

The usually stolid *N.Y. Times* critic was out of his skin giving kudos to the film, the single departure from which was to pan La Marr's "very heavy panting" in one scene. (The same thing appears in *Thy Name Is Woman*. Rather than "panting," however, it is meant to be a laughter-tears hysteria not quite carried off by the actress and therefore misinterpreted by the critics.) Aside from that, predictions for the film's success were universal.

Her marriage to Dougherty already in trouble, on October 6, 1923, Barbara received yet another jolt: Ben Deely filed for divorce naming Jack Dougherty as co-respondent. Deely died before the thing was resolved, but the shock of events associated with it may well have fatally affected Barbara. Deely's lawyer, Herman Roth, with or without his client's consent, secretly told Barbara that, unless she gave him a large sum of money, he would amend the divorce suit to name 26 more co-respondents. Ruinous to her career as such courtroom revelations might prove to be, she would not stand extortion and in February, 1924, successfully prosecuted the shyster.

It's all downhill now.

Declining Years

Miss La Marr's nineteenth film was 1924's *Thy Name Is Woman*. Already our heroine's star had flashed and begun to fade when this film was issued, as proven by comparing its cheap sets and hurried production to the sumptuous background of *The Eternal City*. The picture was stillborn according to the 5 March

1924 *Variety* survey of it: "The story is a tragedy and film fans do not particularly care for this type of tale. The happy ending is something that they must have in their film fare, and without it, they aren't happy. Ramon Navarro plays the soldier lead while Barbara La Marr is the wife. The two handle themselves fairly well, but the honors for acting go to William V. Mong. His elderly Spaniard is a work of art."

The story line is so much like *Carmen* that, short of the music, a viewer might think it to be one and the same.

Another reviewer calls the film a "sorry mess," but on the distaff side Mildred Martin of the *Philadelphia Public Ledger* opined that, "though the ending of Fred Niblo's picture is marred by being too abrupt (or too much censored), the tale is nevertheless an interesting one . . ." Important to our study she adds, "Barbara was her usual efficient and beautiful self." Today it only seems boring and unsophisticated.

Irving Thalberg often visited the set of *Thy Name Is Woman* to see that Barbara's drinking habits did not interfere with the production schedule. A pattern gels right here: the addiction must have affected this and other performances and accounts at least partly for her stunted artistic growth.

Sandra was also released in 1924, Barbara's disastrous year. The *Variety* scribe's words reinforce what we already know of a fading career by telling us that *Sandra* ". . . bears all the earmarks of a feature made with an economic perspective . . . not resorted to when one is making a picture for release by one of the bigger organizations. The Saturday night audiences at the Picadilly . . . laughed at two of Barbara's love-making scenes, both of which were enacted in the same manner."

The next paragraph notes that "Miss La Marr incidentally seems to be putting on some extra weight." What a contrast to the La Marr of '20–'23! What caps the chronicle, though, is this dab of irony: "In some of the big towns, there may be a chance in the neighborhood houses, but it doesn't appear to be a small town picture at all."

In *The Heart of a Siren*, 1925, Barbara played the Parisian Isabella Echeveria. *Variety*, on April 8, 1925, treated this picture as "nothing less than ridiculous other than in production. Lavish sets and clothes, but the story direction, subtitling, and acting drew laughs from a Sunday matinee audience while this nonsensical tale unwound."

The story tells of the leading vamp of Paris who is pursued by an American millionaire, snubbed by an Englishman, and who scorns a fellow Parisian into shooting himself. The Britisher (Conway Tearle) is eventually won over so that he breaks with his betrothed, but Isabella, the all-devouring, relinquishes claim on him upon appeal of his mother. To find whether he did go back or not would have interfered with a dinner date, much more important. (He did.) As to the acting, *Variety* only noted, ". . . Clifton Webb . . . gives this film its one genuine performance."

La Marr's last film, *The Girl from Montmartre*, was written for her by Paul Bern in 1925. During World War I, Emilia, a Spanish girl of good family dances in a Paris cafe to provide small luxuries for her brothers, who are fighting for the Allied cause. After the armistice, Emilia returns to her home on the island of Majorca, taking up her old life. Jerome, an English officer who knew Emilia during the war, comes to Majorca and renews his acquaintance with her. Ewing, a crooked thespian, persuades Emilia that she cannot marry Jerome because of her high social station, and she takes a job dancing in a low dive in order to discourage the romantic Englishman. Ewing abducts Emilia and Jerome rescues her, wounding Ewing. Emilia and Jerome are married.

The February 24, 1926 *Variety* reminds us that "this picture was made before Barbara La Marr's death and marked her return to West Coast productions after having made a series in the east—most of them flops. Following Miss La Marr's death her name was taken from all billing, . . . and the screen announcement has Lewis Stone as the sole name . . . Certainly Miss La Marr has the important role. It is probably the first time a firm has taken the star's name off of any product following death . . ." To such depths had the name Barbara La Marr sunk in two years! The notoriety already associated with her life was strengthened by a debauchee's death. The film's producers panicked, fearing that her name would keep people from buying tickets, though a review predicts that ". . . [the film] will do fairly, as Miss La Marr while alive was never an outstanding drawing card. Stone's popularity may also be expected to help considerably." While perhaps not the country's top "drawing card," the lady made plenty of millions for the studios. That they saw fit to expunge her name from the billing is firstline callousness that, even now, raises hackles.

Barbara La Marr died on January 30, 1926, aged twenty-nine after a life of work, drive, eat, drink, diet, and above all else, hurry. Her reputation had been ruined. Her beauty had been sacrificed. All the money that she had earned—up to $250,000 a picture—was gone. Why did she throw it all away in a banzai attack on life? Answers have to include that she suspected her life would be short; disillusionment merely made it shorter.

To die so young, still sitting on top of the pile, is an awesome waste. And when we realize that her beauty—the thing that most women covet—caused her only grief, the sadness associated with studying this lady's life compounds itself; for, to Barbara La Marr—Reatha Watson—beauty was a beast that she couldn't tame. Close to the end she told her dad, "it's better this way." She'd had enough.

She lay in state while 40,000 people milled around the mortuary. She was beautiful, prepared as she was by makeup artist Perc Westmore, who had labored long and hard to ready this last show. The truth was that without cosmetics the wasted face would have been unrecognizable to those who had come to see Barbara for the last time.

Her remains are in a Hollywood Cemetery crypt provided by Paul Bern. The inscription on it reads, "WITH GOD IN THE JOY AND BEAUTY OF YOUTH."

You can't stop thinking about it.

Ephraim Katz's Film Encyclopedia *(1994) states that La Marr was born in Rich-mond, Virginia, on July 28, 1896.*

A Countess in Hollywood

ELISSA LANDI

John Roberts

Originally appeared in vol. 8, no. 1 (1984)

If Hollywood ever boasted an aristocratic blueblood among its ranks, it was Elissa Landi. And, if Hollywood ever produced a highly touted new star who failed to live up to expectations in the 1930s, it was also Elissa Landi.

No one doubted Elissa possessed ability and Hollywood gave her a big publicity build-up, but she did not catch the fancy of audiences or the industry. The actress suffered through a string of mediocre films and when a major picture like *The Sign of the Cross* came along, Elissa failed to follow with another success.

Hollywood usually thrives on free publicity but not the kind Elissa stirred up. She was an intelligent and outspoken woman whose strong personality caused unpleasant breaks with two studios. Once, she left unexpectedly for New York when a studio needed her for post-production work, forcing them to complete the job without her. Elissa also experienced a messy divorce and a suit brought against her due to foolish negligence.

And consider her appearance. Elissa was petite in size with green eyes, reddish-gold hair, and an unusual face that caused a *New York Times* critic to comment in his review of her first American film, "She's certainly no beauty." That thought was echoed by a Twentieth Century-Fox executive's description, "She is too cold and she has no appeal."

Nonetheless, Cecil B. DeMille was impressed by Elissa: "She has a white, radiant sort of glamour that will carry her far." Elissa *was* beautiful yet lacked charisma when photographed. For example, most still shots show Elissa with an expressionless face and poses reflecting her patrician bearing.

Fan magazines liked to tout Elissa as a real live countess, a little stretch of fact. Elissa Landi was born Elizabeth Marie Christine Kuenhelt of Austrian-Italian parentage on December 6, 1904, in Venice. Her father, Richard Kuenhelt, was an Austrian cavalry officer and government official who died early in his daughter's life. Young Elissa formed a close relationship with her mother's second husband, Count Carlo Zanardi-Landi of Italy, and adopted his last name.

As befitting a person of her background, Elissa received an extensive education from private tutors in England and Canada. Besides her soft clipped English, she spoke fluent French, Italian, and German. Elissa studied three years for the Russian Ballet and was an accomplished pianist and singer. In sports, she loved horseback riding and was reportedly good enough at tennis to turn professional.

An interest in writing led Elissa to acting. While still in her teens, she had her first novel published and joined an Oxford repertory company to gain information for a planned play. At 19, Elissa made her stage debut in the Oxford Playhouse Theater production of *Dandy Dick*. A year later in 1924, London saw her in *The Painted Swan* and *Storm*. Elissa would continue on the English stage until 1930.

To enter films was inevitable. Elissa's motion picture debut was a small role in *London* (1927), a silent film starring Dorothy Gish and directed by British film giant Herbert Wilcox. *Bolibar* (1928), known as *The Betrayal* in America, recalled the occupation of a Spanish fortress by Hessian troops employed by France during the Napoleonic Wars.

Elissa joined Brian Aherne in *Underground* (1928), the first sole directing credit for Anthony Asquith. This was a thriller filmed on location in the London Underground and Battersea Power Station. It was a box office failure. British audiences preferred comedies and wanted their dramas with a high class setting.

Sweden's Svensk Films was eager to break into the world market and formed an Anglo-Swedish co-production to film *Synd* ("Sin") in 1928 based on August Strindberg's play *Brott och Brott*. Gustaf Molander, one of Sweden's greatest filmmakers, directed and Elissa was the leading lady in an all-Swedish cast headed by Lars Hanson. She returned to England in 1929 for *The Inseparables*.

Children of Chance (1930) told of London's backstage life and provided Elissa with a dual role as a lowly showgirl and artist's model. Next, she journeyed to France for a society film *Mon Gosse De Pere* (1930) which was released a few years later in America as *The Parisian*. For leading man Adolphe Menjou, the film came during a lull between his silent and sound careers in Hollywood.

Knowing Men, and *The Price of Things*, both 1930, were directed by a wealthy American authoress, Mrs. Elinor Glyn, who financed the films herself to retain artistic control. Mrs. Glyn was impressed by Elissa's sophistication and personality and signed her to a two picture contract. There were high expectations for *Knowing Men* due to Mrs. Glyn's reputed knowledge of the upper social class, but the critics were disappointed with her account of British society.

After fulfilling her obligation to Mrs. Glyn, Elissa was asked by director Rouben Mamoulian to read for the part of Catherine Barkley for a Broadway play of Hemingway's *A Farewell to Arms*. Mamoulian's favorable reaction was good enough for the play's producer and Elissa left England for New York.

A Farewell to Arms was a flop for the 1930 Broadway season. However, the play served as a showcase for Elissa who garnered favorable reviews for her performance. She had earlier refused an offer to sign with Twentieth Century-Fox but after *A Farewell to Arms,* she signed a long-term contract with the studio and headed for Hollywood.

Her American film debut, *Body and Soul* (1931), was a routine American flyers-involved-with-spies plot with Elissa on hand as Charles Farrell's love interest. She achieved first billing in *Always Goodbye* (1931) playing opposite Lewis Stone as a down-and-out woman caught up in a diamond theft and falling in love with a Scotland Yard detective.

For Allan Dwan's *Wicked* (1931), Elissa was an unwed mother who makes the mistake of associating with criminals and is sentenced to prison. Russia was the setting for Raoul Walsh's *The Yellow Ticket* (1931) with a very young Laurence Olivier as a journalist learning about the brutalities of the Czarist secret police headed by Lionel Barrymore. Elissa was the Jewish woman who provided that information. *The Yellow Ticket* was Elissa's personal favorite of all her films.

There was nothing special about *The Woman in Room 13* (1932), a murder mystery, and *The Devil's Lottery* (1932), a gambling story. A better part came in Frank Lloyd's *A Passport to Hell* (1932) as Elissa played a Sadie Thompson type exercising her wiles on German officer Paul Lukas in German West Africa.

During this time period, Elissa received the full support of the studio's publicity department who dubbed her the "Empress of Emotion." Fan magazines featured the usual interviews and the reporters found Elissa to be quick and animated, a chain smoker refusing to discuss her age but willing to speak her mind on other subjects. The fanfare did not help. Her first six films had bombed. *A Passport to Hell* did generate some business but the studio had given up on Elissa and decided to give her supporting roles and loan her to other studios until the contract expired.

Cecil B. DeMille proved his skill at blending religion and eroticism in *The Sign of the Cross* (1932). To play the part of the heroine in his spectacular production about the coming of Christianity to Rome, DeMille chose Elissa. When asked about his choice, the director replied, "Because there is a depth of the ages in her eyes, today in her body, and tomorrow in her spirit."

DeMille based his film on a famous play by Winston Barrett. As usual, he spared no expense in staging the burning of Rome and the climactic feeding of the Christians to the lions. Karl Struss contributed some handsome photography that flattered Elissa and Claudette Colbert.

For Elissa, the Christian maid Mercia would be the most important role of her career. Mercia is desired by Roman Fredric March and her refusal to give in results in his giving her to a lesbian. Eventually, March sees the light and joins Mercia before the lions. Elissa brought an appropriate, quiet dignity to her performance.

Elissa and March received top billing but the supporting players stole the show. Ian Keith was an evil and swaggering villain and Charles Laughton gave his famous performance as the mad emperor Nero. And Elissa could not compete with Claudette Colbert taking a bath in ass's milk. *The Sign of the Cross* is the only Landi film shown frequently today.

The Masquerader was a famous play and silent film starring Guy Bates Post and United Artists made a sound version in 1933 with Ronald Colman taking the dual role of a member of Parliament and a journalist. Elissa had the thankless part of his wife. In Henry King's *I Loved You Wednesday* (1933), she was a Parisian dancer in love with a construction engineer working on Boulder Dam.

The most ridiculous role of her career was as the sister of the Queen of the Amazons in *The Warrior's Husband* (1933), a tale of Greeks and Amazons living in 800 B.C. She was a feminine knight in glittering steel coming home from a day's battle to homemaker, David Manners. Needless to say, the reviews were bad.

1933 brought a much publicized break with Twentieth Century-Fox. The studio wanted her to accept a part in *I Am a Widow* and she refused because she did not like the film's "Hollywood sophistication." Elissa took a walk leaving behind a furious studio. The affair concluded with a so-called mutual agreement by both parties to dissolve her contract. The wrath expressed by studio executives in early accounts leads to the suspicion that Elissa, who was not a major star, was fired.

The actress moved on to a contract with Columbia. After her first film for them, *Sisters Under the Skin* (1934), history repeated itself. Elissa refused to do *The Party's Over* and took another walk. Columbia did not hesitate in releasing her from the contract.

Elissa now worked in support of strong male leads. For Universal, there was James Whale's *By Candlelight* (1934) starring Paul Lukas as a butler impersonating his master and Elissa as a ladies maid taking her mistress's identity. Paramount teamed her with Adolphe Menjou as two Hungarian stage actors in the comedy *The Great Flirtation* (1934).

Francis Lederer played an Eskimo in his American film debut, *Man of Two Worlds* (1934) with Elissa as an explorer's daughter. *The Count of Monte Cristo* (1934) boasted Robert Donat making his American film debut as Dumas' hero and Elissa as his beloved Mercedes.

Ill publicity and a divorce suit plagued Elissa in 1934. The Schulberg-Feldman Theatrical Agency sued her for 10 percent of her recent earnings owed them. The court ordered her possessions attached and Elissa lost the case, having to pay $7400 to the agency. Why she put herself in this predicament is puzzling and another example of a personal action that damaged her career. In 1928, Elissa had married John Cecil Lawrence, an English lawyer, and after her move to America, the inevitable problems of time spent apart and a clash of careers arose. Lawrence sued for divorce in 1934 which was followed by her countersuit. The press feasted on the suits when she testified Lawrence had had affairs and even encouraged her to see other men. The divorce was not granted until 1936.

Meanwhile, films about opera and opera stars were popular in the 1930s and Paramount made a contribution with *Enter Madame* (1935). Elissa took billing over Cary Grant as a temperamental opera singer whose frantic lifestyle has driven her husband to divorce. Elliott Nugent directed the farce and Nina Koshetz provided Elissa's singing voice. She finished off 1935 with *Without Regret* for Paramount.

Elissa returned to England to star with Douglas Fairbanks Jr. in *The Amateur Gentleman* (1936), the first venture for Fairbanks' newly formed production company. Irving Thalberg took an interest in reviving her career with an MGM contract. For the Lion, Elissa took supporting parts in three minor efforts, *Mad Holiday* (1936) and *The Thirteenth Chair* (1937), both directed by George B. Seitz, and *After the Thin Man* (1936) billed after William Powell, Myrna Loy, and James Stewart. In France, she made an obscure film called *Koenigsmark* (1936) with John Lodge and Pierre Fresnay.

By 1937, Elissa did not have much of a movie career left. Fortunately, she found other media with which to express herself. She did *Michael and Mary* and *The Swan* in 1935 for Lux Radio Theater hosted by Cecil B. DeMille and continued to appear regularly on the stage until 1945. Elissa also continued her ambitions to be an author with six novels in all, notably *The Pear Tree,* and scored a success on the lecture circuit.

Hollywood lured her back one final time. *Corregidor* (1943) was a cheap little film from Producers Releasing Corporation finding Elissa caught in a love triangle with Otto Kruger and Donald Woods set against a wartime background. In 1945, she returned to radio as a moderator for a talk show, *Leave It to the Girls,* broadcast over the Mutual Network.

In the post-war years, Elissa was an almost forgotten film actress. She lived quietly with her second husband Curtis Thomas, whom she married in 1943, and their baby daughter and continued to write and lecture. On October 21, 1948, after a 10-day battle at a hospital in Kingston, New York, Elissa died of cancer. She was 43.

The Birth of a Sex Symbol
JAYNE MANSFIELD

James Robert Haspiel

Originally appeared in vol. 1, no. 6 (July/August 1977)

Anyone with an awareness of the impact of the legendary Marilyn Monroe image is also aware of the existence of Monroe's chief emulator, Jayne Mansfield, whose diffusion of her own identity, by a concerted effort to be like Monroe, became the motivation of her entire career.

The story goes that in 1954 she dropped a coin into a pay phone for a call to Paramount Studios. "Hello. My name is Jayne Mansfield . . . I've come from Texas because I want to be a movie star." The Paramount operator replied, "Thank you, but we already have a movie star." Humor aside, the call was transferred to another line and the resulting appointment for a personal interview was all that mattered to the twenty-one-year-old beauty.

It was Paramount Pictures Interview Pass #23306, dated the 30th of April, that officially welcomed 1954's unknown Jayne Mansfield onto the studio's lot. For all her future boldness, her highly visible sense of security, Jayne's signature on the pass was written with an obviously shaky hand. She said, "Well, I made this test at Paramount. *Joan of Arc*. Crazy? And the man who saw it said I was a good actress but my figure was taking his mind off the character. And if it would take *his* off it, it would take everybody's. I had brown hair then." Jayne was given another test scene script to study and filming was set up for Saturday, May 8th, 1954. "Then they tried me in a bit from *The Seven Year Itch*. The piano bit." Jayne's *Itch* test failed to impress.

During the final days of November a newly blonde Jayne garnered a screen test at Warner Brothers. She filmed the "piano bit" scene she had tried at Paramount earlier. Ironically, this time, on a soundstage not far away, the same scene was being recorded for cinema history by Marilyn Monroe for the 20th Century-Fox production of *The Seven Year Itch*. "I thought I had a contract when they gave me the screen test," Jayne said. "Days passed into weeks . . . Warner Brothers didn't call me back." (Subsequently, as the direct result of a

131

publicity break Warner Brothers took another look and signed JM to a beginner's contract—terminating same six months later, in July of 1955.)

Jayne went to New York and auditioned for a role in an upcoming Broadway stage comedy, *Will Success Spoil Rock Hunter?* The play's pivotal character was Rita Marlowe, a platinum blonde movie sex symbol; a thinly disguised surface burlesque of Marilyn Monroe. Jayne got the part disclosing: "From the first day of rehearsal I became Rita Marlowe. The role gives me a chance to act on stage the way I would like to behave off-stage."

Mansfield was quotable and colorful. Her name, face, and figure became daily phenomena in newspapers and magazines. It has been said with authority that she achieved more notoriety in her year's stay on Broadway than most actresses do in a lifetime. "When I was in Hollywood I was just a starlet. They ignored me. Now all the studios are giving me the rush."

While Marilyn Monroe was Topic A throughout the media for wanting to extricate herself from her existing contract with 20th Century-Fox, Jayne zeroed in on what would once have been an unimaginable target—to be the blonde successor to Monroe at her own home studio! Marilyn's self-imposed exile from Fox was causing the studio financial headaches; they had been in litigation for almost a year in hope of retrieving their number one star. In Mansfield Fox suddenly saw the possibility of creating a "Super Monroe," so they gave Jayne a screen test. She tested in a scene from John Steinbeck's *The Wayward Bus.* It was filmed in early 1956, at Fox's New York City headquarters on West 54th Street.

As a frequent companion of Jayne's at the time, I found myself in the unusual position of being asked by her for assistance with the challenge presenting itself. Jayne was slated to sing "Put the Blame on Mame" in the test, which she realized had been done with memorable effect by Rita Hayworth (dubbed) in *Gilda*—thus we searched for days in vain in the hope of locating a local movie house revival of the movie she so desperately wanted to study. On the eve of committing the test to film Jayne handed me the script and asked me to rehearse it with her. I was not impressed by her histrionic ability. In fact, at a point in the test script where she recited the line, "You men are all alike—you take one look at a girl and your buttons go pop-pop-pop!," her emphasis on the words "pop-pop-pop!" caused me to break up. With great embarrassment I passed the script to someone else present and excused myself. It can be assumed that Jayne fared better with professional direction the next day when she was tutored for the actual filming of the test by George Axelrod, the author of *Will Success Spoil Rock Hunter?*

It was reported that *The Wayward Bus*/Jayne Mansfield screen test played the Bel Air party circuit "long before Jayne arrived at Fox. Josh Logan said it was the first time he had ever seen a film in which the actress rubbed her bosom against the camera lens."

If there hadn't been a Marilyn Monroe there might never have been a Jayne Mansfield. Jayne's very existence beckoned the comparison. Hollywood's Sidney Skolsky commented on the phenomenon in his first column on Fox's new blonde: "Jayne Mansfield is getting the star treatment. There's no doubt that when Jayne acts, walks and talks, you are reminded of Marilyn Monroe."

In all, Mansfield was to make twenty-seven films before her life ended tragically in an automobile accident on June 29th, 1967. Thrice wed, the mother of five children, she was then thirty-four. It is a comment of sorts on just how transitory fame can be to recall that Jayne Mansfield was, during the latter half of the 1950s, one of the most publicized personalities in the entire world—such was her ability to command attention, to excite the public. Today, not infrequently, a younger generation of movie buffs are more apt to confuse her with the one individual she tried so unsuccessfully to be like, Marilyn Monroe.

Marilyn

A PERSONAL REMINISCENCE

Del Burnett

Originally appeared in vol. 5, no. 2 (March/April 1981)

Frank Radcliffe danced with Marilyn Monroe in three pictures—Gentlemen Prefer Blondes *(1953),* There's No Business Like Show Business *(1954), and* Let's Make Love *(1960). Radcliffe grew up in the shadows of the Hollywood sound stages and decided at an early age on a dancing career. He studied with Lester Horton and got his first job as a native dancer in* White Savage *with Maria Montez. This led to a career in a variety of films where he danced with most of the leading ladies—Betty Grable, Cyd Charisse, Mitzi Gaynor, and many others. He says his favorite dance jobs were in* Kismet *with Ann Blyth,* Meet Me in Las Vegas *with Cyd Charisse, and* The I Don't Care Girl *with Mitzi Gaynor. He has studied under many well-known choreographers, including Jack Cole, Hermes Pan, Nick Castle, and Lester Horton. He talks here briefly about some recollections concerning his most famous dancing partner, Marilyn Monroe . . .*

ॐ

The magical presence that was Marilyn Monroe endures even today due to her films. What was the secret behind her magnetic appeal? I think it was, basically, her simplicity, an honest and sincere simplicity that engaged the viewer directly. And still does. But what of the informal Marilyn, the Marilyn who worked with choreographers, who practiced lines, who worked hard on the set . . . ?

One afternoon recently I interviewed Frank Radcliffe, well-known Hollywood dancer and performer, who has worked in a multitude of Hollywood musicals—usually as a support for featured stars in musical sequences. Frank talked at length about Marilyn Monroe and his work with her in three of her big musicals at Twentieth Century Fox Studios.

"All the fellows who danced with Marilyn were big guys," said Frank, who is a big guy himself, over six feet tall and bulging with muscles. "They planned it that way in order to make Marilyn appear smaller—she always said she felt like a football player with small men. Marilyn had a tendency to put on weight readily and was not the easiest person to lift."

Frank recalled the first picture he worked on dancing with Marilyn was *Gentlemen Prefer Blondes*. The choreographer was Jack Cole. Jack had Gwen Verdon as his assistant, and Gwen was always working out routines with Marilyn, who was a very hard worker and perspired profusely. "When she wasn't doing dance rehearsals she was working with her drama coach. When they had the dance routine 'set' they would incorporate it with the other dancers in the entire sequence." Frank went on to tell that Marilyn would sit with all the dancers, never by herself, unless she was worried about a scene coming up; then she would go to her dressing room with her coach and study. "What she did was memorable—the songs she sang, most of them standards, seemed original, as if heard for the first time. She broke the mold of the foxy blonde!" Frank continued, "They always used her own voice. She had a very unique quality. I loved her voice, it went with her. Just like Dietrich's voice fits Dietrich." Frank did the one number with Marilyn in this picture entitled "Diamonds Are a Girl's Best Friend" by Jule Styne and Leo Robin.

One day when Frank was doing a picture at Columbia, again working with Jack Cole, Jack came to Frank and told him that Marilyn's agent had called, and she wanted Cole to do the "Heat Wave" number for her in the movie she was working on, *There's No Business Like Show Business*. The choreographer was Robert Alton, but Marilyn did not feel that he did her justice. Jack Cole was really not excited about doing the job because he felt that Marilyn was not a choreographer's dancer and therefore it was not a challenge for him. So he told them his price had gone up to $6,000 a week for the "Heat Wave" number. The next day they had called him back, and told him he had been engaged as soon as he was available. Marilyn had said in the past, "Jack Cole makes me look better than I am."

It was the summer of 1954, and the entire cast and principals were assembled for the giant finale of *There's No Business Like Show Business*. Many preparations had been made, the set was painstakingly lit, the sound man was ready to start the playback, the principals had been placed in position by the hydraulic lifts, the sound stage was alive with technicians, dancers, extras . . .

When the assistant director was ready to shout, "roll-em," someone noticed that all of the principals, Ethel Merman, Dan Dailey, Mitzi Gaynor, Johnny Ray, and Donald O'Connor were in their positions, but no Marilyn. Everything stopped! The announcement went out requesting Marilyn to come to the set and Marilyn was discovered back at her dressing table having gold dust put on her hair. The announcement went out again and again, "Miss Monroe . . .

Miss Monroe on the set, please." Miss Monroe said, "I'll be right there"—as she turned to her hairdresser and demanded breathlessly, "More gold dust, more gold dust."

The next picture Frank worked on with Marilyn was *Let's Make Love* in 1960 (incidentally, Marilyn's last musical). One day Frank was in rehearsal for the number "My Heart Belongs to Daddy," written by Cole Porter. In this number Marilyn slid down a pole in skin fitting tights and bulky sweater, to join a waiting chorus of boys. Marilyn blew her lines quite a bit. And also her dance steps. They did almost forty takes on eight bars of music. They did a lot of parallels. Jack Cole had her doing almost nothing, but it appeared exciting when finished. Marilyn appeared to be in the middle of a mix-master—the boys were whirling and whirling and falling, a lot of very fast movement, but Marilyn was very static and just doing a little pose here, or grabbing a fellow and singing a line there. Then all hell would break loose and she'd hit another pose and sing another line. "She looked just great, and it was easy for her because she didn't have to dance up a storm," Frank added. *Let's Make Love* was completely rewritten as they filmed it; there were only three pages of the original script left untouched.

Frank went on to explain that there were five to six chorus girls dancing in one of the production numbers. Now, Marilyn was dressed all in green with green tights, and a little on the heavy side as she had put on some weight before starting this picture. Among the dancers was a girl named Bea, a pretty girl with very pretty legs, thinner than Marilyn's and they looked about a foot longer. Marilyn happened to discover that Bea was wearing the identical green stockings. Marilyn went to the costumer and complained, "I don't want anyone else wearing green stockings when I'm wearing them; besides, her legs look better than mine!"

Before they had chosen a leading man for *Let's Make Love*, the studio brought in a couple of actors that she didn't particularly want. Frank heard her on the phone talking to someone about whom they could get; Marilyn said, "Well, if he wants a million dollars, give it to him . . . I want him." She did settle for Yves Montand.

Whenever Marilyn would get hot and tired and wanted to take a break, she would call for a couple cases of cokes and invite all the dancers and people involved to stop and have a coke with her. The dance sequences on *Let's Make Love* took several weeks to stage and again she used her favorite choreographer, Jack Cole.

Frank went on to say, "Marilyn never did display any of the so-called temperament during rehearsals. A lot of her temperament was the fact that she knew what she wanted—she wanted certain people to work with—she would say I won't do it unless I can have them . . . that's really not temperament, I don't think. Jack knew what was good for her and she didn't want to have a bad shot; she'd rather do it again."

She was very friendly to the dancers but kind of shy and insecure. She'd smile and talk if you were in close contact, but never was she loud or boisterous. She knew practically everyone by their first name. Frank said, "When I used to lift her, she would say in a little voice, 'Frank, is there anything I can do to help—am I doing anything wrong?' She was really very thoughtful and nice."

"She wasn't a chatterbox, mostly she would just ask questions. One of the dancer's dogs had been hit by a car and Marilyn was so concerned that two or three times during the course of the rehearsals, she would inquire as to how the dog was doing that day." She had kept her own dog, Mugsey, for 10 years.

Frank said, "Marilyn was a person who was compulsively late; she'd always come in breathlessly and apologize. Marilyn would say, 'I just don't know what is the matter . . . I put my clock ahead and say I'm going to leave an hour early and something always comes up.' She really wanted to get married and be a housewife. I honestly think she had lost her drive for success. I don't think she really was ever happy. I think a lot of people used her."

Marilyn was first married at the age of sixteen. Jim Dougherty, her first husband, claims if he hadn't gone to sea, he would still be married to her and living in Arizona today. Marilyn had a 1935 Ford convertible from her marriage to Jim, and it was later discovered she had 42 outstanding parking tickets, but she had never changed the registration from Jim Dougherty's name.

The studio had her practice expressions in front of the mirror. They taught her how to re-smile so her gums wouldn't show; her own smile was very pretty, but not the big Hollywood smile. Marilyn was simple the way she talked, she talked smoothly and carefully, and chose her words, all small talk.

Frank went on to say, "I don't think she ever wanted success—the studio forced her into it—but she liked to work once she got to know people and felt comfortable with them. She hardly ever attended her premieres, she hated the hoopla."

Marilyn was not wild or extravagant; she led a reasonably quiet life living mainly in apartments and hotels. She paid $70,000 for her home in Brentwood, and wasn't interested in a movie star's palace in Beverly Hills, Frank commented.

"Marilyn liked to associate with people who were the ultimate in power and position; she was well aware of her shortcomings and lack of education. She completed one year of high school; she called herself a waif. She had this burning desire to be someone and made much more of an effort than someone with a normal background—we may have never had her, otherwise."

Frank told how she wanted children; she often talked about it, and said she saw a picture in a magazine she was reading of a deprived child, and it depressed her so much as it reminded her of her own childhood. Marilyn said, "Believe me, if I ever have children they just wouldn't be able to handle all the love I could give them."

Frank finished the interview with, "Her death, when I heard about it, affected me more than anyone else I knew in Hollywood—great, great shock, because to me she was one of the few remaining true Hollywood personalities . . . and yet the girl next door."

Eleanor Powell
BORN TO DANCE

Lisa Capps (additional contributions by Alice Becker)

Originally appeared in vol. 6, no. 1 (1982)

During the eight years between 1935 and 1943 the art of tap dancing was syn-onymous with one name—Eleanor Powell. With her spectacular, precise foot-work she developed a personal style that revolutionized tap dancing. As she flew across the M-G-M sound stages she was magically transformed into a breathless wonder, completely enthralling and captivating her audiences. Her style was unique in her low-to-the-ground footwork that produced clear resonant taps. With her first major film, *Broadway Melody of 1936*, she brought MGM into a new era of successful musical films that lasted well into the '50s, long after she had retired from the screen.

Miss Powell was the first female dancer of the American screen to have vehicles built around her as a showcase for her unique talents. She brought a distinct individualism to all of the dances she created, using her own unique combinations of intrinsic rhythms, acrobatics, and the occasional use of props to lend her creations a degree of character. It was inevitable that she be termed the "World's Greatest Feminine Tap Dancer," a title conferred upon her by the Dance Masters of America, and which she has held since 1929.

She received her first dance training in her birthplace of Springfield, Mas-sachusetts. Never suspecting she would become a dancer, her mother enrolled her in Ralph MacKernan's local dance school at the age of eleven, hoping to cure the youngster of her shyness. MacKernan's school taught a combination of ballet and acrobatics, and dancing proved to be the perfect outlet for Eleanor's creative abilities. She was ultimately "discovered" by Gus Edwards at the age of thirteen, while performing acrobatics on the Atlantic City beach. She then appeared in Mr. Edwards' revue at the Ritz Grill of the Ambassador Hotel in Atlantic City during the summer.

By fall of 1927 Eleanor left with her mother to try her luck in New York. Her first engagement there was at Ben Bernie's Club "Intimes," where she played three months. Shortly thereafter she landed a part in her first Broadway show, *The Co-Optimists* (later retitled *The Optimists*), in which she was the only American in an all-British cast. *The Optimists*, produced by Melville Gideon, was an intimate revue consisting of ten players performing two hours of skits and musical sequences. It opened on January 30, 1928 and played a rather unsuccessful 24 performances during which Eleanor offered an acrobatic specialty.

It was at this point in her career that Eleanor Powell made the momentous decision to learn to tap dance. Heretofore, she had done routines consisting of a combination of ballet and acrobatics, but tap was the new rage on Broadway and to get work in a show, one most certainly had to know how to tap dance. Eleanor signed up for a package of ten lessons at the school of Marilyn Miller's former dancing partner, Jack Donahue. After the first lesson, however, Eleanor was greatly disillusioned with tap because she found the new steps awkward and difficult. After much encouragement and individual help from Mr. Donahue himself, she soon caught on, and by the end of the ten lessons she had moved to the top of the class. As incredible as it may seem, those first ten tap lessons were the only formal tap lessons she had during her entire career!

After the completion of her lessons, she auditioned for the new Schwab & Mandel show *Follow Through* (1929), using her class routine as her audition dance. As a result, she was given a specialty number in the show dancing to "Button Up Your Overcoat," and this show—which ran for nearly a year—represented her first Broadway success.

Thereafter, Eleanor Powell became a familiar face on Broadway, appearing in such shows as *Fine and Dandy* (1930) with Joe Cook; Billy Rose's *Crazy Quilt* (1931) with Fanny Brice; *Hot Cha!* (1932), Ziegfeld's last extravaganza starring Bert Lahr and Lupe Velez; and finally, George White's *Music Hall Varieties* (1932).

Miss Powell also made numerous appearances as a headliner at Radio City Music Hall and the RKO Roxy during the early part of 1933, and by the midyear she was touring in the roadshow of *George White's Scandals*. It was while she was appearing in *Scandals* that Eleanor was first approached with the idea of appearing in films. Producer George White, noted for his countless editions of the *Scandals* on Broadway, was planning to make his second movie edition of the same starring Alice Faye and James Dunn. He felt that Eleanor, who had made such a favorable impression with the audiences during her stage work, would be perfect for a specialty number in the picture. But Eleanor loved the warmth of the stage and was loathe to venture into the unfamiliar territory of filmmaking. It is a credit to Mr. White's powers of persuasion, however, that Miss Powell *did* make that venture, which was to result in one of the most spectacular careers in musical film.

Eleanor Powell's first screen appearance in *George White's 1935 Scandals* was undistinguished at best. Her dance, however, is an outstanding moment in the film. In '35 Fox merged with 20th Century and screen tests of its players were loaned out as a courtesy measure to the other major studios. It was during such a loan out that MGM executives spotted Eleanor Powell and offered her a small part in their upcoming musical extravaganza, *Broadway Melody of 1936*. This had been a pet project of the studio for some time, in their effort to get back into the swing of making musicals. Eleanor was originally given the part of the secretary in the film (later given to Una Merkel), in addition to a dance number which was to be incorporated into the plot. Before filming began, however, the MGM executives wished to test her versatility and asked to see her dance. She performed a variety of tap, ballet, and acrobatic dancing. When she had finished, the MGM officials conferred among themselves, and much to her chagrin, removed her from her small part and placed her in the lead. Eleanor, who felt she knew nothing about the camera and was better suited to the stage, was greatly dismayed at this prospect. However, MGM was convinced that they had finally found their answer to RKO's Fred Astaire in the dancing feet of Eleanor Powell.

By the end of 1935 MGM had a new star. *Broadway Melody of 1936* was successful and the perfect vehicle in which to introduce its newfound young talent. Eleanor was given three breathtaking tap dances, one ballet number with the Albertina Rasch dancers, and the chance to show off her ability as a mimic by performing a splendid imitation of Katharine Hepburn. She demonstrated a very capable acting ability as well, and it was no wonder when MGM began announcing plans for new vehicles in which to star her.

MGM planned to rush her immediately into another edition of the *Broadway Melody*, but a previous commitment to appear on Broadway in the Shubert production of *At Home Abroad* with Beatrice Lillie and Ethel Waters prevented it. MGM reportedly offered to buy her contract from the Shubert brothers for the then staggering sum of $25,000.00, but the offer was declined.

By September of 1935 Eleanor Powell had reached the pinnacle of her success. *Broadway Melody of 1936* opened at the Capitol Theatre on Broadway to rave reviews from the critics, and the following night *At Home Abroad* opened across the street at the Winter Garden to equally strong notices. Within six weeks she was signed to do a weekly radio show for Socony Vacuum with orchestra leader Freddie Rich, entitled *The Flying Red Horse Tavern*. This undoubtedly was the busiest point in her career in which she virtually covered all points of the media from motion pictures to the stage to radio. She continued in this vein until a collapse from exhaustion demanded her withdrawal from both *At Home Abroad* and the radio show.

In June of '36 she was back at MGM and ready to begin work on her next project, *Born to Dance*. She was given a very young and personable Jimmy Stewart as her co-star and was reunited with Una Merkel, Sid Silvers, Buddy Ebsen, and Frances Langford, all of whom had appeared with her in *Broadway*

Melody of 1936. She was again under the direction of Roy del Ruth and was also given a marvelous score by Cole Porter. With its excellence in the script, score, direction, and presentation of musical numbers, *Born to Dance* remains perhaps the most enjoyable of the Powell films. All of the numbers in the film were expertly executed, the two most memorable being the lavish finale, "Swingin' the Jinx Away," and a variation from her usual tap style in "Easy to Love," wherein she demonstrated a style of dancing reminiscent of Great Britain's Jessie Matthews.

By 1937 Eleanor Powell was totally immersed in her film career at MGM. Unlike many dancers, she created all of her routines, and as a result was given an additional twelve weeks off each year solely for this purpose. The studio erected a special bungalow on the lot for her to rehearse in, and in addition to creating her own dances, with the normal amount of rehearsals and filming, she was also required to dub her taps for the screen, and for her own peace of mind sat with the film cutter during the editing of her dance numbers. Just how much care went into all of her dance numbers presented on the screen was particularly demonstrated in her next film, *Broadway Melody of 1938.* All of the numbers in the film were lavishly mounted and carefully discussed between the set designer and Miss Powell herself, to be sure they suited her particular needs with regard to the dances she created. She was teamed again with Robert Taylor, as she was in her first *Broadway Melody,* in addition to a cast that included Buddy Ebsen, George Murphy, Sophie Tucker, and a newcomer to films—Judy Garland. The musical numbers more than made up for any weaknesses in the plot, and *Broadway Melody of 1938* introduced such superb songs as "(Dear Mr. Gable) You Made Me Love You," "I'm Feeling Like a Million," and "Yours and Mine."

Later that same year Nelson Eddy took time out from his work with Jeanette MacDonald to appear in *Rosalie* with Eleanor Powell. A new score was written for the film by Cole Porter. *Rosalie* contains the now famous drum dance by Eleanor Powell, which was truly remarkable in its novelty and size, in addition to two memorable Cole Porter tunes from the score—the title song and "In the Still of the Night." Eleanor Powell's dancing, Nelson Eddy's singing, and comedy provided by Ray Bolger and Frank Morgan (recreating the role of the King which he played in the stage version) made the film most enjoyable.

If *Rosalie* was a journey away from the standard Powell formula, her next film, *Honolulu,* continued even further in that vein. This time the setting was Hawaii instead of Broadway and she was teamed with Robert Young (in a dual role), George Burns, and Gracie Allen in a riotous comedy romp. Film fans saw Miss Powell performing the traditional "Hymn to the Sun" hula, followed by a "hot" tap version, an impersonation of Bill Robinson and his stair dance, plus a dance on board deck of an ocean liner with a jump rope that was a real show-stopper. The script and direction of the film were both marvelous, but it lost the aura of being a real Eleanor Powell vehicle, and it was the first of her films that lacked a "grand-slam" finale.

In 1940 the dream of every dance-loving moviegoer came true—Fred Astaire was united with Eleanor Powell in a film that with nine dance numbers became a literal "dance festival" on film—*Broadway Melody of 1940*. George Murphy, a talented dancer, was also added to the cast along with Frank Morgan, who naturally supplied the comic relief. The main purpose of the film was to give the stars a chance to dance. And dance they did, with probably the greatest abundance of really superior dance numbers of any film made in the '30s or '40s. Being the last in the *Broadway Melody* series, it was more or less a return to the standard Powell musical extravaganza. The film had a fine score by Cole Porter which included such hits as "I Concentrate on You," "Between You and Me," "I've Got My Eyes on You," and the unforgettable "Begin the Beguine." Strangely enough, "Begin the Beguine" was not originally written for the film, but was taken from a rather unsuccessful number used in the 1935 Broadway production of *Jubilee*. In spite of its lukewarm reception from audiences at the time, the number was revamped and used for the tremendous finale of *Broadway Melody of 1940*.

Miss Powell's next assignment was a part in *Lady Be Good*. Although the picture retained the name and some of the score from the Gershwin musical of the '20s, a dull and plodding story line replaced the original script and served as a spotlight for two of its stars—Ann Sothern and Robert Young. It can be assumed that the producers of this film must have intended to cash in on the popularity of Miss Powell's name, while introducing and highlighting other talent. Nevertheless, the outstanding moment in the film is presented by Miss Powell in her superb rendition of "Fascinatin' Rhythm," directed by Busby Berkeley. Other pleasant additions to the film were Miss Powell's dance to the title tune, "Lady Be Good," with a fox terrier named Buttons, and Virginia O'Brien's delightful deadpan comedy style.

With the onset of World War II, Hollywood produced a rash of spy stories. *Ship Ahoy* (1942) can be classified as one of these. The original title of the film was *I'll Take Manila*. With the invasion of the Philippines before its release, however, the title was diplomatically changed to *Ship Ahoy* and the locale to Puerto Rico. Unfortunately, the first title was used extensively throughout the lyrics of one of the film's major production numbers, "I'll Take Manila," which had already been recorded. To keep the rhythm of the original song, the leading character's name was changed from Kay to Tallulah and the number was re-recorded with more suitable lyrics and a new title, "I'll Take Tallulah"!

In this film Miss Powell was somewhat restored to a role befitting her star status, although *Ship Ahoy*, too, was a venture away from the norm. She was teamed, somewhat strangely it must be admitted, with a new and upcoming young comedian, Red Skelton. Two other fine comedians, Bert Lahr and Virginia O'Brien, were given supporting roles. While the critics claimed that Miss Powell did some of her finest dancing in *Ship Ahoy*, the plot was largely geared to the clowning of Lahr and Skelton. A highlight of the film was "Hawaiian War Chant," played by Tommy Dorsey, which introduced Miss Powell's first appearance in the film. Had this number been developed more as a dance number, it could possibly have been one of the finest numbers in the film. Other outstanding contributions by Miss Powell, included her original "Tampico" which was highlighted by her expert use of a large red bullfighter's cape, "I'll Take Tallulah," another lively production number, and finally a soft-shoe number to "Moonlight Bay," in which Miss Powell taps out a message in Morse code to government agents while performing her routine. With plenty of comedy supplied by Skelton, Lahr, and O'Brien and highlighted with some fine dancing by Miss Powell, *Ship Ahoy* was altogether an enjoyable film.

I Dood It marked Miss Powell's last full-length feature film for MGM. She was again teamed with Red Skelton (who this time was given top billing) in a film which was almost exclusively a vehicle for Skelton's comedic talents. As Miss Powell was slowly edged out of the spotlight, the film added insult to injury. Instead of allowing her to create three original numbers, only one was shot and the other two consisted of clips taken from two previous films—her "hot" tap version of the hula from *Honolulu*, and an edited version of the finale from *Born to Dance*. The number shot for the film was entitled "So Long, Sarah Jane," and was a chance for Miss Powell to once again show off her expert ability as a tapster, and allowed her to exhibit an uncanny skill at roping, which she had learned especially for the number. Although this film cheated audiences of her dancing, it did allow a fresh look at Miss Powell's capabilities as a comedienne, which added a new dimension to her performance. But, as a whole, *Born to Dance* was a cut below the usual Powell standard, and must have been a frustrating experience for her.

In 1943 Eleanor Powell announced plans for her marriage to actor Glenn Ford, and soon after took leave of MGM. After her contract expired, however, she did make two more brief appearances for the studio doing single specialty numbers in *Thousands Cheer* (1943) and *Duchess of Idaho* (1950). She was also seen in a clip taken from an earlier film in *The Great Morgan* (1946) but this film apparently was never released in the United States.

In January of 1944 she made her final film appearance in a leading role for Andrew Stone in his *Sensations of 1945*. This somewhat tacky, overproduced picture is one Miss Powell would rather forget. Crammed with musical numbers, vaudeville and circus acts, Miss Powell's "pinball" number is perhaps the most pleasing routine, with Cab Calloway and his orchestra following close behind. Miss Powell looked marvelous and did an excellent job with what she was given to work with. Surprisingly enough, the film was received with generally good reviews from the critics, although today it could hardly be called a classic film of the era.

With her marriage to Glenn Ford in 1943 and the birth of her son two years later, Eleanor Powell retired from the screen. In the 1950s she reappeared for three years on television's five-time Emmy Award–winning religious program, *The Faith of Our Children*. Miss Powell not only appeared on the show, but was involved in quite a bit of the writing and production as well. In 1961 Miss Powell made a brief, but spectacular, comeback on the nightclub circuit. Her dancing was better than ever and she looked marvelous. During this time she also appeared on television on two segments of *The Perry Como Show*, *The Bell Telephone Hour*, and on *The Hollywood Palace*. With her great popularity at this time she was also asked to do a command performance in Monaco for Princess Grace. Her act was successful, but very expensive, and while still at the height of her popularity she decided to retire in 1964.

However, with the advent of *That's Entertainment!* in 1974, in which she appeared in three clips, she has commanded the attention of a new, young audience as well as renewed the interest of those who derived such pleasure from her films upon their release nearly forty years ago. Today, countless people of all ages who see her films in revival theatres around the country continue to be enchanted and amazed by her spectacular dancing. It is regrettable that her film career was a relatively short one, but as long as her films are shown to the public, her dancing feet will never cease to thrill and entertain us.

Today Miss Powell—now a grandmother—leads a quiet life in suburban Beverly Hills. The walls of her den boast many plaques, awards, and citations—souvenirs of her active life in film and in public service. Surprisingly enough, she has few official recognitions for her monumental contributions to dance in musical films. While the public and professional worlds have long acknowledged and applauded the work of Gene Kelly and Fred Astaire, little recognition has been given to Miss Powell. In October of 1981, however, the National Film Society justly presented her with an award named in her honor—the "Ellie." Miss Powell will personally select future recipients of the "Ellie" to be presented annually at the NFS's "All Singing! All Dancing!" musical award ceremonies in Los Angeles. This is a long overdue tribute to a true pioneer in the field of dance on film.

Natalie Wood

John C. Tibbetts

Originally appeared in vol. 6. no. 2 (March/April 1982)

There is a scene in Robert Mulligan's *Inside Daisy Clover* (1966) when a young movie actress (Natalie Wood) is in the dubbing booth recording a song to match her prerecorded screen image. She has difficulty in matching her song to the lip movements on screen. She blows take after take. Finally, we watch in horror as this brightly beautiful movie star collapses into hysteria, her sagging body trapped inside the glass booth.

This scene remains one of the most effective images of breakdown that the American cinema has achieved. I cite it at the beginning of this article not because of any particular significance it might have to the career of three-time Academy Award–nominated Natalie Wood, but because it illustrates quite graphically the hazards that lie in wait for any movie star—especially the child star—who, like the rest of us must grow old and leave youth behind. The image the movie star leaves behind on film does not age, it does not wither, and (barring chemical deterioration) it does not fade. But those images can sometimes become unwelcome monsters that mock the aging process of real life. They invite comparison; and they might even urge us to "try and keep up." But no matter how we try to "match the lip movements," as it were, the effort is doomed.

Like all child stars-turned-adult actors, Natalie Wood's entire life has been recorded on film. She was born in San Francisco on July 30, 1938 as Natasha Gurdin, the daughter of Russian immigrants. At the age of five, she appeared briefly in Irving Pichel's *The Happy Land* (1943). Three years later she portrayed a European orphan adopted by Orson Welles in *Tomorrow Is Forever*. At that time movie producer William Goetz changed her name to "Natalie Wood" (in honor of director Sam Wood) and Orson Welles was heard to observe: "She was so good she frightened me." In 1947 she became an established star in *Miracle on 34th Street*. For the next few years it seemed that Natalie played everyone's daughter in a series of "family" films. She was Fred MacMurray's daughter in *Father Was a Fullback* (1950) and again in *Dear Brat* (1951); Margaret Sullavan's daughter in *No Sad Songs for Me* (1951); James Stewart's daughter in *The Jackpot*

(1951); the (neglected) daughter of Joan Blondell in *The Blue Veil* (1951); and the daughter of Bette Davis in *The Star* (1953).

In 1955, while in her middle teens, she appeared in the legendary production of *Rebel Without a Cause*, directed by Nicholas Ray. Her childlike sweetness, still intact, was infused with the restlessness that was characteristic of the youth of the 1950s. Her range widened a year later when she portrayed a white girl who, after being abducted by Indians, is indoctrinated into their nomadic lifestyle in John Ford's classic *The Searchers* (1956). More restlessness marked her roles as she bloomed into her twenties. She was *Marjorie Morningstar* in 1958, the troubled high school student in William Inge's *Splendor in the Grass* in 1961, the ill-starred Maria in *West Side Story* that same year (her singing voice was dubbed by Marni Nixon), a girl facing an abortion in *Love with the Proper Stranger* in 1964, the troubled movie star in *Inside Daisy Clover* in 1966. As a "sophisticated" adult she appeared in the provocative and highly successful *Bob and Carol and Ted and Alice* in 1969, and in *Cat on a Hot Tin Roof* and *The Last Married Couple in America*, both in 1979.

Now she is gone and with trepidation we await the outcome of the yet-to-be-completed *Brainstorm*, her forty-sixth film. At this writing, director Douglas Trumball has decided to complete the film—although how the remainder of the sequences involving Natalie Wood, Cliff Robertson, and Christopher Walken will be handled is still unknown. Insurers Lloyds of London have kicked in three million dollars to complete the film. And, it is rumored, at least one of Wood's uncompleted scenes will be finished by a stand-in.

It is almost frightening how easily various phases of Natalie Wood's career match both her private life and the changing American temperament over the last thirty years. For example, her initial appearances in films like *Miracle on 34th Street* reveal a rather precocious child whose troubled disbelief in Santa Claus reflected postwar American cynicism. This Capraesque fable balances Natalie's indecision between the worldly bitterness of her mother (Maureen O'Hara) and the eccentric whimsy of Kris Kringle (Edmund Gwenn). The films of her adolescent years reflected the restlessness of American youth in the 1950s—a period torn by a relaxing movie censorship code, youth gangs and juvenile delinquency, the Cold War during the Eisenhower administration, and even the emergence of rock and roll. Not surprisingly, many of Natalie's films from these years—especially *Rebel Without a Cause* and *West Side Story*—were modern allegories based on the "Romeo and Juliet" theme. Private restlessness and public alienation were prime topics. In the first film she falls in love with Jim Stark (James Dean), a youth whose associations with street toughs and violence earns him the enmity of the adult world, particularly his own father. Natalie's character, Judy, is the little girl of *Miracle* now grown up; but she is still surrounded by an uncaring world. As she tells Jim, it is a world where "Nobody, nobody acts sincere." Her fatalism is also brought forth in their very first encounter when she says, "Life is crushing in on us." Verging on the edge of physical and emotional maturity, Natalie cannot even find secure love from her own father, who feels awkward at kissing his daughter since she has turned sixteen. Finally, the young people, pursued by their own insecurities (not to mention the police), escape to a mansion where they set up their own "family." It is a short-lived idyll, however, for Plato's (Sal Mineo) death shatters the momentary innocence. In *West Side Story* violence also disrupts the ill-fated romance between Natalie and "Tony" (Richard Beymer), a gang member of the Jets. Again, the love between Maria and Tony is surrounded by a threatening world, a world of street outcasts alienated from their families and from the law. And again, the only refuge the two lovers can find is in a make-believe marriage (one of the highlights of both play and film) that will soon be disrupted by violence and death.

This sense of the growing alienation of young people was reflected by many other Hollywood films in the 1950s—including *Wild in the Streets* (1957), *Black Board Jungle* (1956), and *Dragstrip Riot* (1958). It even surfaced in another film of Natalie's—John Ford's *The Searchers.* Commonly thought of as a western, it was also a story about a young woman who, at least for a time, cannot relate to her family roots. Since she had been abducted by Indians during a raid on a farm house, her uncle Ethan (John Wayne) has conducted a vengeful search for her. But this world is one of relentless hatred and unbending tradition and when the two characters are reunited, she recoils from him.

As a young adult (she married Robert Wagner in 1957 at the age of nineteen and remarried him later in 1972) Natalie began appearing in films that emphasized the confusions and perils of sexual relationships. She goes insane in William Inge's *Splendor in the Grass* and faces an abortion in *Love with the Proper Stranger.* In *Inside Daisy Clover* the only meaningful relationship that she achieves is with a homosexual (Robert Redford). Her films of the 1960s tackled issues that even films of the 1950s had been unable to confront. Pioneering films that tentatively dealt with drug addiction, racial unrest, and sexual confusion were now replaced by tougher movies. Her roles raised the possibility that one's sensitivity could mark a person as a kind of victim. *Splendor in the Grass* virtually savaged the Romeo and Juliet theme. When Warren Beatty was deprived of sexual love with Natalie in that film he turned to a prostitute while Natalie ended up in a mental institution. The styled violence of *Rebel* and *West Side Story* had changed to the brutal chaos of director Elia Kazan—including numerous bloody beatings and a gang rape.

In spite of some critical brickbats, Natalie's career achieved much recognition. At least one important critic, Pauline Kael, singled her out for a different kind of savagery, marking her sweetness and guile (not to mention her attractiveness) as targets. Kael referred to her as "clever little Natalie Wood," the "most machine-tooled of Hollywood ingénues"; worse yet, she accused her of acting more with her body than with her mind—"Miss Wood probably has the most active derriere since Clara Bow." Another critic described her as being "built like a brick dollhouse." By contrast, however, director Elia Kazan noted that she had a "true-blue quality with a wanton side that is held down by social pressure." As early as 1947, she had been named the "most exciting juvenile motion picture star of the year" by *Parents Magazine*. In 1950 she had been judged Child Star of the Year by the Children's Day National Council of New York. And over the years she had received three Academy Award nominations—for *Splendor in the Grass, Love with the Proper Stranger,* and *Rebel Without a Cause.*

But it was not until films like *Bob and Carol and Ted and Alice* and *The Last Married Couple in America* (which Natalie herself regarded as a sequel to *Bob and Carol*) that the saving leavening of humor was brought to bear upon the many painful dilemmas portrayed in her adult films. Still a sweet rebel, she confronted the sophisticated and sexy controversies of mate-swapping with bemusement and élan. Such films of the late 1960s and 1970s were a far cry from those twenty years earlier that brought former child stars to their first "adult" roles. Remember the hue and cry attendant upon Shirley Temple's first screen kiss and the controversy surrounding the theme of illegitimate parentage in *That Hagen Woman* (1947)?

Over the years the films of Natalie Wood have represented a gradual "coming of age" for both her and for Hollywood cinema in general. She left a lot of images behind, many of which we demanded she live up to because we admired and loved the sweet child that remained in all her roles, young and old. "She clings to things with her eyes," Kazan once remarked of her special appeal. And so our own eyes always found her on the screen. And always will.

Part III

HOLLYWOOD PAIRS

Bette Davis and Claude Rains

TWO "OPPOSITES" THAT ATTRACTED

Anne Etheridge

Originally appeared in vol. 5, no. 3 (May/June 1981)

It was probably inevitable, given the time and place, that Claude Rains and Bette Davis would cross professional paths. They were the natural choices for Napoleon and Carlotta, Alexander Hollenius and Christine Radcliffe, Job Skeffington and Fanny Trellis, Dr. Jaquith and Charlotte Vale. One can hardly imagine anyone else in those parts. Yet it's curious they became friends, these two towering professionals, neither of whom were known for their self-effacing manner.

By the time he got to Warners, Rains had come a long way from Herbert Tree and Her Majesty's Theatre in London. He had every right to be proud of his achievements. Perhaps because it had taken such a long time, perhaps because he had "come up through the ranks," he was very much aware of himself as an actor. His associates, and even his daughter, remember he was always center stage, whether on or off. He was never in someone's living room that he didn't stand in front of the fireplace, hands clasped behind his back, feet apart.

Rains didn't enjoy socializing in the Hollywood sense of the word. Once filming was over, he would retreat to his Pennsylvania farm and spend time in the vegetable garden, perfectly content to be left alone. In spite of his flamboyant actor's demeanor, he had in him all the attributes of a recluse. Few people were invited to the farm. He didn't have many close friends, but Bette Davis was one of them. Their initial meeting, on the set of *Juarez*, was not a harbinger of things to come.

Juarez was another Warner entry in the field of historical biography. The tradition had begun feebly in 1929 with *Disraeli* and gained strength with *The Story of Louis Pasteur* (1935) and *The Life of Emile Zola* (1937). A great percentage of these films featured Paul Muni, buried beneath mounds of makeup and false hair, emoting as one historical figure after another. Jack Warner is once rumored to have said, "I don't know why we pay Paul all that money. We can't even *see* him!" Strictly speaking, *Juarez* was not really the story of the Mexican leader. Much screen time concentrated on the dilemma faced by Archduke Maximilian, who was sent by Napoleon to rule Mexico in the hopes of establishing a Mexican empire while America had its hands full with the Civil War.

It was on the set of this "epic biography" that Claude Rains and Bette Davis met. The first scene they had to play was the one in which Napoleon meets Carlotta, whom he loathes. Davis entered the room, in character, and stormed up to the desk where Rains, as Napoleon, sat. She leaned over menacingly, took one look at his hard, unrelenting stare and stopped short.

"Oh, my God!"

"Cut!" yelled William Dieterle, the director. "What is it?"

"Did you see the way he looked at me? He scared me to death!"

Davis laughs now when she recalls the incident. "It's true. He absolutely scared me to death! That was our initial contact and that I got through it at all was a miracle. When Claude played a character, he was the consummate actor. It was always monumental theatre with him."

Later during production, Rains caught Davis staring at him. He asked if something was wrong and she answered, "Thank God you're married."

"Every now and then, I would kid Claude," says Davis. "I would say to him, you marry all these women, why do you *never* marry me? He would just smile and that was that. I think he was basically enormously sexy. It reeked! He had that in any role he played."

After they became friends, they could joke about marriage to one another, but at the time Davis made the remark to him on the *Juarez* set, Rains was so alarmed he brought his daughter in the next day to serve, one supposes, as proof of wedded bliss.

By the time *Now, Voyager* was in production, their friendship was an established fact . . . one that continued for nearly thirty years. Each had a high regard and affection for the other. "Claude was enormously well read and extremely bright about scripts and his work. He was one of the really great actors. We will never see his kind again. We just never will."

Before they worked together again, Rains went off to make eleven other films, ranging from *The Sea Hawk* to *Here Comes Mr. Jordan.* But then the kind of film Warners did best caught up with him.

As long as Warners could draw on the talents of stars like Bette Davis and Joan Crawford, the studio had a definite edge in women's weepers. Typically, these films were awash in high melodramatics with actors forced to deliver lines like "You'll always be nothing but a cheap, common frump!" with great seriousness. From time to time, though, the genre rose above its own limitations and Rains could be pleased with the fact that, in two out of three instances, he was fortunate to get literate scripts that contained their share of irony and sophistication. They are worthy of closer examination if only for that reason.

Now, Voyager was adapted by Casey Robinson, a master at his craft. Taking Olive Higgins Prouty's five hundred page novel and reworking it into screen size could not have been an easy task. (Richard Corliss points out in *Talking Pictures* that if *Now, Voyager* were remade today by Robert Bolt and David Lean, it would take three years to write, four years to make and five hours to watch.)

Voyager is the story of Charlotte Vale, an over-thirty "spinster" domineered by a mother dripping with evil intentions. The film follows Charlotte as she is sent to Cascades, a mountain sanitarium, to recover from a nervous breakdown after Dr. Jaquith (Claude Rains), the psychiatrist, cuts her mother down to size, saying, "A mother's rights—twaddle!"

Jaquith quotes Walt Whitman to Charlotte ("Now, Voyager, sail thou forth to seek and find . . .") and sends her off on an ocean voyage. Charlotte is transformed from her frumpy self into a remarkably stylish woman with the help of a friend's wardrobe. Alas, the psyche is not that easily healed and she has trouble dealing with the attentions of Jerry Durrance (played by Paul Henreid), a fellow passenger. "These are tears of gratitude. An old maid's gratitude. Nobody ever called me darling before."

Before the end of the voyage, Charlotte has resolved her difficulties and spends a passionate night with Jerry, consummating their affair and ending nearly all her psychological problems. Jerry, already married, returns to wife and family after first suggesting, in a famous scene, that they "have a smoke on it."

Charlotte returns home to her mother, who greets her with "It's worse than Lisa led me to believe. Much worse."

Charlotte responds, "I've come home to live with you in the same house but it can't be in the same way."

At a party, Charlotte meets a stodgy Bostonian who proposes marriage. She accepts, believing she can forget Jerry even though he still sends her camellias every day. On the eve of her wedding, she and Elliot attend a party. Predictably, Jerry is there. A whispered conversation, covered by loud small talk, proves he is still in love with her, so Charlotte calls off the wedding.

Her mother is furious. "What do you intend to do with your life?" "Get a cat and a parrot and live alone in single blessedness," answers Charlotte. They have a heated argument and Mrs. Vale, vindictive to the end, has the poor grace to have a heart attack and die. Charlotte, blaming herself for her mother's death, returns to Cascades and Dr. Jaquith for the support and friendship she needs.

Jerry's child, a young version of Charlotte with all the attendant problems, is also at Cascades. Charlotte takes over as her mother, doctor, mentor, friend— much to Jaquith's pretended chagrin. "I thought you came down here to have a nervous breakdown?" he asks her. "If it's all the same to you, I've decided not to," she says.

Eventually, Charlotte is allowed to take Tina home and give her all the things that were missing from her own childhood. Charlotte, transformation complete, is put on Cascade's board of directors and she and Jerry decide that a platonic relationship is best. As they stand together in the den, he asks her, "Will you be happy, Charlotte?" "Oh, Jerry," she answers, "don't let's ask for the moon when we have the stars."

Writer Casey Robinson managed all this in 117 minutes of screen time. His dialogue is elegantly concise, witty, intelligent and the scenes between the stronger characters of Charlotte, her mother and Jaquith are excellent.

This kind of writing was ideally suited to both Davis and Rains. Rains, especially, was able to give the all-knowing Jaquith just the right touch of gentle irony as he watched his patient move from neurotic spinster to independent woman. His affection for her is only thinly veiled. In their final scene together, as they sit on the floor going over plans for a new wing at Cascades, the electricity between the two is fairly visible on the screen.

"Claude and I used to talk by the hour about the ending," Davis says. "I *know* Charlotte finally married Jaquith because he was strong and she had become strong. Jerry would never have been strong enough for her. Anybody who had any intuition at all felt that Charlotte married Jaquith. That scene where they were planning the new wing together—brother! It was so obvious!"

Davis and Rains may, for whatever reason, have escaped screen matrimony in *Now, Voyager*, but they made up for it in their next weeper, *Mr. Skeffington.*

Skeffington was penned by the Epstein brothers, Julius and Phillip, who had also written *The Male Animal*, *Arsenic and Old Lace*, *The Man Who Came to Dinner* and *Casablanca*. *Skeffington* is an acting tour de force for both Davis and Rains. As Fanny, she moves from innocent girlhood to old age, changing even her speech patterns to match her character. He plays the long-suffering Jewish financier, Job Skeffington, who has the misfortune to be hopelessly in love with a woman who cares only for herself. Rains received one of his four Academy Award nominations for his part in the film.

In a thinly disguised effort to save her brother from the legal consequences of embezzlement, Fanny marries Job. Any doubts he might have that Fanny doesn't really love him are quickly dispelled by her honesty. "You're good and kind. And your eyes are special in a St. Bernard sort of way. Beside the fact that you're very rich."

Unfortunately, Fanny maintains this attitude throughout the first half of the film while her other suitors hotly pursue her in an attempt to win her away from her husband. As Job says, "She has to reject them all on the average of twice a month."

Even pregnancy fails to change Fanny's basically selfish attitude. "Babies grow up," she says, "and everyone expects you to grow up with them." Fanny announces her intention of having the baby in California, away from her friends so they won't see her "swollen and puffy." Job tries to quiet her fears by telling her, "A woman is beautiful when she is loved and only then." In a moment of rare humor, Fanny replies, "Nonsense. A woman is beautiful if she has eight hours' sleep and goes to the beauty parlor every day. And bone structure has a lot to do with it."

The new baby, named after her mother, fails to repair the cracks in the marriage. Fanny pursues other men, while Job turns to his secretaries in an effort to find the love he misses at home. When Fanny discovers his escapades, she sues for divorce and a mutual agreement allows Job to take his daughter with him to Europe while Fanny remains behind with the Skeffington fortune.

The second half of the film concentrates on Fanny's hopeless attempts to maintain the fantasy of youth. As the Second World War approaches, her daughter, now a wise young woman, returns because of Job's fear for her safety in Germany. "I know you had a difficult choice to make," she tells her mother. "You couldn't be both a beauty and a mother."

Fanny contracts diphtheria after a frivolous boat ride in dreadful weather. While recuperating, she continually "sees" Job, who has an ethereal quality as he hovers near sofa and chair while we hear echoes of dialogue past: "You can't really love anyone, Fanny. You'll never be old. A woman is beautiful only when she is loved."

A recovered Fanny returns home to an empty house, pleading with her maid never to leave her alone. On the advice of her psychiatrist, she has a dinner party for all her former suitors and she finds that the fact of age can no longer be ignored.

As filmic fate would have it, Job returns at this point, discovered in the park of cousin George. He brings Skeffington to Fanny, who refuses to see him, saying "Look at what's left of my face." George tells her, "You'll always be the same to Skeffington. He still loves you." Recanting, she goes downstairs to see him. "Is it Fanny?" Job asks. "You don't know me?" "Oh, yes, I do. You're as beautiful as ever." "You're laughing at me again." "No, Fanny, no."

At that, Fanny suddenly realizes Job is blind, the result of a stay in a concentration camp. It causes a sudden metamorphosis in her character and she cries, "Oh, Job, all this time I've been thinking only of myself. Well, you're safe now. You're home with me."

The film ends with a reiteration of the now famous sentiment: "A woman is beautiful only when she is loved."

High theatrics, but nonetheless *Skeffington* is enjoyable for all its melodrama and it serves as an example of Warner craftsmanship at its best. *Skeffington* deserves further examination for one important reason: it marks the only time Rains forgot his character and let his personal feelings interfere with his delivery.

During the scene in which Fanny and Job discuss their divorce and its consequences for their daughter, Rains' tone becomes especially harsh. . .one might
even say bitter.

"Without knowing it, he wasn't going to be talked to that way, even as Skeffington," Davis says. "He forgot his character and I sat there in absolute shock.
My great friend, whom I would have done anything on God's earth for in a
scene, turned on me personally. I shook all over. I was so frightened of him in
that scene, it was unbelievable. He becomes a real male chauvinist. He was not
going to have it, even though that was the way the scene was written."

> FANNY: Won't you sit down? I want to talk to you. I want to thank
> you for the very generous settlement you made on me.
>
> JOB: Twelve years with the wrong husband. It should be rewarded.
>
> FANNY: Well, of course, it was ridiculous of you to settle the for-
> tune on me, but then it would have been ridiculous of me to refuse,
> wouldn't it?
>
> JOB: I'm glad you're going to be reasonable about it.
>
> FANNY: Ah, Job, still laughing at me without moving a muscle.
>
> JOB: I assure you, Fanny, you're no laughing matter.
>
> FANNY: I can't bear to look at you, Job. Your eyes have such a hurt
> expression.
>
> JOB: They have? I repudiate them. I have no right to feel hurt. I
> knew you didn't love me when you married me.
>
> FANNY: I'm sorry, Job. I'm really sorry I can't love you.
>
> JOB: That's all right, Fanny. You can't really love anyone.

One can only suppose at this late date that the scene struck far too close to
home for Rains, who had already been through three unsuccessful marriages.
His marriage to Frances Propper was a happy one and he had become a father
rather late in life. He was sensitive about the age difference between himself and
Frances and it was during the filming of *Skeffington* that they had been mistaken
for father and daughter.

"Frances and Jennifer came on the set," Davis says, "and someone on the
crew actually said that was obviously his daughter and granddaughter. It was one
of the most embarrassing moments I ever went through. You could see it killing
Claude. He was not, rightfully so, enchanted."

That incident, coupled with the underlying reality of the scene, probably
triggered a subconscious fear that one day the scene in *Skeffington* would be
played out in real life. He hated failure and the fact that he had done so poorly
at marriage, through little fault of his own at this point, sorely rubbed him.

The final film Davis and Rains made together was *Deception* and she might have wished he had not been in the picture at all. He walks away with it. The film is an excellent example of the genre in that it has all the flaws characteristic of its type: high-flung melodrama, ridiculous situations and silly characters. But Rains, playing megalomaniac composer Alexander Hollenius, has a field day, romping through his part, tossing off line after line like "There is that about you which suggests one of your peculiar moods."

The film was based on the two-person play *Jealousy*. The character of Hollenius never appeared on the stage. The only saving grace of the film is that he *does* appear. Davis plays Christine Radcliffe, Hollenius' student and mistress. He keeps her in an appropriately lavish apartment the size of Hearst Castle. Her boyfriend, Karel Novak, returns suddenly from war-ravaged Europe and Christine decides it is he she still loves. She has the poor grace to announce this via phone to Hollenius, who is on tour. He returns immediately, making a grand entrance at Christine's engagement party, cape majestically sweeping the air, hands carefully gloved and hair perfectly coiffed.

Christine now lives in fear that Hollenius is going to reveal the truth of their relationship to Karel. She has repeated encounters with the composer, alternately pleading and threatening him to keep the past a secret. In all fairness, there is little concrete indication that Hollenius has any intention of telling Karel about his former mistress. Christine's fears are probably the result of her own insecurities.

Her encounters with Rains over this matter give the film its best moments, particularly as he sits in bed reading the comics spouting sarcastic comments at her and making observations about his own character. ("Pride is more like my weakness.")

Hollenius even goes so far as to allow Karel to play the premiere performance of his new concerto. Christine convinces herself this is merely a ploy and that Hollenius intends to emotionally destroy the already nervous Karel by taking the concerto away from him at the eleventh hour.

She goes to Hollenius' apartment and accosts him while he is getting ready to leave for the concert hall. There is some heavy foreshadowing as Hollenius talks about always being able to picture himself doing things in the future, "But this evening I couldn't." He goes upstairs to finish dressing. Christine follows him and waits at the top of the stairs, gun in hand. He comes out of his room, sees her and responds to the presence of a gun with his usual disdain. Christine fires. Hollenius has time to mutter "You fool!" and clutch his chest before he flings headlong down the stairs.

Christine, having committed the perfect crime, returns to the concert hall to listen to Karel perform the concerto. Once in his dressing room, she confesses. Like the dutiful husband he is, Karel carts her off to the police. Fade out.

"The ending was a mess because of censorship," Davis says, "but Claude was brilliant! Brilliant! If there had to be a third character, he was the perfect choice."

Upon initial examination of the film, one might think that *Deception* was an occasion when the director let Rains have his head. He loved acting so, he was apt to overact at times and he consistently warned directors to watch him so he wouldn't do too much. But, when one considers the character of Alexander Hollenius, Rains' interpretation seems perfect. It gave him an opportunity to return to the expansive acting practiced by his old mentor, Beerbohm Tree. Although critics of the time generally reviewed the film tongue in cheek, they all singled out Rains for his "fascinating portrait of a titanic egotist."

Davis and Rains did not work together again after *Deception*, although they remained friends and saw each other as often as time, distance and conflicting schedules would permit. Even today, Bette Davis will spend hours talking about him and her voice softens when she says, "The biggest compliment I ever had from a very great actor was that Claude Rains wanted me to be his friend."

Cukor and Hepburn

THE STORY OF A CREATIVE PARTNERSHIP
THAT HAS SPANNED FORTY-SEVEN YEARS

Gene D. Phillips

Originally appeared in vol. 4, no. 1 (Fall 1979)

George Cukor's creative association with Katharine Hepburn is one of the most durable professional relationships between a director and an actress in the history of motion pictures. I have discussed Cukor's career with him several times, most recently after the telecast of *The Corn Is Green* (1979), the tenth Cukor-Hepburn film and their second for TV. Their previous telefilm, *Love Among the Ruins* (1975), won several Emmys, including one for each of them.

Their most recent project came into being when Cukor phoned Hepburn to tell her that Alan Shayne, head of Warners TV, wanted them both to do *The Corn Is Green*. Hepburn was impressed, as Cukor was, with the story of Miss Moffat, the spirited spinster who takes in hand the training of Morgan Evans, an intelligent youth working in a Welsh mine, so that he can win a scholarship to Oxford. Their relationship is a rocky one, because Morgan is strong-willed too; but they nevertheless succeed in their mutual endeavor.

Cukor and Hepburn have also succeeded in working together, although they are both artists who possess decidedly independent temperaments. Yet they have learned to collaborate very well together over the years since they first met back in 1932.[1] Katharine Hepburn's first appearance in a Cukor film was in *A Bill of Divorcement*, in which she played a young woman who gives up her own plans for marriage to take care of her insane father (John Barrymore).

Journalist Adele Rogers St. Johns once recalled being accosted by Cukor on the RKO lot one hot afternoon in 1932 and being told, "I've just seen a test of the girl I want for *Bill of Divorcement*. She looks like a boa constrictor on a fast, but she's great!" For her screen test Hepburn chose a scene from the Philip Barry play *Holiday*. In retrospect she feels that her performance in the test reflected how desperate she was to get the part in *Bill of Divorcement*, but Cukor sensed her potential as a screen actress, and the years have proved how right he was.

Among the ten films in which Cukor has directed Hepburn are three in which she was teamed with Cary Grant: *Sylvia Scarlett* (1935), *Holiday* (1938), and *The Philadelphia Story* (1940). The first of these, *Sylvia Scarlett*, was a flop. "That picture had something gallant and foolhardy about it," Cukor comments. "It had interesting and diverting things in it which audiences seem to enjoy more today than they did then. The making of that film was a real group project—as motion picture making always is essentially. I consulted with the producer, the script writers, and the stars; but I never got the film to work. Perhaps the storyline was too complicated as the film unfolded."

Perhaps because the film begins as a frivolous farce and then takes a relatively serious turn as it nears the end, audiences of the time were baffled by it. The film is fundamentally a toast to those who seek to fulfill their romantic illusions in life, and the early scenes in particular are in harmony with this sentiment. We follow the adventures of Sylvia (Katharine Hepburn), her father (Edmund Gwenn), and their companion in skullduggery, Jimmie Monkley (Cary Grant), as they swindle and con their way around England. Since Sylvia and her father already had a police record in France before coming to England, Sylvia dresses as a boy in order that the group will escape detection. But her disguise also betokens the unreal existence that she is living with the other two. The trio becomes further enmeshed in illusion when they become strolling players after they have tired of a life of crime.

A crisis arises when Sylvia falls in love first with Jimmie and then with Michael Fane, an artist. In effect, she has to choose between living in a real world with Michael or continuing to live in the world of fantasy with Jimmie. Sylvia finally faces reality, drops her disguise, and admits her feelings for Michael. She has, however, reluctantly turned her back on Jimmie and the madcap existence which he represents. Cukor seems to harbor some degree of affection for the world of romantic illusion, for there is always a hint of regret in his films when reality inevitably impinges itself on the world of one of his dreamers, as it finally does on the Hepburn character in *Sylvia Scarlett*.

Since Hepburn had done a scene from *Holiday* for the screen test in which she had impressed Cukor so much, it was no surprise that he chose her to play Linda Seton in his film of that play, a role that she had understudied on Broadway a decade earlier. Linda is bored and frustrated by the insulated life of luxury that her stuffy family leads, and she often takes refuge in the nursery room where she grew up in order to get away from them all. Linda's behavior represents an obvious retreat from reality into a fantasy world very much akin to that of Sylvia Scarlett; and, like Sylvia, Linda is eventually shaken out of her unreal existence. She stubbornly endorses her sister's fiancé, Johnny Case (Cary Grant), in his refusal to join the family firm, which he sees as the price of his acceptance by the Seton clan. Johnny does not want to be dominated by the Setons, and his independent spirit inspires Linda to elope with him. Hepburn was to play another Philip Barry socialite in her next Cukor film.

With *The Philadelphia Story* Cukor and Hepburn scored one of their biggest mutual triumphs. As Tracy Lord, Hepburn gives her definitive performance as a strong-willed, super-sophisticated young socialite, who nonetheless retains an undeniable charm and elegance. In the opening scene Tracy throws her husband Dexter Haven (Cary Grant) out of the Lord mansion after a quarrel, breaking one of his golf clubs over her knee for good measure. Dexter gets even with Tracy by inviting himself to her wedding to another man, bringing along with him Mike Connor (James Stewart), a reporter for a gossip magazine. It is Mike who is finally able to melt Tracy's icy exterior and reveal a warm human being underneath. Then he gallantly gives her back to Dexter, whom she is prepared to accept as he really is, now that she has abandoned her unrealistic search for the ideal husband. Like Sylvia and Linda before her, Tracy opts for the real world.

The attempt of individuals to reconcile their cherished dreams with the sober realities of life is likewise reflected in the three Cukor films in which Hepburn was paired with Spencer Tracy: *Keeper of the Flame* (1943), *Adam's Rib* (1949), and *Pat and Mike* (1952). In *Keeper of the Flame*, for example, Hepburn plays Christine Forrest, a young woman who eventually pays the price of having stubbornly nursed private illusions. Christine is the widow of a recently deceased public hero, Robert Forrest, whom reporter Steve O'Malley (Spencer Tracy) suspects was really a crypto-Fascist. Christine does everything in her power to keep the truth about her husband shrouded in darkness—as is quite evident from the shadowy room in which she receives O'Malley for an interview—because she is laboring under the misapprehension that the memory of her husband's spurious greatness can somehow serve as a continuing inspiration to his erstwhile followers.

It is a measure of Cukor's subtlety as a director that he has permeated the film with visual metaphors about the concealing of truth. The tall trees that surround the Forrest estate, for example, signify the way that the late leader had succeeded in keeping the public at large from seeing the real Forrest through the trees. Eventually, O'Malley convinces Christine that Forrest's corrosive influence will continue to do harm if she does not expose him to the world for what he was.

But her doing so costs her her life at the hands of Forrest's henchmen. And so the misguided, though deeply sincere Christine in the end lives up to her name as a feminine Christ-like figure by becoming a martyr in the cause of truth. In *Keeper of the Flame* Hepburn gives one of her most nuanced performances in a role that Cukor calls her last really romantic part. In subsequent Cukor films Hepburn was to play characters who were more likely to help others face reality than to need that assistance themselves.

Thus in *Adam's Rib* Hepburn enacts a no-nonsense lawyer named Amanda Bonner who is defending Doris Attinger (Judy Holliday), a young wife accused of the attempted murder of her husband Warren, whom she discovered with another woman. Early in the film was a long and difficult scene in which Amanda interviews Doris for the first time in her prison cell. Cukor decided to shoot the interview in one seven-minute take, and Hepburn was willing to play the whole scene with her back to the camera while Holliday faced the camera the whole time. Only an actress as professional as Hepburn, Cukor has commented, would agree to give a whole scene away to another actress in this fashion.

While Amanda is serving as lawyer for Doris, her husband Adam (Spencer Tracy) is the attorney for Doris's husband Warren. Adam steadfastly tries to keep Amanda from escalating the case into a crusade for women's rights, and this proves to be quite a challenge. Finally Adam convinces Amanda by a ruse that Doris was not justified in shooting her husband. He threatens to shoot Amanda when he finds her in the company of another man. After she insists that he has no right to shoot her, Adam nonchalantly puts the gun into his mouth and bends the barrel with his teeth: it is made of licorice. This is the perfect conclusion to an inventive, inspired farce. In films like *Adam's Rib*, then, Cukor and Hepburn set the standard for sophisticated light comedy in American movies, as *Time* has rightly remarked.

By the time that Cukor and Hepburn made *The Corn Is Green*, their creative partnership had spanned almost half a century, and they could easily intuit what the other had in mind in approaching the shooting of a given scene. "He has plenty of opinions of his own," Hepburn said while shooting *The Corn Is Green*, "but he gives his actors freedom. He doesn't shut them into his own trap, like some directors who push their actors around like dolls." "Yes, she is full of ideas, and most of them are extremely good," Cukor countered. "There's a complete absence of sham and nonsense between us. A real rapport."[2]

Time's review of the film complimented Cukor's staging of the story against the lush Welsh landscapes as well as Hepburn's commanding screen presence, but wondered why the original play was not opened out more for the TV screen. "When Morgan Evans travels up to Oxford to take his exams, the audience expects to go with him," *Time* noted; but they are left behind in Wales with Miss Moffat.[3] "The transition from stage to screen is always tricky," Cukor has told me. "On the one hand you can't turn out a photographed stage play; on the other hand you can't rend the original stage version apart. If you don't know what was good about the original play, you pull it apart to make a different version for the screen and you have nothing left."

In the present instance I think Cukor was wise in keeping his camera focused on Miss Moffat back home as she frets about the boy's success at Oxford; for the story is ultimately about the renewal of spirit which she experiences in helping this young man to rise above his grim and grimy background, and his success is all the more rewarding for the audience when they learn about it at the same time that she does. For my part, Cukor's artistic intuition was vindicated in this case as it has often been throughout his long career. As he puts it, "If you select material that attracts you and touches your imagination, as I have always tried to do, your originality will come out in the handling of it—if you have any originality. I trust my intuition whenever possible."

Throughout the years, George Cukor, 79, and Katharine Hepburn, 71, have managed to weather the changes in public taste and the pressures of the commercial movie system without compromising their style, taste, or artistic standards. In so doing, they have together created an impressive body of films, spawned by a legendary relationship that will rarely if ever be matched in the history of cinema.

Notes

1. Some of the material on the early Cukor-Hepburn films appeared in a completely different form in my book *The Movie Makers: Artists in an Industry* (Chicago: Nelson-Hall, 1973).

2. Benedict Nightingale, "After Making Nine Films Together, Hepburn can Practically Direct Cukor," *The New York Times,* section 2 (January 28, 1979), p. 29.

3. "Hepburn Shines in Revival," *Time,* January 29, 1979, p. 66.

Making Movies with James Cagney

Mae Clarke

Originally appeared in vol. 7, no. 4 (July/August 1983)

There are at least three different versions of the famous grapefruit scene in *The Public Enemy*: director William Wellman's; star James Cagney's; and mine. Wellman has also accused Darryl Zanuck of horning in and trying to claim credit for that scene.

I can only tell you my side of the story. I was brought to Hollywood in 1929 under a one-year contract to Fox, and made four pictures for them, the first being one with Lee Tracy, *Big Time*, a story of vaudevillians. Seven pictures later, I tested at United Artists for the romantic lead in *The Front Page*. Mary Brian got it, but I had a chance to talk to the director, Lewis Milestone, and convinced him that I was really right for the plum role of Molly Malloy, a prostitute with a heart of gold. I still think I did some of my best film work in *The Front Page*; it was a one-scene part brilliantly written by Bartlett Cormack and Charles Lederer from the Hecht/MacArthur play. It really won me a contract at Universal, playing the lead role for director James Whale in the film version of Robert Sherwood's play, *Waterloo Bridge*.

Jimmy Whale liked me, and I did two other features for him in a row; I played the beleaguered heroine in *Frankenstein* for him, then the lead in *The Impatient Maiden* (from the novel, *The Impatient Virgin*). Then, with everything going my way, I had a nervous breakdown. Columbia had shared my contract with Universal. Both studios dropped me. I was sick from sheer nervous exhaustion.

I recovered in time, and took on a new agent, who was going to see that I came back. There was a good possibility, he said, at Warner Bros. They were making a gangster movie, *The Public Enemy*, starring a new actor of whom they thought highly—James Cagney. It was his fourth picture. I only had two scenes, but they were good ones. The billing was already determined, and I couldn't hope for much in that department, but it was a chance to get back to work, and the money was good. I said that I'd take the part.

166

I did my first scene with Joan Blondell, where we meet two young fellows at a café, played by Cagney and Eddie Woods. Cagney picks me up as his girl, but it was hardly a lasting romance, for the second scene I played with Cagney was the break-up. In it I had fixed breakfast, indicating that I had spent the night with him; he is deliberately contemptuous and snarling, obviously wanting to end the relationship. I try to be pleasant, but he is so mean that I say, "Maybe you got someone you like better." According to the Harvey Thew script, Cagney looks at me ferociously for a few seconds, "then reaches over on the table, picks up a half grapefruit, throws it at Kitty's face, and strides out." That scene was shot as written in the script.

There was a break onset, and I was aware that Wellman and Cagney were on the sidelines, talking quietly and looking tentatively at me while I sat at the table, waiting for the director to okay the take. Cagney came over to me with a smile, and he said that he and Wellman had been discussing the scene, which didn't have a real end, and they wondered how it would be if Cagney snarled, picked up the half grapefruit, and rubbed it in my face viciously before quitting the room. Would I do it again that way? It would be at least a good gag and the scene was already covered, shot as written.

My agent wasn't on the set, so I reluctantly consented, but with the provision that I would only do the scene over once; there would be no other re-take; but I would be a good sport and go for this gag shot. Wellman agreed to that, and I did the scene as re-staged. I can't say that it was anything more than a real shock to feel that grapefruit squashed in my face. I didn't have to make believe about any displeasure I was feeling.

This all happened in 1931, and the picture was released on May 15 of that year. On June 20, 1931, Norma Shearer was first shown as she was roughed up by Clark Gable in *A Free Soul*, and in August of that year *Night Nurse* was released, in which Gable brutally beat up Barbara Stanwyck. 1931 was a rough year for the ladies, but the grapefruit Cagney rubbed in my face made for a scene of humiliation suffered by a woman which no one could forget. Women's clubs protested, and in re-issue prints the grapefruit scene was put back practically in its initial set-up.

In 1934 I played another scene with Cagney in *The Lady Killer*. He played a questionable character who had started out innocently enough as a movie theatre usher; he becomes an underworld hoodlum on the run, gets into the Hollywood scene, and hits it big as a movie star. I was Myra, a gangland sweetheart of Cagney's, whom he's trying to ditch so that he can make time with a society girl. I infuriate him; he pulls my silk pajama–clad figure across the floor, then swings the door open, and continues dragging me into the hallway, where he delivers a swift kick to my posterior, and slams the door shut. Movie critics commented on his rough behavior, but they weren't really shocked. Having a grapefruit rubbed in your face was regarded, I suppose, as more humiliating than any really violent action!

In 1936 Cagney had an argument with Warner Bros. and refused to resign with them, preferring to go to a new fly-by-night studio, Grand National, to make two features. I was selected to be his leading lady in the first of them, *Great Guy*. It was based on several James Edward Grant "Johnny Cave" stories, in which Cagney played a Weights and Measures Department inspector. He sets out to clean up the graft in his own city. I played Janet Henry, who stands by Cagney because she loves him, yet is not above doing some ordering around herself, particularly when it concerns his welfare. It was a pleasant comedy romance, but was not at all in the same box-office league as were the gangster dramas Cagney had made for Warner Bros. He profited from the experience and re-signed with Warners. In the future for him were all the screen classics, *The Roaring Twenties*, *White Heat*, and the great *Yankee Doodle Dandy*, which won him an Oscar.

In March of 1974, Cagney was honored by the American Film Institute, receiving its Life Achievement Award. I was a guest with my mother at the banquet. It was all very grand, with Ronald Reagan, then governor of California, present with his lovely wife, and Frank Sinatra acted as host of the evening. In his acceptance speech, Cagney disclosed that in real life the grapefruit had been an omelette pushed by a gangster named Hymie Weiss into the face of his girlfriend. For the first time, I was grateful for that damned grapefruit! It would have been very messy, as Jimmy reminded me, to have egg all over my face!

Part IV

BEHIND THE CAMERA:
THE DIRECTORS

Charles T. Barton

AN INFORMAL PROFILE

Frank Thompson

Originally appeared in vol. 5, no. 6 (November/December 1981)

Sometimes I think that Charles Barton has seen it all and done it all. In his sixty years in show business he's been an actor, a prop-boy, an assistant director, a writer and a gag man. He has directed about seventy feature films and nearly six hundred television shows.

Nearly as staggering as the list of his own accomplishments is the number (and caliber) of people he has known and worked with: from Broncho Billy Anderson to "Buffy" and "Jody," to Cecil B. DeMille, William A. Wellman, John Cromwell, Eddie Sutherland, James Cruze, Abbott and Costello, Marshall Neilan, W. C. Fields, Cary Grant and scores of others in between.

A child of the "Golden Age" of television will find that Charles Barton directed a goodly number of the most popular comedies of the fifties and sixties: *Amos 'n' Andy, Trouble with Father, Oh, Susannah!, Spin and Marty, Zorro, The Real McCoys, Dennis the Menace, McHale's Navy, The Munsters, Hazel, Petticoat Junction* and *Family Affair*. The quality of the shows may be variable but their popularity can be attested to by the fact that virtually every one is still in syndication today.

With experience like this, one would expect Charlie Barton to be a walking, talking encyclopedia of movie history and one would be right. Charlie's exceptional memory, plus his natural storytelling style, make him a most valuable link to the Hollywood past.

With such vast success in a business where relatively few end up on top, one might also expect Charlie to be aloof and self-important. There one would be quite wrong, for he's the antithesis of the stereotypical Hollywood citizen. Many an aspiring film scholar has turned up at his door to find Charlie unfailingly generous and helpful. In short, Charlie Barton is a gem; kind, funny, warm and completely likable.

Charlie was introduced to a National Film Society audience in October of 1980. He made it quite clear the reason for his success and the evergreen freshness of his best films: he's a fabulous storyteller. I would ask him a question to which I already knew the answer. He had answered the question the night before during our interview in a manner suited to an audience of one or two and his anecdotes were subtle and delightful. Before an audience, however, his timing was masterly. He would punctuate a laugh with an Oliver Hardy–like "audience look" which would bring a bigger laugh. Again and again, he showed that he knew how to get the reaction he wanted. It was a brief but valuable introduction to a man whose works were known to most of the people there, but whose own personality has never been widely known.

After the interview, Charlie, his lovely wife Julie and several friends joined me for lunch. I asked Charlie if he had enjoyed himself. He replied, "Hell, I talked about myself for two hours. How can you enjoy yourself more than that?"

His flippant answer belied his real feelings. His modesty is genuine. There is always at least one "Are you sure you want to hear this?" before he launches into some wonderful story. I guess I wouldn't have it any other way, though. I wouldn't want him to be so sure of his immense value that it would deprive me of trying to convince him of it.

One of us asked him how he had gotten the ambition to direct. Was there an artistic statement that he wished to make? Did he crave the big money? Did he simply want the power? None of the above. It was "Clothes. Boy, Mickey Neilan would come in there dressed to the teeth. And DeMille with those riding breeches. Jesus Christ, I wanted to be a director so I could dress like that."

Whatever fueled them, his ambitions began early. Born in 1902 in Sacramento, he spent his early childhood and teens in various stage-shows in the area, including Oliver Morosco's *The Dummy* and *Young America*. By 1914, Charlie had appeared in a two-reeler with Broncho Billy Anderson and in 1920 played a juvenile role in Maurice Tourneur's production of *County Fair*.

Charlie continued to pursue an acting career for a while, but eventually came to feel that his height (5'2") would be a detriment. After losing a role in Mary Pickford's *Little Lord Fauntleroy* to Jack Pickford, Charlie quit the business and got a job in a drugstore on Lillian Way near the Buster Keaton Studio.

Always active, Charlie played golf regularly with several friends (including avid golfer Babe Hardy). Among his golfing buddies was an office boy at the Lasky Studios. With this connection, Charlie was soon an office boy himself.

Once ensconced in the Lasky studio, Charlie started to learn his way around. He was ambitious and hard working and started a long but steady climb up the ladder of success. He became head office boy and then assistant prop-boy.

This is the job that catapulted him into the thick of the movie-making action. As assistant prop-boy (and later, first prop-boy), Charlie worked with such directors as Joseph Henabery, C. B. DeMille, James Cruze, Herbert Brenon, William K. Howard, William Wellman, Alan Crosland and others. That sort of education in filmmaking you can't get at UCLA.

It was William Wellman who gave Charlie his biggest career boost to date by hiring him as second assistant prop-boy on Paramount's major production of the year, *Wings*. In short order, Charlie was promoted to first assistant prop-boy and then, unexpectedly, he became assistant unit manager of the production.

He recalls, "They found out the unit manager was skimming off the top a little. When he found out we were gonna build a set, he'd go out and buy the lumber and sell it to the studio at a higher price. He was doing pretty good!" He laughs at the memory. "I think they asked him to quit. The assistant, Dick Johnson, became unit manager and, I must say, also the first assistant, because I had very little experience."

It didn't matter much, because Charlie was only passing through the job anyway; he was soon promoted to second assistant director and finally to assistant director. He retained this position at Paramount for the next seven years and worked on pictures like *Beau Sabreur, Legion of the Condemned, Beggars of Life, Dance of Life, Young Eagles, Santa Fe Trail, City Streets, Monkey Business, Horse Feathers, If I Had a Million, Sign of the Cross* and virtually every other important Paramount release of the years 1928 to 1934.

He finally became a full-fledged director in 1935 with a modest Randolph Scott vehicle, *Wagon Wheels*. He was to continue directing features until 1962 and some pictures stand up better than others. He was seldom given major assignments at Paramount and he left in 1939 to go to Columbia.

Before resuming his directing career at another studio, though, Charlie made two brief returns to the jobs of his past. His friend William Wellman hired him to act a brief comedy role in the 1939 version of *Beau Geste*. As a result, Paramount put him under contract as an actor, but no more acting jobs were forthcoming. While he waited for one, he worked once again as assistant director for Cecil B. DeMille on *Union Pacific*. Why he made this curious move in the midst of a pretty successful directing career is something of a mystery. When I asked him about it, he simply replied, "Biggest goddamn mistake I ever made."

At Columbia he launched a brief but successful series based on Margaret Sidney's *The Five Little Peppers and How They Grew*, starring Edith Fellows, Dorothy Peterson, Tommy Bond and Dorothy Ann Seese. The remainder of his Columbia films were comedies and musicals starring such marginal stars (at that time) as Ann Miller, Judy Canova, Joe Besser, Bert Gordon ("The Mad Russian") and the forgotten Jinx Falkenberg.

In 1945, Charlie moved to Universal where he signed on with one of the most popular comedy teams in movie history, Abbott and Costello. They were in a slight decline at the time, but the team was still potent box office. Charlie's films with them are variable; he directed their best films (*The Time of Their Lives* and *Abbott and Costello Meet Frankenstein*) and their worst (*Dance with Me Henry*).

As the 1950s approached, Charlie started to wind down his career in features to work in television. He entered the new medium with a bang; the phenomenally popular *Amos 'n' Andy Show* was being transferred from radio to television with all of its beloved characters intact. The major change was that the radio show had employed white actors and an all new black cast was added for the TV show.

Charlie quickly became one of television's top directors, a position he held through the early seventies when he directed the hit series *Family Affair*. His forays into features were rare but memorable during these years, notably the two features for Disney, *Toby Tyler* and *The Shaggy Dog*. His final film was a Cinema-Scope feature for 20th Century Fox, *Swingin' Along*, with the best-forgotten comedy team of Tommy Noonan and Peter Marshall.

Charlie Barton has had an exciting prolific career. But the first time we met I was almost totally ignorant of it. I only knew that he had been Wellman's assistant director, which is why I visited his Santa Monica apartment to talk with him about his memories of his good friend Wellman.

As might be expected, *Wings* was the major subject of the day; it was such a crucial point in both Barton's and Wellman's career. His memory of that time is vivid and an excitement grows in his voice when he speaks of it.

"That was a big show," he said. "You have no idea. The call sheet would have 3,500 soldiers. 3,500! I tell you it was big." He smiled and leaned forward. "But . . . it worked out fine for me." With that, Charlie Barton reached for the coffee table to knock on wood.

The Elusive Cecil B. DeMille

AN APPRECIATION OF
A HOLLYWOOD LEGEND

James V. D'Arc

Originally appeared in vol. 7, no. 1 (1983)

"I owe him everything I ever learned about making pictures," said film director Mitchell Leisen of his one-time boss, DeMille.[1] "Because DeMille put me in to star in *Reap the Wild Wind*," recounted John Wayne over 30 years later, "I had no trouble holdin' up my head in Hollywood, even though Republic was still tryin' to mess me up with their rotten pictures."[2] Famed Academy Award–winning director Mervyn LeRoy even played a bit part in DeMille's silent version of *The Ten Commandments* in 1923. Said he, "As the top director of the era, DeMille had been the magnet that had drawn me to his set as often as I could go."[3] LeRoy also credits DeMille as having taught him the techniques required to make his own epic, *Quo Vadis*, some 30 years later.

But perhaps the most interesting and touching tribute to DeMille came from the late Edward G. Robinson, who at the time he was cast as Dathan in the later version of *The Ten Commandments* had undergone—and lived with—the scourge of anti-communist investigations of the early 1950s. "No more conservative or patriarchal figure existed in Hollywood, no one more opposed to communism or any permutation or combination thereof," wrote Robinson of DeMille, "and no fairer one, no one with a greater sense of decency and justice." Robinson's blacklisting by the industry forced him to return to the stage which, together with his enormous legal fees, resulted in a great financial sacrifice. However, in considering Robinson for the film 74-year-old DeMille decided that an injustice had been done and industry pressure notwithstanding, gave him the part. "Cecil B. DeMille returned me to films," Robinson wrote shortly before his death. "Cecil B. DeMille restored my self-respect."[4]

But who really was this man whose on-the-set uniform included leather puttees and riding whip and whose passion for flamboyant publicity made him the paragon of the Hollywood director? One might easily start with DeMille's

175

overwhelming popularity. Cecil B. DeMille was one of the most public of men. As a pioneer in early aviation, land development, and banking in Southern California, on radio, and as a civic activist—not to mention filmmaking— DeMille could not escape, nor did he ever try, the preeminence in the public consciousness that he always enjoyed. As such, and probably because he was associated throughout his career with anything "terrific," "colossal," and "spectacular," he was often the object of tales and anecdotes characterizing him as either a whip-bearing tyrant or at other times, touchingly sensitive.

DeMille's whole approach to the business of weaving public myths and fantasies onto film and his profound sense of mission was aptly captured in his first encounter with longtime friend and later associate producer, Henry Wilcoxon on the set of DeMille's *Cleopatra* in 1933. Describing the character of Marc Antony to his modern-day portrayer, DeMille verbally painted a picture for the former stage actor to duplicate on the screen: "He was a man who thought in terms of nations, not of individuals." "He did and thought things on a grand scale. The world was his canvas." Wilcoxon thought on those words for a few moments and replied, "Why don't you play the part?"[5]

As public as he was in his notoriety as the popularly perceived champion of the "epic" film, DeMille has nevertheless remained to this day a little understood figure. To some, his sex-riddled social melodramas such as *Don't Change Your Husband, Why Change Your Wife?*, and *Forbidden Fruit* of the '20s mix uncomfortably with his handsomely produced religious epics *King of Kings*, also in the '20s, plus *Samson and Delilah* and *The Ten Commandments* (including his 1923 original) during the late '40s and '50s. His later linkage with the Deity often made his already questionable status with professional critics even more tenuous. "Perhaps DeMille's survival is due to the fact that he decided in his movie nonage to ally himself with God, as his co-maker," wrote a critic in *The New Yorker* in 1949 after seeing *Samson and Delilah*, "and to get his major scripts from the Bible, which he has always handled with the proprietary air of a gentleman fondling old love letters. In *Samson and Delilah*, DeMille is back on his usual beat, but this time I'm not at all sure that he has produced a work that enhances the glory of him or of his Associate."[6]

While critics on the whole praised DeMille's sense of sweep and spectacle, they rarely credited him with the seriousness accorded to other contemporary directors. And yet, above the lukewarm reactions of critics and the listless enthusiasm of many of his professional peers, the movie-going public could not get enough of films by Cecil B. DeMille. The many thousands of letters in the DeMille Archives at Brigham Young University from fans over a 40-year period attest to the public's intense affection for DeMille and his films. With the possible exception of two or three, all of DeMille's 70 feature films were tremendous moneymakers. Even during the "bad box-office 1950s" when the industry needed a boost to get people unglued from their television sets and back into the motion picture theatres, DeMille was there as successful as ever.

DeMille was simply . . . DeMille. No other filmmaker could duplicate his style. It is also true that not all filmmakers wanted to. However, one who tried was MGM mogul Louis B. Mayer. Mayer, whose studio later made *Ben-Hur*, wished to cash in on the early '50s spate of "spectacle" films with a film version of Thomas Mann's religious saga, *Joseph and His Brothers*, but son-in-law (and distinguished filmmaker in his own right) David O. Selznick cautioned the senior statesman of film not to attempt to enter into creative areas exclusively originated and occupied by DeMille. "I must run the risk of offending you," said Selznick in one of his famous memos, "by saying that unless you have Cecil B. DeMille or his equivalent—and I for one do not know of his equivalent—you must be on guard against assuming that you can deal with equal success in the broad strokes, lack of subtlety, the clichés and convenient situations, in which he revels. Cecil B. DeMille is, of course, one of the most extraordinarily able showmen of modern times. As both professionally and personally he has in many ways demonstrated himself to be a man of sensitivity and taste, it is impossible to believe that the blatancy of his style is due to anything but a most artful and deliberate and knowing technique of appeal to the common denominator of public taste." "But," Selznick concluded, "there has appeared only one Cecil B. DeMille. Nothing is more appalling than second-rate DeMille."[7]

Jesse Lasky, Jr., who wrote screenplays for such DeMille extravaganzas as *Union Pacific*, *The Unconquered*, *Samson and Delilah*, and *The Ten Command-ments*, said of DeMille—after going on at length of DeMille the proud and profane—that, "The devoted attention he paid to wanton debauchery in his movies was always counterbalanced by the final triumph of virtue. He sold the same message as the great illustrator Norman Rockwell, but using Babylon instead of a small-town drugstore."[8]

Moreover, DeMille was successful, repeatedly, in a very difficult genre—the "epic" film—by imbuing his characters and subplots with the historionic vastness of his lofty themes—a Will Durant of the silver screen. Characters in other "spectacular" attempts such as Joseph Mankewicz's *Cleopatra*, *Barrabbas*, *El Cid*, and Samuel Bronston's *King of Kings* either became obscured in the canvas of historical events portrayed or the paralleling stories were too much like other, more conventional films we see merely with an added touch of sandstone desert, palm trees, pyramids, or even a verdant desert oasis. DeMille literally immersed himself into such projects and, not surprisingly, he emerged from the effort to be as miraculous a figure in his productions as his subject matter. Little wonder, then, that one film historian named the hero of *The Ten Commandments* as "not Moses, but DeMille himself, the voice of God and the burning bush and the miracles in Egypt included."[9] Also, what other filmmaker during his own lifetime has been such a persona in the public eye as to be popularly suggested for the governorship of California, asked to run for the U.S. Senate at various times during his career or, as time passed, came to be likened even to God himself?

"DeMille was concerned with Victorian values," said Charles Higham, a DeMille biographer. "He was fascinated by the Bible, fascinated by England in the 19th century. He wasn't of this century at all and managed to sustain a 19th century vision into the 20th century. With the tremendous revolution on campuses, the way that the last shreds of old fashioned idealism were disrupted by Kennedy's assassination and so on, he died actually at a fortuitous moment, because he couldn't really have survived the '60s."[10] We will, in spite of our union with modern society and technology—of progress—and our acceptance with varying degrees of its morality, no doubt often look back with affection and longing for the days of greater simplicity and to the men like DeMille who cinematically dramatized the clear-cut moral struggles in such gargantuan proportions.

DeMille, in that very real sense, is still with us for one of many inexplicable reasons why "old fashioned" idealisms persist. Could it be that while we secretly chuckle at that era's naiveté, that inwardly we somehow envy the resolve and decisiveness in a given situation of DeMille and his generation, or could it be that we've discovered many of those time-honored traditions, no matter how we portray them on the screen, to be true? Nevertheless, while DeMille sought to bring alive the tapestry of men and civilizations for generations to come, he also—perhaps wittingly so—enshrined both his films and himself as an unforgettable chapter in popular Americana.

Notes

1. David Chierichetti. *Hollywood Director* (New York: Curtis Books, 1973), p. 28.

2. Maurice Zolotow. *Shooting Star: A Biography of John Wayne* (New York: Simon & Shuster, 1974), p. 163.

3. Mervyn LeRoy. *Mervyn LeRoy: Take One* (New York: Hawthorn Books, Inc., 1974), p. 56.

4. Edward G. Robinson with Leonard Spigelgass. *All My Yesterdays: An Autobiography* (New York: Hawthorn Books, Inc., 1973), p. 272.

5. Charles Higham. *Cecil B. DeMille* (New York: Scribners, 1973; New York: Dell Publishing Company, 1976), p. 174.

6. *The New Yorker*, 31 December 1949.

7. Rudy Behlmer, ed. *Memo from David O. Selznick* (New York: Viking Press, 1971), pp. 402–403.

8. Jesse Lasky, Jr. *Whatever Happened to Hollywood?* (New York: Funk & Wagnalls, 1975), p. 304.

9. Michael Wood. *America in the Movies* (New York: Basic Books, 1975; Dell Publishing Company, A Delta Book, 1976), p. 1973.

10. Charles Higham. "Interview with James V. D'Arc," 18 July 1977, transcript in Harold B. Lee Library, Brigham Young University, Division of Archives & Manuscripts, p. 11.

Joseph H. Lewis

ASSESSING AN (OCCASIONALLY) BRILLIANT CAREER

Richard Sattin

Originally appeared in vol. 7, nos. 5 and 6 (November/December 1983)

As a feature film director, Joseph H. Lewis' career was confined—with few exceptions—to the ghetto studio 'B' pictures. Lewis' work has remained largely undefined and unexplored, although the now legendary *Gun Crazy* has every frame stamped with directorial presumption, and seems to encourage an auteur-inspired reexamination.

Andrew Sarris' *American Cinema* grouped Lewis, along with twenty-one other directors under the sub-heading "Expressive Esoterica," unsung directors with difficult styles or unfashionable genres, or both: "Their deeper virtues are often obscured by irritating idiosyncrasies on the surface, but they are generally redeemed by their seriousness and grace."[1] Despite the fact that Lewis worked in that corner of the movie industry where small resources, poor material and tight schedules are supposed to produce miracles, away from the over-groomed, committee-made 'A' features, his filmography has been an unprepossessing subject for study. Two practical reasons help to explain why Lewis has remained unidentified. Firstly, because his activity has been restricted to co-features, very few were given press shows. He is now a less familiar name than some broadly comparable practitioners of genre movies, and this situation has been perpetuated by the infrequency with which Lewis' films have been screened on television. Secondly, his career ended in 1958 (excluding programs for television), before he could elevate himself artistically or commercially, out of the straitened circumstances of his beginnings, while directors such as Robert Aldrich or Don Siegel, whose artistic 'independence' was thrown into revealing perspective by their gradual non-alignment from the disintegrating studios. A related difficulty is that Lewis was never grouped with any particular genre, which he might have shaped, been shaped by, exemplified or transcended. To his critics, Lewis' prolific output, forty-one feature films in twenty-one years, remains fairly amorphous, their subjects unclassifiable, except in the basic economic terms of studio scheduling. There seems to be no sense of an artistic personality defining itself in opposition to the checks and compromises of the studio system. Lewis is visual strength without consistency; visual intelligence without conceptual reason; style that doesn't seem to recognize the need for a theme.

In 1971 *Cinema* magazine contained three auteur-inspired evaluations of Lewis' work. The Fall issue, then edited by screenwriter and director Paul Schrader (*Taxi Driver, Blue Collar*), disclosed that only twelve of Lewis' films could be found in Los Angeles. In Schrader's frank estimation: "As the films began to unreel my enthusiasm began to wane."[2] Declaring that he holds *Gun Crazy* to be one of the best American movies ever made, Schrader maintains that only *Undercover Man* and *The Big Combo* "have any real stature," and proceeds to qualify this by unfavorably comparing these films with, respectively, *T-Men* (Mann) and *The Big Heat* (Lang). In the same article Robert Mundy's remarks are also largely devoted to *Gun Crazy* and *Big Combo*, interestingly stressing the underplaying of violence in the latter, but he subsequently ranges rather more widely over Lewis' oeuvre. "In the same year, 1949, Lewis directed one of his most achieved films, *Undercover Man*, and one of his least watchable, *The Return of October*, both with Glenn Ford."[3] The latter movie, according to a rambling, anecdotal interview in the same magazine between Lewis and Peter Bogdanovich, is a comedy about an elderly eccentric who dies and then returns to earth in the guise of a racehorse.[4] Mundy pins down a stylistic continuity in Lewis' predilection for location shooting and extended camera movements and refers to the recurrence of scenes in swamps (*Gun Crazy, Lady Without a Passport, Desperate Search, Cry of the Hunted*).[5] The third article, by Richard Thompson, concludes that Lewis "applies fresh solutions to stock scenes," but that no conceptual slant can be discerned in his work.[6] However he maintains that Lewis found his métier in the film noir, and that all his successful films, among which he places the last Westerns, contained direct or displaced noir elements. He proposed that Lewis "instinctively casts his films in the form of hunter-hunted chases," but again qualifies his admiration in a comparison with Samuel Fuller, claiming that Lewis rarely pursues to their conclusion the outrageous possibilities inherent in his scripts.[7]

The *Cinema* article, as well as being derogatory in many instances, is also contradictory. While Thompson lumps Lewis' Westerns *Halliday Brand* and *Terror in a Texas Town* under the heading of film noir, Schrader insists that: "a Lewis noir is better than a Lewis Western," and draws no connection between the two.[8] With respected authors like Tom Flinn suggesting that the different elements in *Big Combo* and *Big Heat* negate Schrader's unworthy comparison (*Velvet Light Trap*, No. 11),[9] there arises the opportunity to take up Andrew Sarris' challenge about a career that "warrants further investigation."[10]

Film noir is Lewis' generic specialty. The appearance of film noir as a "genre" has generally been attributed to a combination of influences—the arrival in Hollywood of German expressionists and French existentialists, of scenarists schooled on American "hard-boiled" fiction and cinematographers on "ashcan" painting, photo-journalism, newsreels and neo-realism. In particular the list of extra-cinematic influences is almost endless: populism, fascism, anti-fascism, communism, McCarthyism, the Second World War, the Wall Street crash, the Hiroshima bomb, increasing urbanization and bureaucracy.

Specifically Lewis' noir films fall into a sub-genre, the "B Film Noir." To explain Paul Kerr's article in *Screen Education* (32/33) in which he attributed the development of the "B Film Noir" to "a negotiated resistance to a realist aesthetic on the one hand and an accommodation to restricted expenditure on the other,"[11] it should be remembered that the introduction of color in the late 1930s was first appropriated by "fantastic" genres, and color originally signified fantasy. In other words, as well as being reducible to a specific socio-political atmosphere, the noir film can be related to the state of the film industry at a particular time. In the twenty years of transition to the late 1950s, when television and color established themselves ideologically as the presentation of realism, the equation between black and white and realism was primarily evidenced by the low budget noir "B" picture. That period almost exactly coincides with the directorial career of Joseph H. Lewis.

When discussing auteur recognition of Lewis' work it is easy to cite the inconsistencies of his films, supported by Lewis' admission to Peter Bogdanovich that the director by whom he had been most influenced was William Wyler. "I used to look at his films . . . twenty, thirty times . . . I gained a lot from this man because he dealt in people."[12] Leaving aside any stylistic resemblances in terms of deep focus and extended setups, in fact Wyler's filmography shares with Lewis' baffling elements of sheer unevenness. This approach begs the overriding factor of industry determination, a factor commonly ignored by theorists. Working in a sub-genre with as distinctive a strategy and style as the "B Film Noir" imposed a number of constraints. Those constraints should not be considered creatively negative, just that the opportunities for commercial and critical advantage lay in certain directions rather than in others. Countless critics have noted the richness of film noir, but the "conditions for an auteur cinema were deliberately cultivated, in conjunction with certain industrial, political, and cultural developments rather than accidentally propitious."[13] It can be proven, though inconclusively, that Lewis was a victim in an area of filmmaking during the fifties, in which the "B Film Noir" was one specific mode where authorship was institutionally inscribed. Lewis' own testimony subconsciously underlines this proposition. He describes how he and his art director and sketch artist went out on the Columbia back lot looking for a flexible location for *So Dark the Night*

(1946). Columbia had recently completed a war film, leaving a set comprising one-half of a church and several demolished buildings. "I looked at my art director and I said, 'If you took a bulldozer and you made a winding road here, and a dirt road that led past the (church) steeple, and you took a thatched roof in the foreground, just a roof and a side of a building, and over here further back in perspective . . . you know, one in the foreground and one in the background, to cover up all the burned-out buildings and everything, and you had another flat there, and down this sliding road I saw a little donkey cart of some French villager come on an automobile, would I give the impression of a French village?' And the art director leapt for joy, and by the time I had finished, the sketch artist had drawn a French village for me with two flats in the foreground, and out of a field we made a dirt road. That's the French village."[14] The film was shot in under twenty days. Budgetary and scheduling constraints provided economic and other connative solutions to cinematic problems that more expensive films might have solved less expensively. Lewis continues: "In the film a girl is found dead, the little French detective comes running up to the girl's mother and there's a long, tortuous dialogue scene where he tells her mother the girl is dead and she screams and all that. And I got on the set and I rehearsed it and I said oh, no, no, no, impossible. I threw out all the dialogue . . . the little Frenchman runs into the house . . . in extreme long shot two tiny figures you can't hear. He's talking of course but you can't hear it. We're shooting it without sound. And the only noise, shattering noise, that you hear when she drops a silver platter or whatever it was, and that's all you see . . ."[15]

Economy of style is exemplified by the Hampton Bank robbery scene in *Gun Crazy* (1949). Lewis describes how he was presented with forty pages of dialogue, containing scenes of a bank holdup, the reactions of the bank staff, all shot within the bank. The studio estimated four pages per day's shooting. Lewis shot the entire scene in one day, recording the legendary four-minute single take, filmed entirely from the back seat of the getaway car. The camera never sees inside the bank, thereby omitting the necessity for sets. The dialogue was entirely ad-libbed, and even the town where the scene was shot was not informed of the crew's arrangements. The appearance of apparently "directed" extras in the street, were actually astonished local residents who were unaware that the robbery was faked for the benefit of the camera.[16] Lewis directed *Gun Crazy* for the King brothers, and remarked that "they were wonderful to me. They just allowed me to do everything, anything that I desired . . ."[17] The studio maintained that they harbored insecurities about the marketing of "B" product. It was imperative that they were distinct from "A" films, and noir owes a vestige of its origins on a kind of oppositional cinematic mode. Low key lighting styles, for example, were not only more economic than their high key "A" alternatives, they were also dramatically and radically distinct from them.[18]

Lewis' "B Film Noirs" displayed most of the characteristics of the genre. All were under ninety-five minutes, all without major stars and all without rehearsed crowd scenes; their sets and locations, usually only a few used throughout, were often shot from above, below or behind foreground objects to increase atmosphere; their lighting low key and high contrast and the length and number of shots were often of unusually long takes, and few in number, combined with excessive violence and sexuality in key scenes, individualizing the films from their "A" rated competitors. These factors submit a convincing case in favor of the notion of a directorial career determined by the cultivated symbols of the noir genre.

Lewis still remains an enigma. Many avowed auteurists have failed to claim him as an author. His films resist efforts to construct a thematic coherence covering a substantial proportion of his work, locating their pleasure elsewhere, on a more disturbing though fascinating level. Myron Meisel's essay on Lewis in the 1975 anthology *Kings of the Bs,* while subscribing to a few descriptive inaccuracies, suggests Lewis' overall failure lies in not producing an articulated world view, yet suggests, without offering evidence, a thematically structural approach to Lewis' oeuvre via the recurrence of familial situations in disparate films.[19] To extend this assumption, I can offer the heroine of *My Name Is Julia Ross* (1945) who finds herself impressed into a sinister domestic charade. *The Halliday Brand* (1957) evolves around patriarchal domination and boasts a complex series of sibling intercorrections. *Undercover Man* (1949), with a subplot dealing with the mutual dependence of a man and his small daughter, places emphasis on the relationship of the protagonist and his wife, while the conventional implications of love vs. marriage are buried several layers down. Most remarkable is an attempt in *Cry of the Hunted* (1953) to invest the detective and his wife, in the plainest middle-class circumstances, with an animal sexuality the equal of that of the escaped convict and his dark-skinned lover. Finally the relationship of Bart and Laurie in *Gun Crazy* both transcends and parodies the matrimonial state.

Whether or not an approach to Lewis fails on an auteuristic, thematic or deterministic level, *Gun Crazy,* Lewis' own favored film, is recognized in its own right; by French surreal devotees on the strength of its celebration of amour fou;[20] by Richard Thompson as a protonouvelle vague film,[21] and by Robert Mundy as infinitely superior to its imitators.[22] Andrew Sarris rejoices in Lewis' ability to motivate his characters without the superfluous psychologizing in *Bonnie and Clyde.*[23] The weird tension of *Gun Crazy* is that its perfect dramatization of the lunatic escape of guns, sex, and killing, surrounds a perfect hollow. Comparison with *Bonnie and Clyde* is not only instructive because Lewis' anarchic visual style reduces Arthur Penn's to a pedestrian motion, but more that the romantic Lewis isolates as a gesture what Penn places as a symbol.

Lewis' visual style had been clearly observed in his low grade action films for Universal in the late 1930s, despite the meager values of the plot, and in addition to rough edges, definite and original conceptions of how to use a camera were coupled with the ambition to experiment on low budgets. His four films for Monogram (*Boys of the City*, 1940; *That Gang of Mine*, 1940; *The Invisible Ghost*, 1941; *Price of the Bowery*, 1941), all based on the adventures of a hoodlum gang, The East Side Kids, contain creative uses of the camera, with the close-ups and their deployment of special note. "The appeal to the eye was more than sufficient to offset some banalities of the scripts, and drawbacks brought on by production defects."[24] Large portions of *Ghost* and *Bowery* were shot out of doors, not only saving money but giving scenes a "clear, sharp look, adding considerably to the realism." Apparently when Lewis left the series the reversion to routine was evident.[25]

His use of the long take was employed as early as 1942. In *Bombs over Burma* the camera tells the story pictorially; the final scene—played in long stretches without dialogue, depicting a German agent meeting his death surrounded by Chinese guerillas—was "graphically constituted."[26] The extended set-up serves as an incitement to audience involvement. In *Gun Crazy* the rhythmic variations between long take and short cut are designed to form a system, in operation throughout the film, which discreetly introduce the three moments of crisis which punctuate the development of the relationship between Bart and Laurie. First, the crummy hotel room in which Laurie persuades Bart that crime is the only solution; the second, the elegant hotel room in which Bart finally faces the fact that he is being dragged into killing by a killer; third, and last, the oasis of the swamp, cut off from the rest of the world by fog even when the darkness lifts, a resting place from which there is no escape, and where Bart kills Laurie to protect her from the guns of their pursuers. Robert Mundy has suggested that the tonal qualities of *Gun Crazy*, "white and stark as the couple run into the street from the bank robbery wearing trench-coats and sunglasses"[27] must have influenced Godard, inspiring the quick-slow-quick tempo in *A Bout de Souffle* (*Breathless*).

Gun Crazy, with its three defined stages, can be likened to Lewis' overall noir career. The film itself, the zenith of his output, linked to the elegant hotel room in the second stage of *Gun Crazy*, where Lewis recognized that the permanent yet inextricable grasp by the noir genre would be destructive to his long term prospects. The first stage, the seedy hotel room, can be paralleled to his first celebrated encounter with the style in *My Name Is Julia Ross*, where a stronger force persuades Lewis to continue. The final scene in the swamp can be compared to his final noir film *The Big Combo* (1955). Even when the darkness of critical reviews subsided, Lewis extracted himself from the genre and effectively ended his creative career. The studio system had forced him into a style he grew to be synonymous with, and like Bart in *Gun Crazy* he became an unwilling accomplice. *Big Combo* was a gangster film with "sock, shock and brutality,"[28] and "grim, sordid, sexy and candid. . . . likely to satisfy adults but in no sense a film for children."[29] Describing the torture scene, *Variety* commented: "The moronic fringe of sadists will enjoy this and all the little kiddies will be sick to their stomachs," and ascribed the film "for the action trade."[30]

By the middle fifties, however, the action trade had turned to other things, and so Lewis turned to television, destined by the excellence of his noir work to be referred to for innovation, but resigned by material inconsistency to the "elephants' graveyard."[31]

Notes

1. Andrew Sarris, *The American Cinema*, Dutton, New York, 1978, p 132.
2. Paul Schrader, "Joseph H. Lewis," *Cinema* (U.S.) Vol. VII, No. 1, Fall 1971, p 43.
3. Robert Mundy, "Joseph H. Lewis," *Cinema* (U.S.) Vol. VII, No. 1, Fall 1971, p 45.
4. Peter Bogdanovich, "Joseph H. Lewis," *Cinema* (U.S.) Vol. VII, No. 1, Fall 1971, p 48.
5. Robert Mundy, op cit.
6. Richard Thompson, "Joseph H. Lewis," *Cinema* (U.S.) Vol. VII, No. 1, Fall 1971, p 46.
7. Ibid.
8. Paul Schrader, op cit.
9. Tom Flinn, "Film Noir," *The Velvet Light Trap*, No. 11, p 26.
10. Andrew Sarris, op cit, p 133.
11. Paul Kerr, "Out of What Past?," *Screen Education*, Autumn 1979, No. 32/33, p 47.
12. Peter Bogdanovich, op cit.
13. Sheila Johnston, "The Author as Public Institution," *Screen Education*, Autumn 1979, No. 32/33.
14. Peter Bogdanovich, op cit.
15. Ibid.
16. Ibid.
17. Ibid.
18. Paul Kerr, *Joseph H. Lewis and the B Film Noir*, Edinburgh Film Festival, 1980, p 3.
19. Myron Meisel, Lewis, *King of the Bs*, Dutton, New York, 1975.
20. Paul Kerr, "Out of What Past?" op cit p 46 from Borde and Chaunston, *Panorama du Film Nord Americain*.
21. Richard Thompson, op cit.

22. Robert Mundy, op cit.
23. Andrew Sarris, op cit.
24. Don Miller, *B Movies*, Curtis, New York, 1973, p 130.
25. Ibid.
26. Ibid, p 304.
27. Robert Mundy, op cit.
28. *Hollywood Reporter*, 10th February 1955, p 3.
29. *Motion Picture Herald*, 19th February 1955, p 329.
30. *Variety*, 16th February 1955, p 16.
31. Wicking and Vahimagi, *The American Vein*, Talisman, London, 1979, p 131.

Seastrom

THE HOLLYWOOD YEARS

Herman Weinberg

Originally appeared in vol. 4, no. 1 (Fall 1979)

By the time Victor Seastrom left Sweden for Hollywood and a contract with the
Goldwyn Pictures Corporation in 1923 he was not only the foremost film director of Sweden but one of the finest in Europe. He had already made over forty
films including the famous *Korkarley* (*The Phantom Chariot*, 1920), perhaps his
best work, after a novelette by Selma Lagerlof, in which he also starred—he was
not only a fine director but also a fine actor, from the very beginning to the end
(view *Wild Strawberries*, 1957)—and was as eager to see what the "New World"
held for him as was his colleague, Ernst Lubitsch, who came over from Germany
that same year. Both eager to test their mettle in Hollywood, both disappointed
in their initial American works—Lubitsch with *Rosita* for Mary Pickford and
Seastrom with *Name the Man*, from Hall Cain's novel, *The Master of Man*,
adapted by Paul Bern. Yet this was the same Paul Bern, the same year, whose
adaptation of Lothar Schmidt's play, *Only a Dream*, resulted in the Lubitsch
miracle, *The Marriage Circle*.

But fortune smiled on Seastrom and his next picture (he had a three-picture
contract) was made under the aegis of Metro-Goldwyn-Mayer (the separate
Metro, Goldwyn and Mayer companies having merged the preceding year),
whose production chief was the young Irving Thalberg and who suggested that
Seastrom do Leonid Andreyev's play, *He Who Gets Slapped*. Andreyev was a pes-
simist and his play about a scientist whose happiness and success are destroyed
when a friend steals the product of his lifelong research, making the scientist
an embittered cynic, had been successful on the New York stage. And although
Seastrom was persuaded to give the film a happy ending (of sorts)—the original
ended most unhappily—the picture was a success both artistically and financially and Seastrom was now launched on his American directorial career. Hans
Pensel, in his biography of Seastrom, points out that Andreyev's original "had
a lot in common with the later German picture *The Blue Angel.* . . . Sternberg's

film being based on the pre–World War I novel *Professor Unrath*, by Heinrich Mann. There is the same theme of degradation and humiliation of an intellectual man. In both films there is an almost sadistic fascination with the pain and anguish of the main character who, in both cases, is a professor." Of course, Lon Chaney, as the professor, was a "natural" for the role. "It was like making a film back home in Sweden," said Seastrom. "I had no interference and the shooting went quickly and without complications, being finished in a month." The cost was a mere $140,000. If you want to know the difference between filmmaking then and now, think that over.

The New York Times had compared Seastrom to Chaplin and Lubitsch and the film as "the most flawless" they had ever seen. He was off to a good start. *Confessions of a Queen* followed, from Alphonse Daudet's novel, *Les Rois en Exil*, starring Alice Terry, about a king who is forced to abdicate and finally discovers, rake though he is, that he really loves his queen best of all. And since the beauteous Alice Terry was the queen, she fitted her role perfectly. And that was about it. The adaptation (not by the director this time) betrayed the book and nothing was left of it save for the elegant sets and costumes. Lots of hand-kissing and bowing, etc.

This was exactly the opposite of *He Who Gets Slapped*, where the betrayed scientist—to spit in the face of a world that had betrayed him and ruined his life—joins a circus as a clown whose act consists of being slapped in derision over his melancholy by the other clowns. He falls in love with the girl bareback rider (Norma Shearer) but loses her to her riding partner (John Gilbert). He is finally killed by her father. He who gets slapped, indeed. And it wouldn't do, not the Hollywooden sort of thing *Confessions of a Queen* turned out to be. *The Tower of Lies* was closer to what Seastrom was. Again he had turned to Sweden's Nobel literature prize winner, Selma Lagerlof (authoress of *The Atonement of Gösta Berling*, which introduced Garbo) for her bitter novel, *The Emperor of Portugalia*, about a peasant farmer who escapes into insanity when he learns that his daughter (Norma Shearer) has become a prostitute in the city. She is not the fine, cultivated lady he had thought her. The father ends his days walking around the countryside wearing a paper crown and dressed in peacock feathers, announcing to everyone he meets about his beautiful princess in the city. Lon Chaney was, of course, the devastated peasant farmer.

A month before *The Tower of Lies* was released, M-G-M signed Seastrom to a new contract and first off came *The Scarlet Letter*, Lillian Gish's idea, after the churches and Will Hays Production Code office were appeased. And Thalberg chose Seastrom as the only director for it, to which Gish wholeheartedly agreed. And the result was wholeheartedly Nathaniel Hawthorne too, with Gish as Hester Prynne and Lars Hanson (also Gish's choice) as the Reverend Dimmesdale, both giving their all. I once chose it as one of the all-time best American films.

Seastrom now took off for a month's holiday in Sweden and came back to direct Garbo, who by this time had arrived in Hollywood with Mauritz Stiller. Her mentor had presented her to the world in *The Atonement of Gösta Berling*, and now also sought a directorial career in America, along with his star, Garbo. Stiller's is another story and a sad one.

The Divine Woman was Garbo's fifth and Seastrom's sixth picture in Hollywood. She was now a big star and got whatever she wanted—in this case, Seastrom as director and Lars Hanson as her *vis-a-vis*. The story began as an episode in the life of Sarah Bernhardt and ended, after Seastrom gave up quarreling with Frances Marion, the film's scenarist, as a nothing story about a shopgirl who is "romanced" (Hollywood-style) by a soldier. "We made him a soldier," said Seastrom wryly, "because uniforms suited Hanson." Typically, it was a success but after the premiere, Seastrom and his wife rode home in a cab silently and he murmured, "Well, come on, go ahead and say it." So she said it. "You shouldn't make pictures like that, Victor."

In that same year, Lars Hanson appeared in the title role of F.W. Murnau's *Faust* for UFA. Almost more than anything else, if you ever want to know what is meant by the difference between Hollywood and UFA (not between Seastrom and Murnau—they were almost equals)—see *The Divine Woman* and follow it with UFA's *Faust*. (Only you can't see the former anymore—it's lost, alas.)

When Hollywood would sometimes let a director have his own way (if that director *had* a "way" of course), the result could be not only pretty good but sometimes even spectacularly good—like *He Who Gets Slapped, The Tower of Lies, The Scarlet Letter* and *The Wind.*

Curiously, it was M-G-M's idea to make *The Wind,* from Dorothy Scarborough's novel of that name and Gish was to be in it, which meant that once again both Lars Hanson as her co-star and Seastrom, as her director, were engaged. You wouldn't think Hollywood would do a film about the effect of environment on the mind but that's what *The Wind* was. In the novel, the young woman dies on the windy prairie, alone and insane. In the film she adjusts to her surroundings and finds contentment and happiness with her husband—"let the wind blow, as long as we have each other," etc. *Sic semper Hollywood.* But Seastrom had a sense and feeling for landscape. The wind, and endless sky of the western prairie, were vividly evoked. As Pensel put it in his biography, "In few early American westerns, save some of Ince's short films, have natural settings been used so dramatically and meaningfully."

The picture was greatly admired in Europe, especially in France. To one critic, Rene Jeanne, "It was the film of all films by Seastrom that best survived the decades."

In a way it was even a "breakthrough," like *Greed* was a breakthrough—both were unprecedented, both showed how far you could go if you had to. Seastrom now began thinking of returning to Sweden. He had proved himself as spectacularly in Hollywood as he had done in his native country. He didn't need any more proof. But he had two more pictures to do under his contract—*Masks of the Devil* and *A Lady to Love* they were called. The former was based on the novel, *The Masks of Erwin Reiner* by Jacob Wasserman, a variation on the *Dorian Gray* theme: a sinner sees his face in a mirror and realizes he has an evil soul. The sinner, an arrogant, cynical Viennese baron, steals his best friend's girl while keeping up the pose as his good friend.

The idea was to reveal the double identity of the sinner (John Gilbert), to show him as a two-faced being but it didn't quite come off for all its attempt at psychological involvement. *The Masks of the Devil* (note how frequently Hollywood titles are "childish" in comparison with their sources, which shows what the producers thought—and still do—of the movie-going public). *The Masks of the Devil* was Seastrom's last silent American film. After another three-month holiday in Sweden he returned to Hollywood in 1929 to make his last American film and his first sound film—*A Lady to Love* adapted from the play, *They Knew What They Wanted*, by Sidney Howard, about a mail-order bride, set in a farmhouse milieu, with Vilma Banky and Edward G. Robinson. That picture was lost in the big noise that attended the coming of sound to the screen and it was just as well. Seastrom had done his work and he could go back once more, this time for keeps, resume his real name, Sjöström, and relax in the bosom of his family. In a letter he wrote to Lillian Gish in 1952 he said that "getting older, one's thoughts travel more and more back to the days of happiness—and you belong to perhaps the happiest days of my life."

Part V

BEHIND THE CAMERA: THE CRAFTSMEN

Walter Plunkett
DRESSING RIGHT FOR *GONE WITH THE WIND*

John C. Tibbetts

Originally appeared in vol. 6, no. 5 (September/October 1982)

The year 1939 was one of those "best of times, worst of times" that Charles Dickens wrote about. While the storm clouds of war lowered over Europe and little men strutted their way across political battlefields, Hollywood was in the midst of its most glorious year. This was the silver lining we had heard so much about. . . . as a group of films appeared whose like we will never see again. There were the burning sands of Fort Zinderneuf in Beau Geste, *the tryst at the Empire State Building in* Love Affair, *a stagecoach headed for a rendezvous with* The Ringo Kid, *Dorothy's trek toward the Emerald City in* The Wizard of Oz, *Henry Fonda's memorable footrace in* Drums Along the Mohawk, *farewells to* Mr. Chips, *and a smile for* Ninotchka *. . . 1939 burst with all the potency and vitality of the pomegranate seed. It gave shape to some of our best dreams. It gave us all a chance to laugh and wonder in the face of coming war. And it gave us* Gone with the Wind. . . .

We all owe a debt of gratitude to Katharine Hepburn for first urging costume designer Walter Plunkett to read Margaret Mitchell's *Gone with the Wind* late in 1936. Plunkett's costumes for *GWTW* have become a permanent part of Hollywood legend; they constitute a contribution to the film that cannot, perhaps, be overestimated. Just as there are devoted fans of the film's actors, its source novel, and its production crew, so too are there those who have long since consigned all the costumes to memory. They can tell you how many times Scarlett's calico dress was changed in different scenes; why Scarlett's opening lines to the Tarlton twins at the Twelve Oaks barbecue are inappropriate for the dress she wears; what the controversy was behind Gable's ill-fitting Rhett Butler clothes; and what character resorted to thorns as buttons for one of the gowns.

Niggling details? Of course. Trivial? Not at all. It's all a part of a growing consciousness we feel towards the magnificent studio films of Hollywood's

Golden Age. In their costuming, as much as in their scripting and direction, we see evidence of an almost obsessive demand for total control over every stage of the filmmaking process. *GWTW*, of course, brought the studio film to its apogee. It marked the summation of everything that we treasure in that long-vanished time of production autocrats like David O. Selznick. So let others argue about the complicated genesis of the screenplay (see *ACS*, Nov/Dec '81), or the definitive directorial screen credit (Sam Wood, George Cukor, Victor Fleming), or the historical context of the story; in these pages we will be content with the contributions of one man, Walter Plunkett, who, like Beau Brummell of an earlier day, did so much to influence the way Hollywood wore its clothes.

Fans of the *GWTW* saga are notoriously like baseball fans: They love to recite the time-honored statistics of their subject. The book had been published in May of 1936 and had sold 201,000 copies by July. By September it had made history as the fastest-selling book of all time, with 370,000 copies in print. Many book stores reported their windows broken as copies of the novel were stolen. Katharine Brown, the story editor for Selznick International in New York, had been among the very first to see the cinematic potential in the novel. By December 15, 1936, when the millionth copy of GWTW was printed, her telegram had already been received in Selznick's offices: "WE HAVE JUST AIRMAILED DETAILED SYNOPSIS OF GONE WITH THE WIND BY MARGARET MITCHELL, ALSO COPY OF BOOK, I BEG, URGE, COAX AND PLEAD WITH YOU TO READ THIS AT ONCE. I KNOW THAT AFTER YOU READ THE BOOK YOU WILL DROP EVERYTHING AND BUY IT."

On January 13, 1939, the final casting plans were released by Selznick, ending months of speculation about who would play Scarlett O'Hara. Thirteen days later George Cukor called "Action" on the first day of shooting. Finally on December 15 of that year the film premiered at Loew's Grand Theatre in Atlanta. Four days later it was premiered at two major Broadway houses—the Astor and the Capitol. The most massive "premiere" of all, however, came on December 28 when *GWTW* was screened at the Fox Carthay Circle in Los Angeles.

Six months later it had been seen by 25 million people in North America alone.

More statistics. *Variety* reported that *GWTW* grossed an unprecedented $945,000 in a single week—an accomplishment which remained without parallel for several decades to come. The movie became everyone's conversational topic. MGM mounted a "Traveling Tour of Costumes" as advance publicity for openings elsewhere in the country. You could see at first hand Gable's "Bazaar" tuxedo, Leigh's green sprigged muslin dress, the "evening prayer" dress, Leslie Howard's officer's uniform (upon which he commented, "I looked like a fairy doorman at the Beverly Wilshire."), and little Cammie King's riding habit. At the Academy Awards dinner in 1940 it garnered ten awards, more than had any previous film. Oscars went to Vivien Leigh, Victor Fleming, Sidney Howard (the only writer given script credit), and Hattie McDaniel.

But in 1939 there was no category for Costume Design. The public at large probably knew very little about the man who designed for and clothed everyone in the film. But the industry knew. Walter Plunkett became the most famous designer of his day—especially for films that had historical backdrops. Interestingly enough, Plunkett in later years declared that *GWTW* was not his own favorite effort. "I did a film for Lana Turner in the 1950s called *Diane* and I consider that my best work. But it had a terrible script and nobody remembers it. I thought my clothes for Elizabeth Taylor in *Raintree County* were better also. But you see you get the recognition for the big moneymakers in Hollywood. It's a money town." This comment from the *Los Angeles Times*, August 22, 1976, reflects a lifetime of being tagged as "the man who dressed *GWTW*." The artist in him rejected that kind of "typecasting," and we can't blame him. But Plunkett's achievement here can never be minimized. Almost three years of actual work and a lifetime of experience in the movies went into *GWTW*. We can do no less than pay tribute to that. . . .

At first, characteristically, Plunkett thought of *GWTW* as "just another project." In 1976 he recalled: "Oh, I knew the novel was glorious and I was pleased as punch when Selznick told me I would design the clothes for the picture. But as far as I was concerned, the picture was just another job. None of us expected it to be the biggest box-office smash of our time." By October of 1937 he was under a fifteen-week contract with Selznick. He ended up staying 162 weeks. The nature of Plunkett's working agreement with Selznick remains a bit controversial to this day. Reportedly, wrote Roland Flamini, after Plunkett's contract had expired, Selznick offered him the chance to continue on for nothing. An emotional and highly artistic man, Plunkett refused. After this, Selznick accepted costume designs from other designers—including Adrian, Milo Anderson, and Howard Greer. Plunkett was then recalled and told he could come back at $400 a week instead of the $600 a week he had been originally making. "Plunkett was made to feel he had no choice but to accept if he wanted to stay with the project." Plunkett commented in the *Velvet Light Trap* (No. 18) that he confronted Selznick about these tactics. "He told me he never had intentions of replacing me," defended Plunkett, "only that he wanted me to work harder, and that my work was splendid. I said, 'Thanks a lot,' and went back to work." According to Ron Haver in his book on Selznick, another aspect of Plunkett's contract was that he was to work on the research and designs for three months with no compensation. Only after production actually started would he receive $750 weekly.

Anyone who says that filmmaking in Hollywood—even in those days—was a picnic, is talking through his proverbial hat.

While completing his work on the costumes of Hepburn's *Mary of Scotland*, he began in earnest to pore over Margaret Mitchell's sprawling masterpiece. "I read the book two more times, making notations of every line and passage containing a reference to clothes or related subjects," recalled Plunkett to Ron Haver. "Then my secretary read the book to catch any items I might have missed, then we made a script of these notes, and it worked out that there would be almost 5,500 separate items, all of which would have to be made from scratch."

Some of Mitchell's costume descriptions were of sufficient detail to be of great value to Plunkett; on the other hand, some barely suggested the requisite appearance. For Rhett's daughter, Bonnie, Mitchell had conceived a ridiculous riding habit that represented Rhett's indulgence toward the ill-fated child: "So Bonnie had her blue velvet habit with a skirt that trailed down the pony's side and a black hat with a red plume in it." No problem for Plunkett there. But for one of Scarlett's most famous dresses, the green muslin gown (that was to have been originally seen in the first scene of the film), we have only this spare note in the book: "Her new green flowered muslin dress spread its twelve yards of billowing material over her hoops." Plunkett quickly noticed from his readings that Scarlett seemed to be wearing the color green most of the time. While in Atlanta, he obtained Mitchell's permission to introduce more variety into Scarlett's wardrobe. She said, according to Roland Flamini, that Selznick was entitled to dress Scarlett in any colors he pleased. Green was merely her own favorite color.

Always the indefatigable researcher, Plunkett traveled to many locations in his quest for period authenticity. In November of 1937 he was in Paris researching hoop-skirts and bustles. Women's fashions had undergone two visable metamorphoses in *GWTW*—from the prewar plantation days with the distinctive billowing hoop-skirts, to the austerity of Reconstruction garb, to the bustles that soon followed. His knowledge of the "architecture" of the hoop-skirt, for example, saved Selznick from at least one embarrassing blunder. Selznick had insisted that for the "Twelve Oaks" sequence the camera should pan across six ladies' frocks "which stand stiffly in a prim row like so many headless bodies, on their crinoline petticoats." Plunkett objected to this preposterous notion in a memo to Selznick's technical adviser, Susan Myrick: "As you know, neither hoops or crinolines could stand by themselves. If they were rigid vertically it would be impossible to sit in there. I have called Mr. Selznick's attention to this but find myself ignored. . . ." Plunkett finally prevailed and the scene was eliminated.

At his own expense and initiative, Plunkett also journeyed to Atlanta and Philadelphia seeking the swatch books from mills of the 1840s. With pictures from the *Godey's Lady's Book* publications of the day as guides, he finally found a mill near Philadelphia that had been producing some of the same patterns since 1840. He also found that Atlanta ladies had used materials at hand for their dresses during the Union blockade. Most of the gowns were made of cotton and were dipped in butter-nut dyes. The hats, moreover, were adorned with chicken feathers!

If Plunkett became obsessed with authenticity, it was no worse than the costume mania that gripped Selznick himself. He was adamant that Plunkett design the costumes with complete authenticity. For example, he insisted that the petticoats for the Southern ladies be made of costly Val lace. "Nobody will know it's there," complained Ann Rutherford. Selznick replied in his best Von Stroheim manner, according to Bob Thomas in his book on Selznick: "But you'll know it's there." Questions constantly came up that even Plunkett couldn't answer. Margaret Mitchell was startled during the production schedule to receive a wire from Hollywood demanding to know how Hattie McDaniel should tie her kerchief! Mitchell deigned to let Hollywood have its own way in the matter.

In all, Plunkett was responsible for all the costumes and changes of the fifty-nine principal characters. He set up his own cottage industry at Selznick's to make the costumes out of the material supplied from the Philadelphia mill. Seamstresses made the dresses and uniforms by the hundreds. Weavers reproduced the homespuns of the Blockade period on two old looms. Ironmongers soldered the skirt hoops. Assistant sketch artists constantly were at Plunkett's elbow, laboring at the thousands of drawings conceptualizing every possible variation in the costume.

Problems inevitably arose. There was the "Gable Controversy," for example. It seems that Selznick became quite upset when it became apparent that Gable's costumes didn't fit him properly. Plunkett's wardrobe department had not allowed for the changes in Gable's posture when he stood relaxed and when he held himself rigidly. In one of his famous memos, Selznick complained:

"I spoke today to Walter Plunkett about Gable's costumes. I think there is no excuse for their fitting him so badly, especially around the collar. . . . I think it is very disappointing indeed to have the elegant Rhett Butler wandering around with clothes that look as though he had bought them at the Hart, Schaffner, and Marx of that period and walked right out of the store with them." As a result, Selznick assigned Eddie Schmidt (Gable's Beverly Hills tailor) to tailor a new set of principal costumes for the rugged star. This rebuff was more than compensated for by another problem involving the fitting of Vivien Leigh. Director Victor Fleming demanded more visible cleavage from Scarlett—particularly in the scene when Rhett forces Scarlett to appear at Melanie's birthday party in a décolleté burgundy gown. To get the voluptuousness Fleming wanted, Plunkett had to resort to desperate measures. . . . He had to tape Leigh's breasts tightly together, thrusting them forward and upward while Leigh complained about being unable to breathe. One can only imagine the astonishment of her soon-to-be husband, Laurence Olivier, who was present at the proceedings.

One problem extended beyond Plunkett and involved Selznick himself. It concerned the presence on the set of Natalie Kalmus, the Technicolor consultant. She had veto power over any color scheme she felt inappropriate to the Technicolor process—whether it involved a costume or set decoration. This meant that she was able to toss out costumes whose color schemes dissatisfied her. She especially was distrustful of yellow and turquoise color schemes which, she insisted, tended to look smudged on film. This kind of supervision may have had some validity back in the early days of Technicolor when it was a bi-pack process. In the filming of *The Black Pirate*, for example, Douglas Fairbanks in 1926 had had to resort to color charts to ensure that colors photographed reliably and correctly. Generally, the use of bright and vivid hues was discouraged in favor of more pastel varieties by the time Selznick was making *GWTW*. Selznick's memos objected to Kalmus' domination over Plunkett's color schemes; they also showed his appreciation for a vivid and dashing use of color. In a memo distributed generally, he noted: "I have tried for three years now to hammer into this organization that the Technicolor experts are for the purpose of guiding us technically on the film stock and not for the purpose of dominating the creative side of our pictures as to sets, costumes, or anything else." Ultimately, Selznick and Plunkett won out in their preference for vividly hued costumes. In the first third of the picture, the costumes were generally bright and rich; in the second third, they were more of a neutralized color (representing the poverty of Reconstruction), and in the final third the contrast was emphasized between Scarlett's extravagant costumes and those of the other actors. Plunkett would employ such strategies often—most notably in his conceptions for *Raintree County* (see *ACS*, vol. 6, no. 4).

There are many memorable costumes to be seen in *GWTW*. Choosing a favorite among Scarlett's green sprig dress, her white "Evening Prayer" dress, one of the many calico variations (Plunkett claimed that there were twenty-seven versions; Herb Bridges says only five; Ron Haver says six), or the décolleté burgundy gown (a Plunkett original) becomes a frustrating—but fascinating—exercise. Indeed, these and so many of the other costumes become almost characters in themselves. This is certainly true of perhaps the most famous Plunkett dress in *GWTW*—the "drapery dress." Facing imminent eviction from Tara if she couldn't come up with an additional $300 in tax money, the desperate Scarlett resolved to seek out Rhett Butler in Atlanta for a loan of the money. Scarlett fashioned a dress made from green velvet portieres for the trip. This green velvet masterpiece, in Plunkett's hands, became the spectacular gown of the film and a striking emblem of Scarlett's fierce determination. Even if it did not impress Rhett enough to aid Scarlett with the tax money, it did sweep Frank Kennedy off his feet so that he married her! It is now known for all time as the "Scarlett Costume #16."

Plunkett designed for other Selznick films, including *The Adventures of Tom Sawyer* (1938) and *Duel in the Sun* (1946), but it was in *GWTW* that these two complex personalities best and most completely merged. It is sometimes easy to forget that Plunkett also designed costumes for other films in 1938 and 1939—*The Hunchback of Notre Dame*, *Stagecoach*, and *The Story of Irene and Vernon Castle*. In their own way, they were just as formidable in their demands as *GWTW*. It is a testament to Plunkett's art that in that one year, films appeared displaying costumes from 18th century Paris, the American West of the 1880s, the fashionable drawing rooms of the Belle Epoque, and the Civil War and Reconstruction periods. It is small wonder that when Plunkett finally retired in 1966, he noted that it was singularly dispiriting at the time to consider designing t-shirts and blue jeans. The Old Guard was changing. The man who had once designed Beau Brummell's cravat could no longer be content with torn undershirts. Unlike the Beau, however, Plunkett never went into exile. He remained in the public eye, a gentle yet seasoned professional who was the best at what he did. He wore his age and his retirement as gracefully as Rhett would wear his riding clothes.

ॐ

The author wants to thank Ms. Stacy M. Endres of the Herrick Library of the Academy of Motion Picture Arts and Sciences for her invaluable assistance in the research and preparation of this article.

"Mr. Electricity"
THE MULTI-VOLTED CAREER OF KENNETH STRICKFADEN

William Ludington

Originally appeared in vol. 7, no. 1 (May/June 1983)

Picture Fu Manchu (Boris Karloff), the Frankenstein monster (Karloff again), and Chandu the Magician (Bela Lugosi)—all bathed in electronic nimbuses of light. Think of all the death rays of departed Saturday afternoon matinees that destroyed a thousand cities. Remember the exotic laboratory of the villainous Emperor Ming in the *Flash Gordon* serials. Think of those and a host of other electrical marvels and you have the work of one man—Kenneth Strickfaden. His was the mind of a thousand volts . . . and some of the most "highly charged" special effects Hollywood has ever come up with.

Most dabblers in the realm of electricity have probably, at one time or another, constructed what is known as a Tesla coil. Named for its inventor, Nikola Tesla, the Tesla coil is simply an induction coil used to develop a high-voltage, high frequency, oscillatory discharge. Kenneth Strickfaden, a veteran of the First World War and an electrical hobbyist, made these things in his Santa Monica, California home for the amusement of himself and his neighbors. He also built other electrical effects, all of which had been originally discovered and perfected by Tesla before the turn of the century. These included the "Jacob's Ladder" effect with its ever-ascending tiers of electric flames between two diverging wires; electric pinwheels with their exciting gyration of sparks; electrostatic generators demonstrating lightning and St. Elmo's Fire; and on and on. As with Tesla, his spiritual mentor, this young hobbyist always strived for bigger and better effects. The way in which they were constructed displayed a certain sculptural quality reflecting the Art Deco style of the period. And so it was, that around the year 1930, the great megaphone of Hollywood called his name.

When Strickfaden arrived in Hollywood, his peculiar talents were immediately put to use for minor electrical effects in a number of movies. The advent of sound in the movies certainly opened the door to many creative and exciting possibilities for such effects as those presented by Strickfaden. His first film job was to produce a realistic sound of a condemned man being executed in the electric chair. Two thousand volts repeated four times, with five hundred volts in between, has been the grim procedure required for this execution. To obtain this sound he passed a high frequency current through a block of wood. The wood offered a resistance to the current and made a sizzling noise with a resulting wisp of smoke that drifted lazily across the set. After this ominous debut he was then assigned to blow up a tree with a bolt of lightning. This was relatively simple. He ran some wire up a prop tree. The wire was connected to a high voltage generator. When it was turned on there was a flash of light and the tree crashed, demolishing in its path a native hut. For another film he rigged up a rotary spark gap for a wireless station sound effect on board a ship. An appropriate sound resulted when he condensed a high voltage spark. The electrical stunts became more difficult when he was called upon to build a machine supposedly capable of emitting a ray that would interfere with the ignition of an automobile. The ray machine was a boxlike cabinet composed of various lenses, bulbs, coils, and dials. Although it was only a prop, it appeared as though it was capable of strange activities such as emitting all kinds of rays.

In early 1931 a film version of Mark Twain's *A Connecticut Yankee in King Arthur's Court* was released by Fox. This was the first sound version, with the title shortened to *A Connecticut Yankee*; it starred Will Rogers. Strickfaden created for this film a gigantic and mysterious radio set that supposedly had the power to bring back the sound of past ages. He called it "the retrogressive wave charger." When it was used in connection with a high frequency generator it produced artificial lightning.

The film with which Kenneth Strickfaden has been most closely associated is Universal's classic horror production, *Frankenstein* (1931). The script of *Frankenstein* called for a laboratory where lightning from the stormy heavens would be captured and channeled down into the inanimate monster (Boris Karloff), restoring him to life. For this Strickfaden built an apparatus based on the principle of the horn gap and designed it as the "Lightning Bridge." He was aided in the construction of this and other laboratory gadgetry by studio electricians. The construction of this particular set with its "lightning bridge" and other flashy effects necessitated moving half a ton of equipment over the Monster's operating table. It was very difficult for the three electricians to work up there as they did during the famous life creation scene. According to Boris Karloff, in an article called "Memoirs of a Monster" (*Saturday Evening Post*, November 3, 1962), he was quite uneasy doing this scene. Karloff lay half-naked, strapped to that operating table, and directly above he could see the "special effects men brandishing the white-hot scissors-like carbons that made the lightning." Karloff concluded by saying that he "hoped that no one up there had butterfingers!"

Rumors about this fantastic set and its electrical effects made people curious. As a publicity stunt, Universal invited people from all over the area to come witness the electrical pyrotechnics of the Frankenstein creation scene. This, and Boris Karloff's makeup as the Monster, gave the film its long celebrated trademarks.

Next there was a low-budget film called *Murder at Dawn* (Big 4 Films, 1932), an "old dark house" mystery, where Strickfaden built a device used to harness the sun's energy. It was called a "DXL Accumulator."

After this he worked on *Chandu the Magician* (Fox, 1932) starring Edmund Lowe and Bela Lugosi. This was a silly, but rather artistic, occult thriller directed by the set designer, William Cameron Menzies. Strickfaden's contribution to this production was a disintegrating death ray. Studio officials wanted sparks to appear all over the large ray gun, and as the infernal machine was destroyed, the barrel was supposed to melt and an electrical control handle burn off and fall to the floor. To accomplish this, huge amperages were needed to produce instantaneous heat, and a complicated and delicate resonator apparatus was used to create a spark six feet long. For this scene to be photographed it was necessary to hoist the apparatus overhead, thus making matters very difficult. The ray gun, and its photography, provide one of the most memorable scenes in the movie.

A much more spectacular picture, made with Strickfaden's electrical effects and properties, appeared toward the end of 1932. This was *The Mask of Fu Manchu* produced by MGM. Boris Karloff, on loan from Universal, portrayed the evil Oriental scientist. During a scene in this picture Karloff as "Fu" was to transfer a six-foot 1,000,000-volt arc from the ball terminal of a piece of strange apparatus to the presumed sword of Genghis Khan as a test of its authenticity. Approaching the roaring machine, he was to calmly intercept the awesome spark on his long Chinese fingernails and channel it to the sword. If this was truly the sword of the Great Khan it would not melt but would withstand the high amperage. For this purpose a sword made of brass and another made of gilded wax and magnesium powder were employed.

Strickfaden was required to double for Karloff in the sword-testing scene. Karloff would have no part of this stunt which he considered too dangerous. Trick photography was ruled out for the scene, so Strickfaden, who occasionally doubled actors in handling his electrical devices, dressed up as Fu Manchu, taking every possible precaution. A wire concealed under the Oriental costume was run from long copper fingernails to the resonator apparatus ground through a safety gap. At this point the director called for action. A low hum from the apparatus grew louder as the arc developed from the electrode to the tips of the copper fingernails. The spark was reaching its full intensity and Strickfaden was on the verge of transferring it to the sword when, suddenly, he did a convulsive back flip with the fire still flowing from his fingernails. Immediately the electricity was shut off, the camera stopped rolling, and the stunned man was helped to his feet. The problem was soon detected. It was a smoking cable that carried 10,000 volts from the transformer to the rotary gap. The cable had been punctured. An ensuing arc was formed across the flooring to a pipe underneath. The circuit was completed up through Strickfaden's body along the wire on his arm to the safety horn gap which broke the circuit and averted possible electrocution. After repairs were made and the cable moved, a final take was completed without further difficulty. The only sensation experienced by Strickfaden during this incident was that of a strangely painless flash of light. However, his back became sore and this lasted for some time.

One other spectacular, fantastic prop used in this film was an electrical death ray gizmo. In the climax of the movie, Fu's infernal machine goes haywire and destroys him and his followers. This contraption was very similar to the disintegrating death ray in *Chandu the Magician*.

Then along came the preposterous serial called *The Lost City* (Krellberg, 1935) utilizing such Strickfaden equipment as a large death ray, a machine to destroy people's wills, television, and miscellaneous gadgets.

In 1935 a sequel to *Frankenstein* was released by Universal. *Bride of Frankenstein* made use of practically all the same lab equipment used in the original 1931 production.

During the next year, 1936, Strickfaden did work for at least three productions. He equipped two gadget-laden serials. For the serial *Flash Gordon* (Universal, 1936), he fitted out the laboratory used by Dr. Zarkov on Planet Mongo. More lab equipment and gizmos were in the serial *The Clutching Hand* (Stage & Screen, 1936). And strangely enough his equipment was used to stock another mad scientist's laboratory in a B-western entitled *The Ghost Patrol* (Puritan, 1936) starring Tim McCoy.

There have probably been other films and serials made in the thirties in which Strickfaden and his equipment have been involved. Sometimes his name is seen in the credits and other times it is not. But his equipment is usually recognizable. Among many films with equipment resembling Strickfaden's are the serials *The Vanishing Shadow* (Universal, 1934), *The Fighting Devil Dogs* (Republic, 1938), and features *Son of Frankenstein* (Universal, 1939) and *The Devil Bat* (PRC, 1941).

Strickfaden's initial stint in Hollywood seems to have ended by the Second World War. No sign of him can be discovered until long after that period. With changing styles and the possibility of over-exposure of his equipment in so many films, his services may have been phased out to make way for fresh talent.

While working in Hollywood Strickfaden also carried on a sideline activity. Between pictures he would load up his movie props and high voltage apparatus on a custom trailer of his own design and take them on tour. His electrical circus included music over light beams, electric snow, artificial lightning, photo electric and gaseous tube effects.

Kenneth Strickfaden, now well into his eighties, still travels around California with his collection of electrical gadgets giving lectures and demonstrations at high schools and colleges. His name and reputation grow more popular with film buffs every year. About ten years ago he was called upon by Hollywood to once again render his peculiar talents and equipment in the production of several films. In the lurid, low-budget horror picture entitled *Dracula vs. Frankenstein* (Independent-International, 1971) he created some fresh special effects involving a magical lightning ray ring worn by Dracula. A few years later he allowed his original Frankenstein equipment to be used again for the laboratory scenes in the Mel Brooks comedy, *Young Frankenstein* (20th Century Fox, 1974).

In later years Strickfaden had moved and changed his telephone number. People had been calling and writing to him from all over the country asking him if he wanted to get rid of his machines. This is probably insulting to him since he must obviously cherish these gadgets (as well as his privacy).

The kind of films that incorporated strange electrical effects always made a difficult job for a technician like Strickfaden. These films called for authentic apparatus that would perform sensational displays usually possible only in large electrical research labs furnished with expensive equipment. Not all the gadgets seen in these movies, however, were required to work—many of them just sat around filling in space and looked atmospherically impressive. Strickfaden was expected to have in stock a wide array of every kind of apparatus that might be needed. If he did not have it, he would go home to Santa Monica and build it overnight. Many pieces of apparatus were used over and over again in different films, sometimes slightly altered or disguised. Quite a few of these pieces were originally used in the 1931 *Frankenstein* picture. Strickfaden gave names for some of these things such as the "DXL Accumulator," "Lightning Screen," "Dynascope," "Retrogressive Wave Charger," and the "High Amperage Pyrogeyser." And they've all glowed, pulsated, hummed, crackled, and sparked their way into the hearts of millions of movie fans for over the last half century.

ॐ

When I first spoke with the eighty-seven-year-old Strickfaden, early in March 1983, he told me he had recently moved from his home in Santa Monica and had taken up residence in the electrical lab of a shop owned and operated by a longtime friend named John Foster. The laboratory, or "Musereum," as Ken likes to call it, is located near Los Angeles.

The two men work nearly every day on some new invention or electrical demonstration. Some of the recent inventions born in their lab include a "Gravity Neutralizer," a new musical instrument Ken has dubbed "The Magnetone" (which is operated by a Ford magneto), and a seven-foot-tall transformer/scintillator which makes a terrific spark.

Ken, whose wife died in 1978, has two children and grandchildren. Although officially retired from full-time film studio work since 1961, he has, for over the past twenty years, done much freelance work for movies and TV. His equipment can still be rented.

Kenneth Joseph Strickfaden was born in the mining town of Anaconda, Montana, on May 23, 1896. His father had been a miner and mule driver. In 1908 his father took him to Oregon where they lived for a few years. In 1912 Ken and his father, by then divorced, drove down to Santa Monica, California, where they settled. Here Ken graduated from high school and developed his interest in electricity. In 1916 he joined a traveling vaudeville musical novelty act. He made music by blowing air through holes in his revolving "Melodyne" disc. The act played on the Orpheum and the Pantages circuits and also at Coney Island.

After serving with the U.S. Marines in France, Ken returned to the States at the end of the First World War. He arrived at Coney Island, N.Y. and set up his own electrical laboratory which won him first prize in the November, 1919 issue of the magazine, *Electrical Experimenter.* He then journeyed by Model T Ford across the country back to Santa Monica.

In 1921 he found employment in the electrical shops of various Hollywood film studios. Throughout the 1920s he did electrical work for many studios, eventually leading him into special effects.

During the late 1920s and 1930s, while sound was still new, Ken worked for many studios including Fox, Universal, and MGM. He did sound engineering and effects, visual electrical effects, and supplied strange electrical apparatus for horror and science fiction movies. The first major fantasy film with which he was involved was *Just Imagine* (1930). Some of his equipment was featured in the laboratory scenes of this film.

It was about this time that Ken began his other longtime career of touring the country giving demonstrations and lectures about electricity. When he was not busy in Hollywood he could often be found—using the stage name "Kenstric"—giving a demonstration at schools, fairs, and expositions. Some notable expositions included The Toronto International Exhibition (1936); the San Francisco Exposition (1939–40); the Utah Centennial (1947), and many more. His strange equipment fascinated thousands.

If Ken Strickfaden had done nothing else but create the electrical laboratory equipment for the 1931 *Frankenstein* picture, his fame would have been assured. This film and many other thrillers of this period, including *Mask of Fu Manchu,* were enhanced by the presence of his own designed equipment and special effects.

The irony of Strickfaden's career is that so many of the films on which he worked did not credit his services. A partial listing of these titles include: *Just Imagine* (1930), *A Connecticut Yankee* (1931), *Frankenstein* (1931), *Doctor X* (1932), *Chandu the Magician* (1932), *Bride of Frankenstein* (1935), *Flash Gordon* (1936), *Wizard of Oz* (1939), *Dr. Cyclops* (1940), *War of the Worlds* (1953), *Young Frankenstein* (1974), and *The Man Who Fell to Earth* (1976). He also worked on television series like *Lost in Space, Star Trek,* and *Wonder Woman.*

Other miscellaneous activities over the years include the electrical ballyhoo for the 1933 premiere of a Raoul Walsh film at the Carthay Circle Theater. There Ken projected a special effects cloud in the sky from his "Lightning Torch" which lit up that part of Hollywood. He has worked for Disney Studios on various jobs including work on an animated robot of Donald Duck for Disneyland, c. 1955. In 1976 he built a million-volt generator for the stage show of the "Kiss" rock group, and it produced a spark twelve feet long. Using the old Frankenstein equipment he put on an electrical demonstration at the Academy of Motion Picture Arts and Sciences, in November, 1981.

Strickfaden died in 1984 at the age of 87.

Coming to Light

THE CELEBRITY PORTRAITS OF ORVAL HIXON

John C. Tibbetts

Originally appeared in vol. 2, no.4 (March/April 1978)

I visited the 93-year-old Orval Hixon and his wife several times in the last few months. Their home is a lovely, enchanted place, where the faces of Eddie Cantor, Theda Bara, Ruth St. Denis, Eddie Rickenbacker, and countless others peer out at the curious as if to announce that they are still around, thank you. Down in the basement room Mr. Hixon still operates his private studio—mostly for old customers and special guests. Time has slowed him down a bit but he manages the steep stairway with good humor and his sharp, snapping eyes don't miss a thing. They've missed very little over the years. If most of us see half as much, we will be lucky—and he is color-blind at that.

The world of Orval Hixon lies somewhere behind other eyes, the thousand eyes of the black-and-white portraits that have followed him through the years. They look on as he sits quietly in the living room reminiscing; they still look on as he works downstairs, crouching over the retouching stand or moving among his old cameras, some of them survivors from the turn of the century.

He got his first camera in 1898. It used glass plate negatives about 2½ inches square. He tried to become a news photographer in Kansas City but ended up working in other capacities, such as apprenticing himself to a portrait photographer and shooting the Kansas properties belonging to the Union Pacific Railroad. He preferred faces to railroads and established his own studio in 1914 on Main Street, between 11th and 12th in Kansas City. In 1920 he moved to the Baltimore Hotel where he began his famous series of celebrity portraits.

Hixon has kept the records and the memories of those years. He estimates his photographic output at something like 37,000 photographs. He can show you the books that list his clients, the number of poses, and the number of prints ordered. Alongside famous names like Al Jolson and George Arliss are other entertainers of lesser ilk, like Trixie Friganza and Grace La Rue (a dancing co-medienne who traveled with a group of Black children called the "Inky-Dinks") and Hazel Flint and Evelyn Nesbit Thaw (the scandalous "Girl in the Red Velvet Swing" whose lover, architect Stanford White, was killed by her jealous husband in full view of hundreds of witnesses).

He knew them all. In those days, freewheeling vaudeville and legit came roaring through Kansas City as part of the fabulous Orpheum circuit. The entertainers needed portraits for publicity purposes. Their future bookings could depend upon the quality and excitement in those portraits. In many cases booking agents had only those to work with for their decisions. So the stars came to Orval Hixon.

They knew his worth. Vaudevillian Joe Page said Hixon's portraits captured the quicksilver temperaments of the performers better than the work of any other photographer he had ever seen. Dancer Ruth St. Denis judged his oriental study of her the best she had ever had and used it in her book of dance (he still owns one of the original 350 copies of that book).

Although some of his most important work was for these itinerant celebrities, he was, is, and likely will remain completely clear-eyed about the whole thing. No fawning star-worship for Orval Hixon. With a gentle candor and obstinacy, he refuses to look upon these people as other than professionals like himself who looked for the light. His memories are not reveries lost in a nostalgic haze, but rather accounts of expeditions with Valeska Surratt to find the right kind of wild flower for a sitting, a spaghetti dinner home-cooked for him by Fanny Brice, a sitting with a young kid from Olathe, Kansas by the name of Buddy Rogers who wanted to go to Hollywood—and did. And so it went. So casually did he take the whole thing that his wife Gladys recalls the many times a star celebrity would show up at the studio only to find Mr. Hixon absent. *They* would have to wait for *him.*

Portrait photography has played an important part in the history of photography. In the mid-nineteenth century one could buy a daguerreotype for anywhere from twenty-five cents to eight dollars. The small image of a frontally posed, stiff-necked, sharply focused, and probably hand-tinted figure would likely be clasped in a case of imitation leather covered with the scallops, cherubs, flowers, and curly vines that were popularly supposed to signify art—an assumption, incidentally, still alive and well today. These little portraits appealed to a public avid for their own images, and photography as a popular and commercial success was on its way.

Now a sitting for a famous portraitist like Richard Avedon might cost in the thousands of dollars, while the portraits of an Orval Hixon might come to you in a heavy, boarded folio at a similar cost. But there are other differences than just price. Over the last hundred years or so, portrait photography has penetrated the sometimes stiff facades of the daguerreotype to the quick-silver ambivalences—to the soul—of the sitter. And an interesting offshoot of the photographic portrait has lurked among the shadows during this time—the celebrity portrait.

Recent studies of the celebrity photographer have virtually ignored the work of Orval Hixon. This is more an indication of the fact that, unlike many of his contemporaries, he did not work in Hollywood. The studios wanted him out there but he refused. Some studies have brought to light such photographic notables as Clarence Bull and George Hurrell, both of whom worked at MGM; and others have afforded recognition to other photographers like Ernest Bachrach, Laszlo Willinger, and Ruth Harriet Louise. But they all worked in Hollywood. Hixon by contrast stayed in the Midwest. These celebrities he photographed came to him in Kansas City—something of a tribute in itself. And unlike these other notables Hixon did not confine himself to celebrity portraiture. He lent to the faces of the street, so to speak, the same sensitivity and burnished touch that he lavished on the stage and screen greats like Theda Bara and Wallace Reid.

The work of Hixon and the others owes a great debt to the classic traditions of the nineteenth century portrait and theatrical portrait. This refers mainly to the inculcation of painterly techniques into the photographic plate. An early daguerreotypist, Carl F. Stelzner, was typical of the photographer who treated his work to resemble hand-painted products. From its beginnings in the 1830s and 1840s, as a matter of fact, photography was itself considered as a kind of artistic handmaiden, its value lying in how it could aid—or imitate—painting. The Englishman Fox Talbot regarded photography as "the road to drawing." His calotype process was an early paper process that, unlike the daguerreotype, had the "failing" of unequal textures and a consequent lack of detail which made the photographs look more like drawings (the "imperfect work of man," as was noted at the time) than the precision product of a mechanical device. The heavy, unpredictable, soft grain of the calotypes split the photographic world in half. There were those who saw them as merely smudges; but there were others who saw in them a union of the painterly and the photographic. Artists like the Scotchmen David Octavius Hill and Robert Adamson excelled in this kind of portraiture, as did the Victorian Julia Cameron. Their works are seen today as mid-nineteenth century marvels as painterly "tones" and "impressions," penetrating documents of personalities like Lord Tennyson and Longfellow. The move to take portraits away from the photographic precision of the daguerreotype toward the painterly suggestiveness represented by the calotype resulted in methods such as retouching negatives, painting directly onto plates and prints, utilizing soft-focus lenses, printing on special papers, etc.

Such photographers were called "artist-photographers" and historian Van Deren Coke has pointed out how they merely catered to a public eagerly seeking photographs that resembled painted likenesses. I might add that, paradoxical as it seems, these photographers were not just imitating painterly models, they were developing the resources at their disposal. They were learning to treat photography as an artistic medium in the traditional sense, which is to say that they were exercising the artistic prerogatives of manipulation, selection, alteration, and construction. One of the chief publications dealing with this in the nineteenth century is the book by the celebrated Victorian photographer, Henry Peach Robinson, *Pictorial Effects in Photography*, in which he not only instructs the erstwhile photographer in how to imitate painterly models and techniques, but how to manipulate the elements of his medium.

Modern-day masters of the celebrity photograph like Hixon, Hurrell, and Bull owe much to this period and to the early celebrity photographers practicing then, men like O. G. Rejlander and the two Americans, William Kurtz and Napoleon Sarony. Rejlander photographed actor John Coleman and his company in the early 1860s. Coleman, a "dramatic artist and manager," had introduced *Belphegor* to the British public at Coventry in 1855. Rejlander caught him in the role and later as Richelieu. He even made a combination print to the man—a picture called "An Actor's Day-Dream." Sarony and Kurtz introduced celebrity portraiture of the stage to America with the establishment of their respective studios in New York in the 1860s. One notable result from Sarony was his portrait of actor Joseph Jefferson in his most famous role, Rip Van Winkle. In the foregoing examples it was realized the importance of capturing the actor in his role and creating in any way possible the essential atmosphere embodied in both actor and role. Often his work featured low-key lighting because it stimulated the artificial lighting of the stage; and often the photographic plate itself is subjected to the manipulations described above, whether it be combination printing, retouching, focus diffusion, etc.

Orval Hixon's work, particularly the celebrity photographs from 1918 to 1930, reveal the fruits of this theatrical tradition in portraiture. He has shown me the glass negatives dating back to that time. They have been carefully worked over with the artist's brush and etching tool and pencil. The plate for him was only so much raw material with which he could work. These plates, old and now fragile, are paintings in themselves, ghostly images in negative possessing the haunting quality of music half-remembered. They demonstrate the elusive union of the artist's brush and the mechanical fidelity of the plate. All of which accounts for the unique mixture of dream and reality in Hixon's best work. Look at such portraits as the Annette Kellerman and the Ruth St. Denis series.

Hixon's work is part of that body of work over the years that embodies a resounding response to the now-famous criticisms of photography of Charles Baudelaire in 1855. Baudelaire complained that photography's allegiance was to external reality. Photography, he implied, reveals only visual evidence, not the dreams of the artist. The artist-photographers at their best, from Sarony and Rejlander to latter-day dreammakers like Bull, Hurrell, and Hixon, retained that capacity to dream within the mechanical confines of the photographic medium.

They could look out from between its mechanical bars and still fancy what lay beyond.

"It used to be a glory to express what one dreamt," said Baudelaire, thinking his words sounded the death knell of the imaginative artist. Looking at the work of one such as Orval Hixon we now know those words to be narrow and premature. As his subjects came to the light, so now in a sense do we.

Index

Seven Keys to Baldplate, 42–44, 48, 52, 55
The Seven Year Itch, 131
Seventh Victim, 62
The Shadow Box (play), 90
The Shaggy Dog, 174
Shakespeare, William, 68
Shark's Treasure, 84
Sharky's Machine, 66
Shaw, George Bernard, 93
Shaw, Victoria, 83
Shayne, Alan, 161
Shearer, Norma, 167, 183
Shelley, Mary Wollstonecraft, 61
Shelley, Percy Bysshe, 61
Shepherd of the Hills, 100
Sheppard, Gene, 18–85
The Sheriff, 12
Sherman, Lowell, 14
Sherwood, Robert, 166
She's in the Army, 115
Ship Ahoy, 143–144
Shipp, Cameron, 5
Shockproof, 82
Shoemaker, Dorothy, 27
The Shootist, 72
The Shop at Sly Corner, 62
Sidney, Margaret, 173
Siegel, Don, 72, 180
Sign of the Cross, 126, 128–129, 173
Signoret, Simone, 90
The Silent Comedians (book), 7
Silvers, Phil, 80
Silvers, Sid, 141
Sinatra, Frank, 168
Singer, Stan, xiii
Sirk, Douglas, 82
Sisters under the Skin, 129
Six Hours to Live, 29
Skelton, Red, 144
Skidoo, 71
Slave Ship, 30
Smiley, Joseph, 42
Smith, C. Aubrey, 30
Snow, Marguerite, 39

Snow White and the Seven Dwarfs, x
Something Wicked This Way Comes, x
Sometimes a Great Notion, 66
Son of Frankenstein, 61, 205
Son of Fury, 83
The Song and Dance Man, 52–53, 55
A Song to Remember, 80
Sothern, Ann, 143
Soule, Helene Vivian, 61
Spin and Marty, 171
Spitfire, 34
Splendor in the Grass, 147–149
Spoor, George K., 38
St. Denis, Ruth, 209–210, 212
St. John, Al "Fuzzy," 10
St. Johns, Adela Rogers, 117–119, 161
Stagecoach, 201
Stahl, John M., 80
Stairway for a Star, 81
Stanwyck, Barbara, 33, 167
The Star, 147
Star of India, 83
Star Trek (TV), 208
State of the Union (play), 35
Steinbeck, John, 132
Stella Dallas, 74
Steltzner, Carl F., 211
Sten, Anna, 36
Sternberg, Josef von, 20–25, 188
Stevens, George, 98
Stevenson, Robert Louis, 30
Stewart, Gloria, xvi
Stewart, James, xvi, 70, 82, 139, 146, 163
Stiller, Mauritz, 190
Stine, Dorothy, 61
The Sting, 65
Stone, Lewis, 26, 70, 124, 128
Storm (play), 127
The Story of Irene and Vernon Castle, 201
The Story of Louis Pasteur, 153
Stranger's Return, 99–100
Street Scene, 96–97
Strickfaden, Kenneth, 202–208
Strike Up the Band, 70
Strindberg, August, 127

About the Editors

John C. Tibbetts was educated at the University of Kansas (B.A., Ph.D.) and has worked as an artist, illustrator, editor, writer, teacher, and broadcaster; for eight years he was editor-in-chief of *American Classic Screen* and sat on the board of the National Film Society. He is an associate professor of film and theater at the University of Kansas and the author of several books, including the two-volume *The Encyclopedia of Filmmakers* (2002), *Composers in the Movies: Studies in Musical Biography* (2005), and *All My Loving? The Films of Tony Palmer* (2009).

James M. Welsh is emeritus professor at Salisbury University in Maryland and was educated at Indiana University, Bloomington, and the University of Kansas (M.A., Ph.D.). The founder of the Literature/Film Association, and the co-founding editor of *Literature/Film Quarterly*, Welsh was East Coast editor of *American Classic Screen*. He now serves on the editorial board of *The Journal of American Culture* and *The Journal of Adaptation in Film and Performance*, published in Britain. His most recent books are *The Pedagogy of Adaptation*, co-edited with Laurence Raw and Dennis Cutchins, and *The Francis Ford Coppola Encyclopedia*, co-edited with Rodney Hill and the Rev. Gene D. Phillips, S.J., both published by Scarecrow Press in 2010.

About the Contributors

Frank A. Aversano kept the occasional column "Sidelong Glances" for *American Classic Screen* magazine.

James Bawden was television critic for *The Spectator* in the Province of Ontario, Canada, and became a contributing editor for *American Classic Screen* in 1977.

DeWitt Bodeen (1908–1988) began as a stage actor and playwright before becoming an RKO screenwriter for the films *Cat People* (1942 and 1982), *Curse of the Cat People* (1944), *Night Song* (1947), and *Billy Budd* (1962). A Hollywood historian, he wrote for *Films in Review, Classic Images,* and *American Classic Screen* and was the author of three books: *The Films of Cecil B. DeMille* (1969, with Gene Ringgold), *From Hollywood* (1976), and *More From Hollywood* (1977).

Del Burnett was a Hollywood actor and friend of the choreographer Frank Radcliffe.

Raymond G. Cabana Jr. was the author of *The Films of Peter Lorre.*

Lisa Capps, a paralegal secretary living in Los Angeles, was a devoted, longtime fan of Eleanor Powell.

Mae Clarke (1910–1992) had a long career in acting, extending from her co-starring with James Cagney in several films, including *The Public Enemy* (1932), to later roles in *Big Hand for a Little Lady* (1966) and *Watermelon Man* (1970). She appeared in numerous lead and supporting roles in films, serials, and television shows.

James V. D'Arc is curator of the Harold B. Lee Library Archives of Brigham Young University in Provo, Utah, and was a contributing editor of *American Classic Screen.* The Lee Library at BYU houses the Cecil B. DeMille papers.

Betty Dodds was a friend of Diana Serra Cary ("Baby Peggy" on the screen), who worked for the Performing Childrens' Research Project.

Anne Etheridge was administrative assistant for Raymond Burr Productions and manager of the Transition Team for the American Film Institute (West Coast).

Bruce M. Firestone was a freelance contributor to both *American Classic Screen* and *Literature/Film Quarterly* in 1977.

William Hare was appointed associate editor of *American Classic Screen* in 1977 and thereafter became West Coast editor for the magazine.

James Robert Haspiel worked early for *American Classic Screen,* providing profiles with Jayne Mansfield and Kim Novak.

Audrey E. Kupferberg is a film historian and archivist who began cinema studies at Albany College in New York with Professor Arthur Lennig and went on to become film archivist with the American Film Institute in Washington, D.C. Her study of George M. Cohan won a national competition sponsored by the National Film Society. She later became assistant director of the National Center for Film and Video Preservation at the American Film Institute and project director of the American Film Institute Catalog. She is co-author of *Angela Lansbury: A Life on Stage and Screen* (1996); *The John Travolta Scrapbook* (1997); and *Meet the Mertzes* (1999). Contributing editor of *Leonard Maltin's Family Film Guide,* contributor to *Women Filmmakers & Their Films* and *The Whole Film Sourcebook,* film consultant to the Peary-MacMillan Arctic Museum at Bowdoin College, and former director, Yale University Film Study Center.

Michael Thomas Lord was a theatrical producer of the Off-Broadway play *Don't Grow Up Without Me,* by television actress Brett Somers.

William Ludington was a freelance writer living in Silver Spring, Maryland.

Jack Marston is a National Film Society member and freelance writer.

Rev. Gene D. Phillips, S.J., a prolific film scholar, teaches English and film at Loyola University in Chicago. He was a member of the *American Classic Screen* editorial board and has published books on several major literary figures (such as Graham Greene, whom he interviewed) and film directors he was also privileged to know, such as Alfred Hitchcock, Stanley Kubrick, John Schlesinger, Ken Russell, and Billy Wilder. He is the co-editor and co-author of *The Francis Ford Coppola Encyclopedia,* recently published by Scarecrow Press.

John Roberts is a North Hollywood freelance writer interested in film history.

Richard Sattin, upon graduating with honors from a university course in film and television production, left his native London to take up permanent residence in the United States.

Gene Sheppard, film collector and enthusiast from Edison, Georgia, profiled both Cornel Wilde and Lana Turner for *American Classic Screen* in 1982.

Frank T. Thompson has worked as an editor, archivist, and television writer in Los Angeles, Chicago, Atlanta, and elsewhere. A multitalented film buff, Frank has written several books, including *William A. Wellmann, Robert Wise: A Bio-Bibliography* (1995), *Lost Films* (1996), and *The Alamo: A Cultural History* (2001).

Herman G. Weinberg (1908–1983) was a friend and contributor to *American Classic Screen*, journalist, translator, raconteur, and feuilletonist. He wrote for the *New York Times* and *Variety* and kept a regular column, "Coffee, Brandy & Cigars," for the Canadian magazine *Take One* before joining *Films in Review* with his column "The Weinberg Touch," named in honor of his popular book *The Lubitsch Touch*. His other books include *Josef Von Sternberg* (1967), *The Complete Greed* (1972, on the Erich Von Stroheim film he considered "the Holy Grail of the Cinema"), and his memoir, *A Manhattan Odyssey* (1982). The cover photo for his last book, *Coffee, Brandy & Cigars* (1982) was taken by Stanley Kubrick.

Robert Young Jr., a freelance writer based in Sacramento, was associate editor of *American Classic Screen*. He was a former New York magazine editor and advertising executive.